"The True Bones of My Life"

Dread and all her improbabilities are an inevitability we must make our lover. It is singularly stupid not to make yourself ready for anything that could happen. In my own memory, time has never stopped.

—Jim Harrison, "Fording and Dread"

To look at the world: and when we have learned once more to look, we see the possibility of renewal, of an implied order, in every aspect of the life around us. In the stillness of leaves floating in a forest pool; in the flight pattern of a flock of birds obedient to an invisible current of air; in the twilight folding of a particular hillside. . . . Sometimes I think that is all we are really here for: to look at the world, and to see as much as we can.

—John Haines, "Notes, Letters, and Reflections,"
Fables and Distances

If I do not deny my origins, it is because it is ultimately better to be nothing at all than a pretense of something.

—E. M. Cioran, *The Trouble with Being Born*

[Michel Foucault's] deep mistrust of series, criteria for periodization, levels of hierarchy, and stratification, as well as associations that lead to causality, prompts him to question how written documentation has been used to create unities and totalities—monuments of history. He even questions the facts upon which assumptions are based because facts cannot, he suggests, be seen as separable from their interpretations.

—Gordon E. Slethaug, *The Play of the Double*
in Postmodern American Fiction

I recently came upon a book by a sixteenth-century Japanese swordsman, Musashi, where he speaks of fording, of the opportune time to make a critical move—the metaphor of crossing water at the right time and place. I used to enjoy reading about how the pioneers and settlers managed to cross these enormous rivers. Musashi on the surface is involved with warrior strategy, adding "You must research this well."

—Jim Harrison, "Fording and Dread"

It is not down in any map; true places never are.

Herman Melville, *Moby-Dick*

But how alien, alas, are the streets of the city of grief,
where, in the false silence formed of continual uproar,
the figure cast from the mold of emptiness stoutly
swaggers.

—Rainer Maria Rilke, "The Tenth Elegy," *The Duino Elegies*

"The True Bones of My Life"

*Essays on the Fiction
of Jim Harrison*

PATRICK A. SMITH

Michigan State University Press

East Lansing

∞ The paper used in this publication meets the minimum
requirements of ANSI/NISO Z39.48–1992 (R 1997)
(Permanence of Paper).

Michigan State University Press
East Lansing, Michigan 48823–5202

Printed and bound in the United States of America.
07 06 05 04 03 02 1 2 3 4 5 6 7 8 9 10

Library of Congress Cataloging-in-Publication Data

Smith, Patrick A., 1967–
   The true bones of my life : essays on the fiction of Jim Harrison /
Patrick A. Smith.
      p. cm.
Includes bibliographical references and index.
   ISBN 0–87013-612–7 (alk. paper)
   1. Harrison, Jim, 1937—Criticism and interpretation. 2. Michigan—
In literature. I. Title.
   PS3558.A67 Z88 2002
   813'.54—dc21   2002002061

Book design by Bookcomp Inc.
Jacket by Heather L. Truelove
Cover Portrait is *The General* by Linda Welsch © 2001. Oil on canvas,
24" x 30". From the private collection of Beef Torrey.

Visit Michigan State University Press on the World Wide Web at:
www.msupress.msu.edu

For Lori Chorey,
simply

Contents

Acknowledgments

I am humbled by the support that I've gotten in the course of researching and writing this collection. A mention to all of those individuals here is the smallest token of my appreciation. Still, the following is only a partial list of those who were instrumental in helping me to bring this project to fruition: my mom, Martha, whose own love for literature was my best possible influence; my dad, Gerald, who taught me to understand and fully appreciate our own little piece of wilderness; my brother and friend, Matthew, whose astute and occasionally unconventional insight always puts things into perspective; and my extended families, who have offered kind words and respite on occasions too numerous to count.

Also, Jim and Linda Harrison, who invited me into their home and without whom this study would never have been given voice; Guy and Terry de la Valdéne, for their uncommon generosity and friendship; Bob DeMott, whose *aficion* for literature and nature is outstripped only by his willingness to pass that passion along to his students; Joyce Bahle, Jim Harrison's longtime assistant; Martha Bates, Julie L. Loehr, and Annette Tanner at Michigan State University Press; Peter Berg, director of Special Collections at Michigan State University; Dr. Gordon Schanzenbach, without whom I would never have begun the journey in the first place; Dr. Beef Torrey, a fine traveling companion and a steady influence; the faculty and staff in the English Department at Ohio University; and the unsung multitudes in the libraries at Ohio University, Michigan State University, Florida State University, and around the country for making the world of ideas so readily available.

My thanks go out to Leon Anderson, Joseph Bednarik, Susan Crowl, Jim Fergus, Roy Flannagan, Don Foss, Dan Gerber, Tracie Church Guzzio, Rich Hayes, David Heaton, Charles Hodge, Charles Lewis, Pat Martin, Patti McSteen, Ronald Primeau, Lilli Ross, Douglas Seifert, and the FSU Photo Lab.

I would also like to thank Bill Barillas and Keith Comer, who joined Bob DeMott and me on the panel of the inaugural meeting of the Jim Harrison Society at the American Literature Association conference in Boston, May 2001.

Introduction

The Contexts of Jim Harrison's Fiction

There is a not quite comic schism inherent in the idea that on a daily basis The *New York Times* and "All Things Considered" tell us everything that is happening in the world, but neglect to include how we are to endure this information. If I had not learned to find solace in the most ordinary preoccupations—cooking, the forest and desert— my perceptions and vices by now would have driven me to madness or death. In fact, they very nearly did.
                    —Jim Harrison, "Dream as a Metaphor of Survival"

There's something almost eery, tremendously uncomfortable about the will to change, because we're never quite sure what precipitated it, let alone what might become of us in the process.
                                        —Jim Harrison, "Fording and Dread"

"Sure he's a good writer but ninety-nine point nine percent of all writers are forgotten within a month after their last book."
                                        —Jim Harrison, *Westward Ho*

I

As he writes from his cabin in the Upper Peninsula of Michigan in a 1982 essay, "Fording and Dread," Jim Harrison understands in a way that few writers will what a modicum of popularity can do to the creative impulse: "I've managed a recent humor about success which I treated badly with the attitude of my father which involved deep pessimism, the maudlin, a sense of 'this too is martyrdom.' . . . It's probably a little too late to be anonymous. Being recognizable is certainly the most disabling accoutrement of success but I'm now sure it doesn't have to be."[1] Despite his wish to the contrary, Harrison will never be anonymous again after a thirty-year roller-coaster ride through the American literary landscape, though that hardly implies that his is a household name in American letters. Most people recognize Harrison's name only in the context of the film version of *Legends of the Fall.* The author's first appearance on a best-seller list was in France, where *The Road Home* (1998) rose to the number two spot more than thirty years after *Plain Song,* his first collection of poetry, was published.

Perhaps Harrison's refusal three decades ago to participate in what he still dismisses as the politically motivated rites of passage that characterize the academic writer-teacher who has become the mainstay of American letters has helped his reputation as an "outsider" who steadfastly refuses to compromise his notions of what literature should be.[2] In fact, Harrison had an eminently short and unfulfilling career as a writing teacher at SUNY Stony Brook (he was there for not quite two years beginning in 1965, the year that *Plain Song* came out; the collection was coaxed to publication by the late Denise Levertov, who became an early poetic influence and mentor to the aspiring writer), and he claims that when he left the job the only thing he took with him was a trunk full of student papers that he had neither graded nor returned to his students.[3] Despite betting his future on the long shot of becoming a literary writer who makes his living solely on his craft, Harrison has managed to survive and prosper. In retrospect, the decision was easy for the author, who "wanted to be a painter when I was growing up. . . . I wanted to be Gaugin, but I was no good at it. All I can do is write. I've failed everything except immediate acts of the imagination. That's what I do well, so that's what I do."[4] After suffering a dry spell during which he averaged $10,000 annually, Harrison realized popular success with the novella collection *Legends of the Fall* and, by his own admission, made and spent a fortune in a haze of dissipative living. About the reversal of fortune, Harrison has only to say, "I didn't know how to handle it; I behaved badly."[5]

Since then, Harrison has had time to write fiction and poetry in part because of his prolific work in writing screenplays and essays, the author's alternative to teaching. In all, he has sold seventeen screenplays, including *Carried Away,* an adaptation of his novel *Farmer; Cold Feet,* which he co-wrote with Tom McGuane; and adaptations of his novellas *Revenge* and *Legends of the Fall.* He has also been a frequent contributor of essays to a variety of magazines and journals, including *Sports Illustrated, Sports Afield, Smart, Men's Journal, Antaeus, Psychoanalytic Review, Playboy,* and *Esquire.* A monthly food column that ran for two years in *Esquire* in the early 1990s offers an intimate glimpse into the author's passion for food and drink.

His obsession with writing has paid off: the author is sixty-four now, and his life has assumed the veneer of stability which most of his characters seek. Although he chooses to separate himself these days from the glitz and glamour of Hollywood, instead splitting his time between his home on the Leelanau Peninsula of Michigan, a cabin in the Upper Peninsula, and a winter home in Arizona, he claims a devoted core of fans who have kept all of his fiction in print, a fact about which Harrison is understandably proud at a time when books hit the remainder racks almost as quickly as they come off the press. The bibliography of Harrison's work—fiction, poetry, and essays— grows larger by the day as reviewers and critics have begun to take notice of the work of the man whose words typify the Midwestern sensibility that has so profoundly influenced him.

I was introduced to Jim Harrison's fiction when I read *Brown Dog,* the first appearance of Harrison's irreverent, lusty title character who somehow seemed out of place in a collection of novellas that includes a sensitive portrayal of a woman's dissolving marriage in the title story *The Woman Lit by Fireflies* (1990). This study of Harrison's fiction has forced me into the sort of contradictions that Harrison presents in his disparate characters: to articulate, with a healthy dose from what T. S. Eliot dubbed "the lemon-squeezer school of criticism," what a writer of such strikingly visceral prose so often allows the reader of his fiction simply to *feel.* For anyone who has seriously read and studied Harrison's fiction, the need to feel along with him is part of the inexorable and often difficult journey toward understanding ourselves that has drawn us all to the words on the page in the first place. Still, despite his immense talent, increasing critical support, and a growing popular audience, Harrison remains elusively in the margins of American letters.

II

A full-length critical study of Harrison's work (to date, Edward Reilly's Twayne Series book and *Jim Harrison, de A á W,* a quirky encyclopedic biography by French critic Brice Matthieussent, are the only others) is valuable for illuminating the diversity and range of Harrison's genres, protagonists, settings, and themes: from novel to novella; comically macho picaro to psychically scarred female protagonist; wilderness to city; and from food to sex to alcohol to psychosis. Harrison's greatest strength is an uncanny intuition for the vast scope of human experience and his subtle articulation of other more intangible elements that elude expression in many writers (one critic perceptively notes that "[j]ust who Harrison is gets to be a complicated issue, but in the end, it all comes down to passion").[6] That intuition is complemented by Harrison's ability to form in our minds the well-rendered concrete object, a vestige of his consistent production of poetry for nearly four decades and the provocation for the unequivocal attention, both positive and negative, that Harrison's fiction has garnered in the last three decades.

Perhaps the most telling assessment of the author's talent outside the works themselves is in his reviews, which simultaneously delimit the work under review and Harrison's own versatility. In a 1972 review of Larry McMurtry's *All My Friends Are Going to Be Strangers,* Harrison extols the same "memorable" qualities that mark his own fiction, ones that are "central in terms of esthetics to any good novel. It is simply the viable cornpone that good art sticks and draws us back to life while the bad is easily forgotten. . . . I could remember at will nearly every incident in the novel, that the whole book was disturbingly back there in my brain with the rest of my sainted heroes whether I wanted it to be or not."[7] Harrison also finds that the best fiction works when it reaches a middle ground between sensuality and violence—a combination that is quite often tempered in his own work with an undeniably comic (albeit often dark) impulse. The author treats the themes of fragmentation and alienation and the tenuous relationship between wilderness and an ever-encroaching society with an eye toward the inevitable humor in our words and actions. Reinforcing the themes of alienation and lost identity in all of Harrison's fiction is the morphology of the narratives themselves, which take on an organic, free-form life of their own and rely on the author's own experiences and pastiches of the best American writing since the mid-nineteenth century. A vast store of knowledge that comes from his years of close attention to our history and its tragic and ironic consequences rounds out the author's formidable arsenal.

Harrison is, above all else, a writer who refuses to shy away from his own history. The biographical details of his life are not unusual in themselves, although he has turned the most memorable events in his life into building blocks that surface repeatedly in his fiction: he was born in Grayling, Michigan, 11 December 1937, and has spent his adult life living and writing in northern Michigan; his left eye was blinded by a friend when he was eight (Harrison's accounts of the incident vary, though there is invariably a sexual overtone in the retelling); his father and sister were killed by a drunk driver in 1962; he is an avid sportsman whose hunting and fishing friends include artists and literati Russell Chatham, Guy de la Valdéne, Dan Gerber, and Thomas McGuane.

Harrison comes by his passion for nature and a curiosity for objects honestly: his father worked as a state agricultural agent in Michigan and encouraged his young son to hone his observation skills, a trait that would become vital in all of Harrison's future work. The author's parents also encouraged him to read, and the writing life seemed as likely as any for a young man of Harrison's native curiosity and imagination. After receiving a typewriter as a gift from his father, Harrison began writing poetry because "I had an attention span like Richard Nixon's, very brief; poetry is a young man's form in a sense."[8] His penchant for immersing himself in topics by researching and experiencing them firsthand is legendary among writers, and in an age of word processors and Internet searches for information he still relies on a capacious memory and a legal pad for the writing of the manuscripts. (Harrison's fiction-writing career was nearly derailed before it began when the only copy of the manuscript for his first novel, which Harrison typed and sent to his brother John, was lost in the mail for a time during a postal strike.) Typically, the stories have fermented in his mind for several years before they see the light of day. The granary where he writes in Leelanau is littered with esoteric books on subjects ranging from dam building to Native American history to comprehensive tomes on the flora and fauna of North America. The wall in front of his writing desk is covered with pictures that recall many of Harrison's characters and his favorite historical figures, and hanging from one of the rafters is a collection of objects with totemic importance for the author, including a pinecone from the forest where Garcia Lorca was murdered and the compass that his friend Doug Peacock carried with him in Vietnam.

Harrison's fiction, nurtured by a voracious appetite for both American and international writers and poets, recalls Thoreau, Twain, Hemingway, and Faulkner in all the evocations of the icons of American literature (Pico Iyer, a consistently astute reader of Harrison's work, also compares the author's eye for detail to that of the more sophisticated social observers Vladimir Nabokov and Evelyn Waugh). In *Wolf*, Harrison's first novel, Swanson wanders the wilderness in an attempt to transcend the banality of a society at odds with itself, all the while recalling and reconstituting his reality in terms of the books he has read. One of Harrison's later protagonists, in the novella *The Beige Dolorosa* (in *Julip*), is a retired English professor who realizes that the literary knowledge he possesses is useless in the greater context of a struggle with a debilitating disease and the politics of the academy. That novella, like so much of Harrison's fiction and poetry, is undeniably autobiographical. In coming to grips with a life in books and his own mortality, Harrison articulates a sense of the urgent acceptance with which he documents his world. His characters study and emulate philosophers, writers, composers, and great works from Kierkegaard to Bellow to Beethoven to the Bible, and the characters he creates are accretions of everything he has read or experienced.[9]

Because of such varied literary and life experiences, Harrison eschews what he calls a "mono-ethic," a predisposition for everybody to want to do the same thing—"amazing, in a political sense, with all the diversity, to want some kind of unanimity"—which pervades the American conscience and has diluted American literature to the point that characters are neither believable nor wholly human:

> People don't want to know. Most of the people now who eat chicken, beef, or pork have never known an actual chicken, an actual pig, or an actual cow. This is life. So it's really kind of cultural snobbism. They don't want any real nastiness to enter fiction. They think it's really a polite game, and that's what it usually is and fiction should all be written by fucking Michael Ireland or Ronald Fairbanks. It certainly isn't from the depths. . . . But I'd rather in Neruda's sense have the sloppiness that can grab my gizzard than any kind of anal compulsive fiction. The sad thing in writing schools is when all the young writers are trying to write like Milan Kundera but none of them have had any of his experiences. It's kind of hard to be that distraught in Iowa City.[10]

In an analysis of Harrison's third novel, *Farmer,* an unnamed reviewer writes that "it is appropriate that Harrison, a man who can choose a learned word like 'fetor' over its synonym 'stench,' should also enrich his rustic hero's thoughts with some basic details of rural life: oiling an old harness, butchering hogs. Moreover, Harrison's dialogue is true to its setting—flat, almost toneless, yet still expressive."[11]

Still, Harrison's current selective academic appeal, in which critics often fail to separate the author from his fictive creations, stems in part from a concern in the academy for what some scholars see as a recurring misogynistic disposition in his writing. One review of *Legends of the Fall,* Harrison's greatest mainstream triumph, posits that women do not enjoy the novella because it celebrates a "fantasy of masculine self-sufficiency," and that while women are essential to the plot, they never understand why a "man must blaze his path in a solitary world."[12] In a 1986 interview with Jim Fergus, Harrison refutes the charge of machoism, a "particularly ugly peacockery, a conspicuous cruelty to women and animals and children, a gratuitous viciousness."[13] He also recalls in his own essays that the men in his family,

> though they all fished and hunted strenuously, would never describe these particular activities as "manly." That idea seemed to derive from writers of city origin like the tortured Hemingway, who, though a very great writer, seemed to suffer from a prolonged struggle with his manhood. Faulkner was a bit more nonchalant and colorful on the subject, what with his lifelong fascination with the "pelvic mysteries of swamps."[14]

The distinction between "macho" fiction and fiction written from a man's experiences (although, to be sure, Harrison has not confined his perception to that of men, as evidenced in his taking on the female persona in *Dalva, The Road Home, The Woman Lit by Fireflies,* and *Julip*) is an important one. In one of the few critical pieces that deals directly with the issue, William H. Roberson points out that "Critics who immediately delimit Harrison's work by a preconceived notion of macho are in effect attempting to dictate the subject of the works. Moral concerns become synthesized with aesthetic ones."[15] Julia Reed writes that "In this era of the literary starlet, when publicity has become a stand-in for talent, Harrison's relentlessly low profile seems suspect, almost perverse. His devoted readership has grown steadily, organically, spurred on the old-fashioned way, by the writing itself."[16] Certainly, even in his presentation of characters who are pushed to the margins of society or unlikable (or perhaps both), Harrison never loses the grain of truth that lodges itself in our national consciousness until the raw nerve of self-analysis is exposed, our dreams juxtaposed with the elegies. Harrison is self-critical to the point of being confessional, but at no point does his disdain for what he sees in society become overwhelming or absolute. Rather, he works within the contradictions of his own imagination.

The articulation of those contradictions is a result of a profound identification with Keats's "negative capability," the ability of "being in uncertainties, mysteries, doubts, without any irritable reaching after fact and reason," or, as Harrison writes, "the capacity a poem or novel must have to keep afloat a thousand contradictory people and questions in order to create the parallel universe of art."[17] Harrison has harbored the idea since his initiation into poetry as a teenager:

> When I first read Keats whom I loved very much even in high school, the hairs on my neck rose when I read about the *"Negative Capability"* because that's obviously what a novelist has to have more than anything else. The best example of this is Shakespeare or Dostoevsky—that's what their work is. Nothing human is alien to them. Nothing can't be examined. They never limit themselves to sexual neuroses like many Americans.[18]

Indeed, the author examines Keats's notion repeatedly in his essays and fiction. That portrayal is especially poignant when Phillip Caulkins, the same academic who battles academic politics, writes,

> I've been making literally cartons of notes since my book was published just short of twenty years ago. I daresay many of my notes are brilliant but I lack the ability to connect all of their disparities. The vaunted *"Negative Capability"* that Keats ascribed to Shakespeare is a curse to a scholar who is then liable to delay his conclusions to the grave. We catch ourselves frozen and stuttering in incertitude.[19]

The passage applies equally to both Harrison the writer and to his characters.

III

Though the currents of myth, place, and history run deep in all of Harrison's fiction and are inseparable from any discussion of the work, the seven chapters of this study are meant to be as varied in their scope and their themes as the novels and novellas themselves. From the symbolic and literal uses of food and drink in *Warlock* to a reading of *Farmer* as a regional novel, I give an open critical forum to the dominant ideas and most appealing stylistic quirks of Harrison's fiction. The study is not meant to be all-encompassing—Harrison has written twelve novellas, for instance, and a rigorous critical analysis of each is beyond the scope of this book—but rather an initial ingress into the mind of a writer whose work bears the weight of close scrutiny well and will be viewed in retrospect as integral in the canon of late-twentieth-century American literature. Because of the diversity of themes and styles in Harrison's fiction, I present these essays chronologically in order to give the reader of this collection a sense of Harrison's evolution as writer of fiction.

The limitations that Harrison sees in contemporary American literature manifest themselves through the critics' insistence on classifying Harrison's work, particularly his fiction, in order to package the author's ideas for mass consumption. In an explanation of the ghazals published in his third book of poems, *Outlyer and Ghazals* (1971), Harrison posits that in order to maintain the integrity of the artistic vision, a writer must

> . . . *choose what suits us and will not fairly wear what doesn't fit. Don't try to bury a horse in a human coffin, no matter how much you loved the horse, or stick some mute, lovely butterfly or luna moth in a damp cavern. I hate to use the word, but form must be an 'organic' revelation of content or the poem, however otherwise lively, will strike us false or merely tricky, an exercise in wit, crochet, pale embroidery.*
>
> *Ghazals are essentially lyrics and I have worked with whatever aspect of our life now that seemed to want to enter my field of vision. Crude, holy, natural, political, sexual.*[20]

For Harrison, the theory is equally true in all writing (it is also worth noting, perhaps, that his first novel, *Wolf,* was published the same year as *Outlyer and Ghazals,* a fact that suggests a mind that can deal with both poetry and prose simultaneously). In the same way that the form of the poem depends upon a deeply personal context, Harrison avoids formula writing, instead relying on a mode of expression that best suits the narrative's content and the author's own vision. And although much of the analysis in these essays is New Critical, focusing on the content and form of the works at hand and offering an unobtrusive theoretical grounding through which we can frame the novels and novellas, I break with that textual grounding on at least two occasions in defining specific works as either "regionalist" or "postmodern." Harrison himself would not agree with such a dissection. He has spoken out against classifying literature as "regional," preferring to view it as a series of slice-of-life vignettes that combine—with the right words and a well-directed passion for the material the amalgam is synergistic—to construct our impression of the whole. "What I hate about this notion of regionalism in literature," Harrison tells Fergus, "is that there's no such thing as regional literature. There might be literature with a pronounced regional flavor, but it's either literature on aesthetic grounds or it's not literature."[21] For Harrison, the rubric "regional literature" is itself limiting, the result of the

Urbanists' (read: academics') continued belief that the hub of creative and intellectual thought is in the city, and that whenever the cultured and urbane Manhattanite wanders into Middle America the result is bound to privilege cosmopolitan wit and wisdom over the exaggerated words and actions of one-dimensional rubes genetically predisposed to farming and pumping gas, not creating viable literature from the world around them: "Everywhere you look people are deeply totemistic without knowing it. They have their lucky objects and secret feeling from childhood. The trouble in New York is, urban novelists don't want to give people the dimensions they deserve."[22] Still, I argue, to view a work as "regional" in Harrison's case is to make a necessary and valuable distinction between the novels of American manners (in Updike or Cheever, for instance) that have become the staple of fiction publishing on the "Dream Coasts" and the fiction that derives its understated power from the specific places that define the experiences of "middle America."

In addition, the chapter in which I examine the postmodern elements of Harrison's novellas *Brown Dog* and its sequels *The Seven-Ounce Man* and *Westward Ho* and read the texts as pastiches of Twain's *Huckleberry Finn* poses a similar problem of classification/limitation for Harrison, who finds that "The post-modern novel suffocates from ethical mandarinism. It is almost totally white middle class, a product of writer's schools, the National Endowment, foundations, academia. The fact that this doesn't matter one little bit is interesting. . . . The literary world is one of those unintentionally comic movies they used to make about voodoo and zombies."[23] In deference to Harrison's own distaste for theory, I posit that to read the novellas as postmodern texts gives us an opportunity to conceive Harrison's style in terms of the alienation, fragmentation, and identity-making (and re-making) that are the touchstones of postmodern literature.[24] Such a reading also allows us to trace the evolution of Harrison's vision and to use the push and pull of literary theory to examine the divergence of Harrison's fiction away from the purely postmodern into a mode of narrative expression that amplifies the author's distinctly American literary voice.

While the fiction and the poetry are often the center of attention in Harrison's repertoire, his nonfiction provides us the opportunity to limn the creative process and to cross-reference much of the material that makes its way into the author's fiction. *Just before Dark,* a collection of Harrison's essays culled from a dozen or so journals, offers valuable insight into the creative mind of the author. Those essays contain the germs of ideas that become the characters, vignettes, and philosophical meanderings in his fiction. In reading and re-reading Harrison's work, I have focused my attention several times on a short essay titled "Fording and Dread," which articulates Harrison's passion for writing as a way of reconciling the beauty of literature with the unbearably brief movement of a life through time: "The limitless ambition of the young writer, whose vast, starry, nineteen-year-old nights must come down to the middle-aged man in the northern night listening for more howls, trying to learn what he is with neither comparison nor self-laceration, treasuring that autumnal sensuality of one who has given his life's blood to train his soul, brain and senses to the utmost."[25] Its brevity notwithstanding, the piece offers a cogent discussion of the author's philosophy of writing and his understanding of and appreciation for lived experience. That understanding, Harrison is quick to point out, is very often our single tenuous thread between existence and nonexistence: certain events in one's life come to the fore and inculcate themselves deepest in the places—the native spaces of geography and consciousness—where we protect their memory and where we finally are able to give them voice. Harrison sums up that notion neatly when he refers to writing (though he makes the comment specifically in reference to his poetry, surely the phrase is fitting in the body of his work) as "the true bones of my life." The title of this collection is apt, given the skeleton of words and ideas upon which Harrison hangs the muscles and skin, to extend the metaphor, of intense experience and profound passion.

Underpinning each of the essays in this collection is Harrison's notion that the "American Dream" as our forefathers understood it—that rugged pioneers heading into the wilderness could carve their niche into pristine nature, the fulfillment of some vaguely described and rarely questioned Manifest Destiny—is no longer tenable.[26] The author clearly understands and demarcates the boundaries of such misguided fervor. The "American Dream" in Harrison's fiction hauntingly echoes Faulkner's sense of mortality in *As I Lay Dying*: survive, and feel life at every moment, in every sinew of your being; once you're dead, you'll stay dead a long time.

·1·

" . . . no woods to travel far back into"

Last Great Places in Jim Harrison's *Wolf: A False Memoir*

I recalled a quote from [poet Drum] Hadley's mentor, Olson, in his book on Melville, *Call Me Ishmael,* "I take space to be the central fact to man born in America, from Folsom cave to now." This, whether illusion or reality, is a whopper of a statement, but it was more true when Olson wrote the book forty years ago, and certainly purer truth in Melville's time.

> —Jim Harrison, "The Beginner's Mind,"
> *Heart of the Land: Last Great Places*

Du schnell vergehendes Daguerreotyp / in meinen langsamer vergehenden Händen.

> —Rainer Maria Rilke, "Jugend-Bildnis Meines Vaters"[1]

I

"Everybody has to be somewhere, as the joke goes. We are all deeply colored in our nerve endings by locale," Jim Harrison says, and no theme is more important to understanding Harrison's earliest fiction than his analysis of place and its effects on his characters' states of mind.[2] In *Wolf: A False Memoir* (1971), his peripatetic first novel, the author illuminates both the perceived need for freedom of movement and its consequences on a ravaged American landscape. Although critics and readers alike often view the narrative as another installment in the saga of the Great American Road Narrative, the text strains against such classification, paying homage to the claims for the individual that Emerson, Thoreau, and Whitman espouse, ways of life through which one becomes the "authority about the nature of your most fundamental ties to the world. Your behavior conformed to, was sanctioned by, your innate capacity for moral judgment; no creed or publicly agreed-upon standards were required."[3] The novel recalls the work of many of Harrison's famous literary predecessors—Twain, Faulkner, Joyce, Hemingway—whose narrative structure informs Harrison's first attempt at fiction, and whose presence in the style and plot of the narrative buttresses the author's own search for a literary voice that had dealt exclusively with the language of the poet.

The author's stylistic duality in the production of poetic fiction that relies more on the effect of snapshot vignettes and movie-frame cutaways than traditional linear plot is a controlling frame of reference for the substance of the novel as well.[4] Americans' increased mobility, despite the romantic allusions we make to Kerouac and others in the two decades after World War II, contributed to (and in some cases, was the root cause of) the rapid disappearance of wilderness from the American landscape, a demystification of the wild places that had offered respite from an increasingly complex and alienating society. The expression of such paradoxical impulses ("should I stay or should I go?") results in an eloquent, if often rough-hewn, quasi-autobiographical statement extolling the preservation of last great places, a treatise on introspection and the profound influence that geography and "place" have on our lives.

Wolf is a complex introduction to Harrison's later fiction, a "false memoir" that plumbs the depths of Harrison's fiction-writing abilities. The subtitle suggests that Harrison is experimenting with the constraints of a genre that is relatively new to him and also hints at the play between personal experience and fiction, "the strength of the autobiographical juice" that allows an author to begin "writing about other people."[5] In the "Author's Note" to the novel, Harrison (Swanson) is quick to point out that "This is a memoir dealing mostly with the years 1956–1960 written from the vantage of the present—it is a false memoir at that and not even chronological and its author is a self-antiquated thirty-three, a juncture when literary souls always turn around and look backward. Most of the poisons have been injected, some self-inflicted; how does one weigh mental scar tissue?"[6]

Like the popular Zen way that Harrison's characters intermittently practice (or Harrison himself relates in *After Ikkyu*, a collection of Zen poems), the complexities and contradictions of time and the chain reactions that events often engender in our lives have little effect on

Swanson, whose own existence seemingly is one discrete and aimless event after the next. He is an individual who acts on visceral instincts and has little concern for his interaction with those around him: when a bar patron refers to him as an "Abbie Hoffman commie," Swanson elaborates that "I don't want anyone to adopt my mannerisms, or opinions. If I had those interests I'd run for office. My interests are anachronistic—fishing, forests, alcohol, food, art, in that order." [7] As Swanson's disdain toward the larger world suggests, Harrison is careful to distinguish this narrative from more *real* (not to be confused with more *legitimate*) wilderness tales, in which "The devising of a manner of inscription consubstantial with the place itself serves as correlative to the situated event as original, authentic, 'lived' within and not just 'written' about: a material testament."[8] Harrison is equally careful, despite his own familiarity with much of America's remaining wilderness, to give the narrative a "written about" quality that increases its effectiveness as a "false memoir." The premise gives Harrison a fictional space that allows him to write many of the "real" events of his life in the guise of fiction, the result of which is a narrative that "will paradoxically be truer than those usually called memoirs since, as the writer of an admittedly false memoir, he is free to invent characters and situations that better illustrate the truth as he perceives it."[9]

The novel is important in Harrison's evolution as a writer for the way it bridges the gap between fiction and poetry, the latter which, by the time *Wolf* was published, had won him critical acclaim as a stylist "relentlessly hard on himself: his past life, his present plights, his character in general," and a reputation as an author difficult to pigeonhole into any of the popular molds, as he "redeem[ed] the poems from grimness by a buffoonery of anguish and by something else that is more elusive."[10] In establishing a prose style—an idiosyncratic combination of folksy Michigander-cum-philosopher—Harrison's first fiction circumscribes the duality of our being: an outer world that encompasses physical space and the linear movement of time, and an inner world that shapes our "bifurcated selves, split into considering subject and considered object. . . . It is precisely this capacity for mirroring between the inner and outer dimensions that makes possible the 'inward voyage,' an archetypal form in which movement through the geographic world becomes an analogue for the process of introspection."[11] Harrison's ability to "mirror the inner and outer dimensions" of being is imperative to his continued success as a fiction writer, and the importance of the journey and an extraordinary sense of history, as well as the author's own keen sense of a literary past and his knowledge of the earlier masters of American literature, provide a "thick" American context within which he writes.

Despite the apparent success of his fiction (after all, Harrison's eleven works of fiction spanning thirty years are all currently in print), critics did not agree on the degree of success with which Harrison initially "crossed over" from poetry to fiction. Reviews of the book were mixed, and Harrison's own popularity as a poet undoubtedly worked against him for the reviewers who saw him as merely another "poet-turned-fiction-writer." Joyce Carol Oates questions the seemingly desultory organization of the narrative, positing that *Wolf* is a "small-scale, Americanized, pop *Remembrance of Things Past,* another tender chronicle of the road and the city, the unfocused young man with infinite adventures and no way of comprehending them." Her assessment of the novel as "the kind of diarylike work many writers publish before they can write their first significant books" is not unfair.[12] Clearly, Harrison is working outside the comfortable realm of the purely poetic here; while the novel does contain certain "diarylike" aspects, the real value of this novel comes from its themes and its primacy in the oeuvre of Harrison's fiction. Jonathan Yardley's words for the novel are more kind, and he seems to better understand what Harrison has accomplished in his "raunchy, funny, swaggering, angry, cocksure book. It's also a poignant, handsomely written self-exploitation that deserves comparison, if it does not reach such heights, with Frederick Exley's *A Fan's Notes* and Frank Conroy's *Stop Time.*"[13] Christopher Lehmann-Haupt's astute review of *Wolf* takes into account Harrison's poetic sensibilities and the difficulty of transforming the poetic vision into fiction, asserting that simply because the narrative is a "poet's novel," "does not mean it will prove inaccessible to readers who look for the meaning of novels in their action; it is only that in this case the action is as simple as a clothesline . . . and the meaning lies in the past incidents and the present observations that are pinned to the line like so many scrubbed rags hung out to dry in the fresh light of memory."[14]

The novel's working between two worlds, always with one eye on a distinct literary past, has become Harrison's modus operandi, and he admits that the narrative was an attempt at something new, and an "extremely direct, non-therapeutic attempt to come to terms with my life in the present."[15] During his stay in California, the protagonist

Swanson echoes Harrison's own writing life to this point: "From the vantage point of 1970 it appeared that all my movements since 1958 had been lateral rather than forward. I had printed three extremely slender books of poems. . . . A succession of not very interesting nervous breakdowns. The reading of perhaps a few thousand books and the absorption of no wisdom at all from them."[16] The love of books shared by the author and his protagonist is an important subtheme in the novel and much of Harrison's subsequent work. That love is also intertwined with the notion of the "false memoir," Harrison implies, in that the narrative should be read primarily as a fictive construct, like the "few thousand books" to which Swanson refers, and not as an autobiographical account, although several important events in the book parallel events in Harrison's own life. Through Swanson, Harrison references the death of his own father and sister, and many of Swanson's travel sequences parallel Harrison's own traveling back and forth across the country in the late 1950s and early 1960s.[17]

The exaggeration and deliberate falsification that Harrison mingles with biography in his own loose interpretation of the road narrative are inherent in the writing process, even in ostensibly "factual" nature narratives such as Wendell Berry's or Annie Dillard's, writers both known for their incisive interpretations of wilderness and its symbols. Randall Roorda cuts to the heart of the "big dilemma" in writing wilderness when he posits that one must choose between the wild and the text.[18] The site of writing for many apologists of nature, both literally and figuratively, is the windowless room, the ebullient, violent, or poignant scene remembered in the tranquility of a favorite writing venue. For Harrison, that site is a hospital bed, a place to contemplate home, to reconstruct his memories through Swanson, and to underpin those recollections with the remembered journeys of three decades in the Upper Peninsula wilderness and several years on the road.[19]

The experiences of place, then, become intertwined with the author's writing process (in fact, without the "textualizing," we would never know the experience at all), and for Harrison to write the narrative through the prism of writing-about-nature is doubly appropriate, given his love for, and knowledge of, wild places and an untimely confinement to bed. Berry's distinction between "writer" and "creature" in terms of the sites and senses of nature writing are especially important for Harrison's protagonist in *Wolf.* The lack of distinction between the two—the writer, on the one hand, who has inserted himself into the narrative but maintains his autonomy by constructing a "false memoir," and the creature, on the other hand, who remains symbolic, elusive, and only tangential to the story—recalls Keats's "negative capability," an attempt at reconciling the writer and the creature in the nature narrative by mustering the "capacity to structure oppositions without collapsing them, to raise issues without settling them."[20] Swanson's story *is* Harrison's story; Harrison's most difficult task as a writer is to bring Swanson to life through the guise of a "false memoir."

II

The narrative uses a complex, disjointed structure—a "freewheeling chronology"—to convey Swanson's struggle for control in his life.[21] The protagonist's recollections wash over him in random waves when he spends a week in the Upper Peninsula wilderness, and his remembrance of adventures in cities on both coasts and the encroachment of civilization on the intervening spaces intertwine with his experiences during his enlightening, if uncomfortable, retreat. The contradictions of writing nature are inherent in nature itself, a myriad of often strange, wondrous sensory impulses that can be articulated only as the accretion of lived experience. Explicit in Swanson's admission that he lacks a keen sense of nature is his own attempt at ordering his relationship with nature, Swanson's primary reason for returning to the wilderness: "There's more than a small portion of shabbiness to my love of nature; on most pack trips I've been on I've loaded cumbersome fifths of bourbon, so heavy but necessary."[22] He admits that in his quest to accept whatever nature has to offer him, "The only points in my favor were nonchalance and reasonably good health but I had none of the constant wariness owned by all good woodsmen."[23] The paradoxes Swanson raises in his internal monologue, a cursory and feeble rationalization for the failures he has orchestrated in his life, are at the heart of the narrative. Swanson wants to experience the mystical healing powers of wilderness, but he cannot purge himself of the habits that lead him back to the wilderness in the first place.

Physical death, which might occur in the unforgiving wilderness that Swanson describes, does not have the same attraction for him as the many spiritual and psychic deaths that he has already suffered. "It occurred to me the other morning," Swanson writes as he contemplates stray cats or skunks or killers or ghosts moving through the labyrinthine spatial and temporal matrix that underpins the narrative, "that people don't talk about [physical] death because even to the simplest of them death isn't very interesting"; he muses later after a night of "twelve double Jim Beams and a few steins of beer" in a pub in Boston that "I've had hundreds of intuitions of death and none of them, fortunately, were accurate."[24] That understatement, tinged with a hint of truth and philosophical depth, sets the tone for a narrative that treats its objects roughly and with contempt and runs its subjects through an intellectual wringer. Swanson's trek into the wilderness is not unlike the Native American vision quest or the forced solitude of the ascetics who isolate themselves in the wilderness to overhaul their spirits and who "routinely described a transcendent sensation of elation, oneness with the universe, and an appreciation for natural grandeur contrasted with their own smallness."[25] Indeed, Swanson experiences all these things, and he advocates the experiential wonder of youth and expresses his disdain for anyone who would take away his freedom and his mobility—two key components of a uniquely American mindset.

Swanson is thirty-three years old, situated nearly in the middle of the young liberals and the war-hardened conservatives who constitute the society-at-large. The reference to the author's (and protagonist's) age is clearly an allusion to Christ and implies the author-as-Christ-figure. Still, the narrative's religious symbolism should not be overstated: simply put, Swanson's own repeated crucifixion and resurrection, spiritual only in the sense of the protagonist's self-realization brought about by his external and internal changes of place, is central to the narrative; but the tenuous and unfulfilling closure he attains at the end of the narrative in his return home makes the memoir more introspective than ironic. Any parallels to the return of the prodigal son and any offhand or irreverent parallels to the persecuted and crucified Christ are undoubtedly little more than wordplay on the author's part. Indeed, in later works, Harrison expresses his disdain for irony, which he sees as an easy out for any writer of serious literature. As with many of Harrison's declarations on literature, however, this one seems to be a bit disinguenous and wholly negotiable.[26]

Swanson's singular ability to distance himself from others physically, to cast himself as the symbolic loner if not a true Christ figure, allows him to fulminate on his position in life and his intimate connection to the past. The way he vividly, if falsely, remembers the past allows him to connect memories of death to place: After his father's death, he throws his father's broken false teeth "in the swamp we had planted years before with multi-flower rose for game cover."[27] Swanson crisscrosses the country in five acts, in five different places, which only nominally detail his search for an elusive wolf, a symbol for the search itself, and the protagonist's halfhearted belief that is his cross to bear: "I felt that if I could see [a wolf] all my luck would change. Maybe I would track it until it stopped and greeted me and we would embrace and I would become a wolf."[28] Once, in fact, he imagines that he sees a wolf in the light of a full moon, but dismisses the sighting as a chimera, if only to extend his journey. His tacit realization that he has journeyed into the wilderness for much more than a glimpse of a wolf moves the narrative on to its logical conclusion: a return home. Unfortunately, Swanson is unable to see clearly, either in the present (the sighting of the wolf) or the past (the events he recounts as "false," but only reassuringly so). He is an outcast, a victim of his inability to adapt to place, whose concurrent appellation of community and culture runs counter to the notion, especially important in a "false memoir," that "solitude need not recapitulate an ethos of individualism, complicating easy equations between the person alone and the culture of loners. In certain of its moments, nature writing shows another permutation: solitary writerly invention associated with resistance to elaborated technology and a critique of modernist individualism."[29]

The five different places that form the five acts of the narrative—the Huron Mountains, in which the search for the physical wolf takes place and through which the protagonist recalls in depth his boyhood and early manhood; Boston and New York City, juxtaposed against the purity and seclusion of the wilderness, which allows Swanson his introspection; the West, as in much of Harrison's work, an invocation of Huck Finn's "lighting out for the territory"; and Swanson's home, where he visits his grandmother and reminisces about his childhood—run the gamut of geographical and cultural milieus and haunt Swanson's own restive search for a codifying point in time and of place in his life. He admits that "The argument at bedrock: I don't want to live on earth but I want to live."[30] For Swanson, man and nature, not time and the traditional linear course of events, are inseparable, and man's forced presence in nature, which manifests itself most violently in westward expansion and man's violence upon man, will ultimately destroy its resources, its last great places.

The personality trait that allows Swanson to maintain his tenuous grasp on the present is his dubious ability to rationalize others' roles in his own failures, psychological wounds infected by the disintegration of the physical world around him. The public library is one place of respite for the hyper-literate Swanson, who "had spent so much time reading magazines and writing my history of pain and grief" in the library, and he remembers "standing in a bookstore and reading the entirety of *Lolita* in two hours, then walking out onto the street with glazed eyes, a full-fledged nympholeptic. The power of literature."[31] He has read the Bible, Rimbaud, Dostoevsky, Faulkner, Mann, and Joyce, and he admits to having "fashioned myself on one of those young men [he has read about]."[32] Yet the present outside literature holds no attraction for Swanson, who wonders, "What would happen to me if there were no woods to travel far back into—or when there is no more 'backcountry.'"[33] He broadens his search for a niche in a society that becomes increasingly more confusing, unnecessarily complex, and destructive, environments that offer "a reduction in the quantity and quality of our experiences, as well as the erection of social barriers and hierarchies that relegate traditional communal responsibilities to bureaucracies."[34] Swanson's distinct advantage in his assimilation to the city is that he understands his relationship to place and can masquerade himself well, if only for a time, in almost any situation—many of which he has read about and cast himself as the protagonist. But Swanson's fantasies are not the stuff of the traditional bildungsroman.

Likewise, Harrison's wilderness is not the Edenic backwoods we might expect to find in fiction that often denigrates the impersonality, crowdedness, and aspirituality of the city. Rather, he juxtaposes the wilderness with "civilization" in much the same way that the first settlers of the New World made the distinction between paradise and wilderness: "If paradise was early man's greatest good, wilderness, as its antipode, was his greatest evil. In one condition the environment, garden-like, ministered to his every desire. In the other it was at best indifferent, frequently dangerous, and always beyond control."[35] The chaos and unpredictability of the unknown that denotes the settlers' inability to control wilderness is the same aspect of wilderness that draws Swanson back for healing, the pupil who returns to the master with the knowledge that the answer to his question is neither easy nor, in all likelihood, a tenable remedy to his problems. He explains, in a statement that echoes Harrison's own views of the fated interconnection of technology and environment, that "There is no romance in the woods in opposition to what fools insist. The romance is in progress, change, the removing of the face of earth to install another face. Our Indians were and still are great anti-romantics. Anyone who disagrees should be parachuted or landed by float plane in the Northwest Territory for a dose of romance."[36] Although Swanson implies an anti-romantic stance ("There's no romance in being alone,"[37] he writes, and for much of the narrative he is alone, most often of his own accord), "Writing may be as prone as any activity to the romance of self-sufficiency, which figures in nature writing's appeal from *Walden* on; there may be inscriptional equivalents to 'living off the land.'"[38] Swanson muses that "though I'm barely over thirty I come from the nineteenth century and a somnolent world with a top on it. I feel destined not to do anything about anything."[39] He bemoans the absence of the "far field" that he had read about from the great outdoor writers in his adolescence, instead substituting his own nostalgia for such romantic notions of the unbridled wilderness. Those sentiments recall Leslie Fiedler's encroachment vision and the American response, in which "the American boy becomes for a little while the Indian, the trapper . . . [and] finds it easy to think of himself as somehow really expropriated and dispossessed, driven from the Great Good Place of the wilderness by pressures of maturity and conformity."[40]

Swanson's sense of dispossession comes not only from the nature/civilization binary, but also from the question of his own identity: Swanson can trace bitter disavowal of romance as far back as his grandfather's passage through Ellis Island and the origin of his surname, which was changed without his grandfather's permission. The question of Swanson's true ancestry forces him to reassess his identity and allows him to write the "false memoir," the only life he is capable of writing: "Here is the story, the fiction, the romance—'My frame was wrenched by a woeful agony which forced me to tell my tale,' someone said a long time ago. I've never seen a wolf. . . . Perhaps I'll never see a wolf. And I don't offer this little problem as central to anyone but myself."[41] In coming to terms with his past (both his own genealogy and the broader European history that informs the world around him in the present), Swanson collides head-on with the two visions of wilderness that have come down to us from our first encounter with the New World: "The Great Good Place," which is both "erotically seductive virgin landscape or the maternally comforting lap or bosom of Mother Nature"; and the "cultural imperialism that softens the killer by making him a mediating force sympathetic to Indians, while villains of both races effect the work of genocide, and greedy white bullies tear down the forest and slaughter its wildlife."[42]

III

Swanson's venture into the wilderness, the place within which the recollections that make up the "false memoir" are given life, is the Huron Mountains, the rugged and isolated mountains in the Upper Peninsula of Michigan.[43] Even though he appreciates the beauty of unspoiled wilderness, the protagonist's view of the landscape that surrounds him is bleak and cynical. He remains in the place, in one sense, to rid himself of society's inertia, "to resist what will be a gathering temptation to return to more certain comforts. It will not quite be fear, but it will be next to this: a kind of existential humility born of a sense of all the life that surrounds and includes us and that will go on without us."[44] Swanson's is an attempt at "connecting" with the wilderness in return for solace, and he seeks out the "truly unimproved natural setting" that will facilitate that connection.[45] The protagonist takes great care in his description of the gateway to "the comparatively vast, the peopleless Huron Moutains" to delineate the destruction of the wilderness that once covered the Upper Peninsula, "a land with no appreciable history and a continuously vile climate."[46]

The contrast between what Swanson hopes to find in the impenetrable wilderness and the reality of the place is stark. Harrison's own perception of wilderness seems not to impose limits on the remoteness of the place, but rather on one's ability to come to terms with place without outside interference. The fact that so few wolves remain for Swanson to sight is an analogue to the alarm that many of Harrison's protagonists, who often wish only to experience "wilderness" in something that approximates a pristine state, feel when they come to grips with the reality of the situation. The depth of the true wilderness does not bother Swanson nearly as much as the notion that the wilderness is grudgingly acceding to the hand of man. The encroachment of man on the last remaining pure wilderness is an eloquent statement of Swanson's need to keep moving, and only when he wanders deep enough into the trackless wilderness that he becomes lost, using his map as a gauge of his retreat from humankind rather than a means of finding his way out, does he realize that there are, in fact, areas still unscarred by logging roads or other signs of human violation. The

seclusion he discovers provides him the opportunity to attune his
senses to his new surroundings in order to better recollect his experiences in the past—the reason, after all, that he has journeyed this far.
"Seeing new country or a new city has always wiped the immediate
past clean," Swanson writes of his conception of place and time that
helps to organize his many aimless journeys, which become blurred
and embellish the falseness of the memoir, the "false conclusions about
everything" that become the basis for the narrative.[47]

Swanson's quest for a glimpse of a wolf, itself perhaps one of the
protagonist's "false conclusions," is subordinated to his recollections
and made symbolic in light of his habitual searching for something
(anything) that might put an end to his restlessness and that could
order his past. One thought leads to the next in random associations
of place and the sensory impulses—both in the present and the past—
that Swanson collects and catalogs. The seeming insignificance of the
events that spawn Swanson's quirky behavior underscores the chaos
within which he recalls his past, and the accretion of several such
events on Swanson engenders his loss of innocence to the city, a sharp
contrast to the interaction of the protagonist in his Upper Peninsula
wilderness, in which the protagonist surprises a bear and falls into a
Faulknerian stream-of-consciousness pastiche conjured from his sense
of guilt at having encroached on the wilderness. The rush of memories encompasses the whole of Swanson's life: the random and sudden
destruction of his family, the inefficacy of religion to order his life, his
own inability to come to terms with his past and his future.[48]

Swanson's detailed description of a maid recalls the miscegenation
of Faulkner's characters in *Light in August* and *Go Down, Moses* and
gives importance, like Faulkner's Yoknopotawpha County, to a specific place in which time is often distorted to mark the interconnect-
edness of the past and the present. But Swanson cannot reconcile his
past with the present and the future until he rids himself of the visions
that poison him during his time in the wilderness. Out of boredom,
cruelty, and stupidity, Swanson shoots a turtle off a log with his rifle,
an act that prompts another flood of memories held together not by
temporal concerns, but by their evocation of place and the senseless-
ness of the act itself. His thoughts are drawn to death, a notion he earlier disavows. The thoughts actualize the crux of Swanson's story and
provide one of the few contextual groundings, elements of "plot," that
Harrison allows in the narrative: "When I got back to the tent I dozed
in the late afternoon sun. I wanted *one place*. Lost all character in

travel; in one thousand miles, even less, *one could become something because there was nothing to displace.* Stay here" (emphasis mine).[49] The individual case becomes the rule for the cynical Swanson; one traveler becomes the next, one experience blends into another and all experiences become the same—violence in the streets of Laredo, stabbings in the streets of Boston, police brutality in the streets of New York, and a safe place to eat in Utah all mean the same thing despite their very different denotations of the "American experience." Experiences repeatedly and forcefully become fictionalized as they come closer to articulating a reality (although the center of that reality is always elusive) that Swanson would rather not recall. All that remains is Swanson's ordering of the past in terms of place.

That place, the Upper Peninsula wilderness, repeatedly forces itself into Swanson's consciousness—a coyote's thin and dog-like bark reminds the daydreaming Swanson of his search for a wolf. More importantly, the sound prompts memories of his boyhood and the potency of mindless physical labor, which freed his mind for other imaginings, the introspection that he will hone into the fictive reveries of his profligate adulthood, the work that "dulled the brain, left the brain elsewhere seeking a sweet place to forget tiredness."[50] Harrison relates that his idea of turning inward during physical labor comes from reading Richard Slotkin and his anti-romantic accounts of westward expansion and Harrison's own notion, fueled by the fact that he is "not very evolved" and that his "brain is nomadic," that something must be done to occupy the brain during long periods of intense physical labor.[51]

Swanson's brain is likewise "nomadic," clearly both a manifestation and a symptom of his past life and its profound effect on his present. Even the smell of smoke on his body is enough to goad him into an uncomfortable half-waking reverie, "Asleep on the skin and awake at center," and he disingenuously attempts to lessen the importance of recalling past events: "Nothing more tiresome than the idyll of someone's youth. . . . How hopeless to live it over and over again, to savor only the good parts, forgetting the countless wounds which seemed to lie deeper and were kept masked with force."[52] But the theory does not fully explain his obsession with the past as he continues his nominal search for a wolf. Such thinking does, however, privilege the protagonist's place in the wilderness over the more confusing and dangerous city, a dichotomy that he will visit time and again in his seven-day journey.

Undoubtedly, Swanson's contention that he is not wholly comfortable in the wilderness but prefers it to the city characterizes his unease with his present life and the past with which he attempts to reconcile himself: "Not that I am competent at [living in the wilderness] or feel truly comfortable. It is after all an alien world still existing, though truncated, in many places but its language nearly forgotten."[53] Swanson exhibits two distinct personalities in the narrative—one in the present and one in the past—that are affected by both geographical and temporal concerns. That split is accentuated by the two worlds through which he roams. That the recollection ends with his father's death is significant: the three past journeys in the narrative before the final chapter, "Home," emphasize the increasing disorder of Swanson's life and his continuing search for the wolf that is his own "macerated brain" mulling the tortured events of a past that Swanson only wishes was inaccessible.

IV

Swanson's memories of Boston are not unlike his recollections earlier of New York, or later of the West Coast, and he says simply of the city, "I'm not very interested in my opinion of Boston" with a nonchalance that reinforces his preference in the present for the wilderness.[54] Swanson's recollection of Boston is written with the same regression and return as in the other journeys (he is, after all, confined to one place for all but the last section of the narrative). The Huron Mountains underpin Swanson's various recollections and create an immediate present that holds the narrative's "plot" together. Naturally, the city's filth and human presence have displaced the relative calm of the vast and unspoiled forest and the rolling thunder, a juxtaposition that Harrison uses in this novel and in his later fiction to great effect. Swanson's memories of Boston are intimately connected to place names and streets in the city, and the visceral images and scatology suggest Leopold Bloom's journey through Dublin.[55] The protagonist's remembrance comes as he sleeps in the cold summer air, several years and many places removed from Boston, the past and present connected by sensory perceptions both remembered and felt. At the same time that he begins to lose his grasp on the mythical and symbolic aspects of his journey, Swanson becomes intertwined in the two very different worlds of the story. The past and present lose meaning for him; linear time becomes irrelevant, and what is palpable for him at the beginning of the narrative becomes something that he can experience only through the developing "felt sense" that wilderness nurtures. The transition, however, is not tidy, nor can it be complete. Swanson comes to realize

> what many of Harrison's heroes will also learn: that while he is certainly not "of the city," and does not espouse the values of modern society, he is also not "of the wilderness." As much as he might embrace wilderness values, aspire to wilderness virtues, and long for mythic wilderness in America, he is nevertheless like the hanging man of the Tarot card, caught between heaven and earth, or like Adam after the fall, never truly part of either world.[56]

V

Swanson's first remembrance of his travels west orients the narrative solidly in terms of geography: "If you look at a map of the American West closely (I mean by West all land on the far side of Kansas City) you'll find an unequivocal resemblance to the topography of Siberia or the Urals. But television of course has proven this notion untrue—those thin blue and black and red lines on maps indicating rivers, roads and boundaries tell us less than the whole story."[57] His concern at the simplification and demystification of geography by television, which eliminates our need to travel in order to know and understand our country—a homogeneity that makes one place the same as the next and parallels Harrison's notion of the "mono-ethic"—is echoed in Richard Reeves's *American Journey,* in which the author posits that "I had found the differences in Americans, no matter how fervently celebrated locally, overwhelmed by the similarities. The sameness of tract homes, shopping centers, and hamburger stands—man's contributions to the countryside, rural and urban, northern and southern, eastern and western—seemed a deliberate, if unconscious, defense against the trauma of mobility."[58] Indeed, Swanson despises the earmarks of suburbia that proliferate and thrive, with their strip malls, pollution, and television towers, on patches of land that once were wilderness. The conspicuous signs of "civilization" that agitate Swanson are, in his estimation, symptoms of an inhibited and invariably hypocritical society. The same sensibility that spawns the suburbs and their trappings, Swanson muses, insinuates itself into our personal lives; we have acceded, finally, to the conservatives who preach that a society's adolescents should live like middle-aged adults.

Swanson's diatribe against conservative cultural mores becomes a dystopian vision in the wilderness when he sees an osprey nest and reflects that "Few of the eggs survive; DDT has somehow affected the reproductive cycle and the eggshells are too thin to withstand the weight of the parent. Might have looked into the fact before marketing."[59] The observation echoes Rachel Carson's seminal *Silent Spring*, which delineates the effects of DDT on humans and wildlife a decade before Swanson pens his "false memoir." Carson uses the chemical destruction of nature as a synecdoche for humankind's war against ecological balance when she observes that "As man proceeds toward his announced goal of the conquest of nature, he has written a depressing record of destruction, directed not only against the earth he inhabits but against the life that shares it with him."[60] Our last great places have been corrupted, and for much of the narrative Swanson is a victim of the inertia that manifests itself in recollections of past events in other places.

As he becomes more comfortable in the wilderness, though, he is not wholly helpless to make modest strides toward fully understanding the importance of place. The simplest acts become the most meaningful for Swanson. The geography of the place where he makes the decision to join with nature, as in Nick Adams's own escape from society in Hemingway's "Big Two-Hearted River," is a wild river that protects its best fishing with a particularly difficult traverse of land and water, a swamp that "abutted the lake. . . . I waded gingerly at first but the bottom was solid though my feet were numbing from the cold water."[61] His wading, a symbolic baptism that gradually washes away the psychic offal accreted through years of experience and the subsequent bittersweet memories, raises the possibility of Swanson's redemption by virtue of the fact that he is quite happy acting *within* nature, not *on* it. His main concern as he wades "around a point of firs jutting out into the water, by this time thigh deep in a patch of lily pads,"[62] is not to fish, but to find an osprey nest and wait for one of the birds to return.[63] Like Thoreau, his favorite bird is the loon, whose "coiling circular wail" recalls time's circuitous path in Swanson's life and his own balancing act between "laughter and madness." The recollection of his childhood conjures memories of a specific place, a manifestation of "a constant urge to re-order memory—all events falling between joy and absolute disgust are discarded. Some even favor leaving out disgust."[64] Swanson evokes the timelessness of memory, and implicit in that memory is the innocence of childhood and the purity of the places recalled—a simulacrum that symbolizes a specific, yet fleeting, node in time more than it recalls in faithful detail the immediate sensuous experiences of place. At this point in his search for redemption, Swanson, like Thoreau, is "not so much concerned with the literary recreation of places as with what lay beneath their surfaces."[65]

Clearly, "the literary recreation of places" is at the center of Swanson's narrative. The attraction of the road for the protagonist is not the superficial and often redundant events that transpire, but the diversity of the landscape, which facilitates the eclectic experiences that he relates and explains Swanson's inability to erase his memories of the past.[66] For Swanson, as with anyone who seeks the solitude of independence, escape means "freedom from schedules, commitments, memberships, and credentials; the highway journey also suspends for a while definition according to one's origins, profession, and geography. Movement also leaves behind restricting ways of looking at oneself and brings at least temporarily a frozen time and ever-changing space where all is possible."[67] Further, dreams and aspirations are realized on the road, and any perceived powerlessness that the traveler feels apart from familiar surroundings "has its compensation in knowledge gained along the way."[68] That knowledge for Swanson is the understanding that one must comingle the superficial realities of the road adventure with the deepest part of one's self that recognizes freedom in the anchor of a specific place.

Swanson's fantasy, however, feeds on a distinctly American notion of freedom, which is itself actuated by his restlessness, and his desultory search for the perfect place also hinders his interaction with nature and, at least for a time, blinds him to the reality that he must reconstruct before he can heal himself. In his travels, one place is confused for another and memory supersedes the reality of the present. As a result, in his present, Swanson has difficulty apprehending the simplest of sensory perceptions: "The hawk was sitting on the nest. I cursed myself for not seeing him land."[69] Swanson is as uncomfortable under the scrutinizing eye of the city as the bird is sure to evade Swanson's sincere, if untrained, gaze in the swamp. In the Huron Mountains, under the controlling gaze of the wilderness, he extols the simultaneous singularity and universality of his interaction with nature, and he "felt exhilarated for no particular reason—for all it mattered on earth the forest I was standing in could have been a far province of China four thousand years ago."[70]

Even as his distaste for certain aspects of the city distances him from fully assimilating to its culture, Swanson easily moves into the language of the road, which changes with the geography much as his attitudes change with his surroundings. He connects the act of forming language to the survival of the animal, a questioning of communication that becomes relevant again in his observation that "New York has the highest concentration of mumblers per square acre in the world. . . . Shirts spittle-flecked from it."[71] He wonders if, away from the babble of the city, he will be able to use the same language he has always used, or if geography will somehow alter communication until it becomes indecipherable:

> I've talked myself into the woods up here and will there be a common language when I return? Or is there a need for one or was there ever such a language in any world at any time? I think so. . . . Off in the dark there is a wolf who speaks his limited instincts to another. I imagine he knows that there are few of his own kind left. On Isle Royale they control their population without help. I'll talk to Villon or Marlowe tonight when the fire goes out.[72]

Harrison's subtle manipulation of time and language points up the complexity of the readable, if disjointed, text. Swanson's own thoughts, which switch back and forth from a murky past to a largely indefinable present (even though we seem to know as much of the story as the protagonist), prefigure Harrison's later fiction, which focuses on discrete vignettes at the expense of a traditional linearity. Here, language's ability to ground his quest is paramount to Swanson, who carves a place in the landscape of communication and attempts to order his life through both remembered dialogues and the events they describe. Implicit in his disdain at the loss of meaning in language is the calling into question the authority of his own memoir, which "springs from its proximity to the truth claim of the confession, a discourse that insists upon the possibility of telling the whole truth while paradoxically frustrating that goal through the structural demands placed on *how* one confesses" (emphasis mine). [73] Swanson's search for people with whom he might exchange the "intricacies of language"—those who, in retrospect, might validate his journey into the wilderness—results in a catalog of places and their people that characterizes his journey: Green Street, the Hanging Gardens, Grant, Geary, the Opera House.

As he nears the end of his week-long reverie, the reality of his present in the wilderness and his recollection of the past converge. In the

Huron Mountains, in the present, he pulls himself from a lake and can tell by the shadows "that I was well behind my schedule, the intended circle only half completed," not unlike the concentric circles he traces in his search for lovers in the streets of New York.[74] Visions of past lovers and his family's own journeys become more readily accessible to the protagonist; the search for lovers becomes comingled with his search for the wolf and his temporary transformation into a wolf when he does "a little dance around the fire and howled as loudly as I could. I howled and howled until I felt sure that all beasts in my area were adequately warned."[75] Now, only in the wilderness can Swanson create chaos from the silence and tranquility of his surroundings, as he had done in one of his breakdown periods when he "would only refer to myself in the third person and change my signature every day." Although his howling has served an important purpose in awakening Swanson to the possibilities of life, he laments that "In six days I hadn't so much as seen a wolf track, only the perhaps imaginary shadow crossing the log road near the source of the Huron."[76] He is astonished at his exhaustive and exhausted assessment of his own relationships, as surely characterized by psychic fragmentation as they are by physical distances.

As Swanson packs in preparation for his trip home, he offers his sincerest attempt yet at finding peace within himself, articulated as an understatement of death. He is careful to leave everything as he found it, to avoid physically scarring the wilderness as he imagines he has begun to destroy his own brain or as he considers the carnage of a shotgun-suicide. He cares for the wilderness—in the abstract and at the point of physical and psychic impact—in a way he has never been able to care for those whose paths he has crossed. Swanson treats his memories much as he treats the wilderness, a smoothing over of the used parts, an acceptance of certain facts as he reorders his existence. He still has little control over his life, and he fantasizes about restoring nature, much as he cannot restore himself, through the use of force.

VI

Swanson's return home is inevitable. After all, his quest for solitude, to see a wolf in the wilderness, and to cleanse himself of the past, is predicated on his involvement with others in that murky past. Swanson too clearly understands the notion that "dramas of solitude, while

defined precisely as sited outside human presence, cannot be understood as sited outside a web of community relations," and he revisits
Reed City, the place of his childhood. [77] The narrative's fifth and shortest chapter, "Home," provides the contextual grounding for the core
of the "false memoir" and gives the narrative closure at the same time
that it posits again the question of the factual and fictive in the retelling
of Swanson's story. Swanson carries his thoughts of the interconnection of nature and an encroaching society, "the romantic and inextricable intermingling of pleasure and violence in memories [that] have
the quality of an alabaster trance," into the final stage of his journey,
and his anxiety leads to an unexpected calm that, sweet as it is after
such a thoroughgoing psychic purging, forces the protagonist to realize that "I had changed my life so often that I finally decided there'd
never been anything to change."[78] He considers his life in terms of a
series of pointless jobs, his alcoholism, his marriage, and for the first
time fully understands the necessity of defining lives as journeys, not
series of unrelated events. Even the wilderness that has endeared itself
to Swanson is, like his relationships, ofttimes inhospitable to him; he
hibernates like a wild animal and dissociates himself from human contact, until he is able to drive back into the truest solitude of all to connect to the "surest of realities," "the human spirit and its dark necessity to realize itself through body and place."[79]

Swanson makes his way past his boyhood home and finds only desolation. His spatial and temporal perceptions have narrowed to this
finite and infinitely weighty place and to this particular point in time.
The continuous recollections and returns to reality that characterize
Swanson's time in the wilderness have brought him to the one place
that could codify his present and point him toward the future. The
homecoming, though, is something less poignant than Swanson
expected when he realizes that "My dad had been born in this house.
I wanted the impact of this to sink in but nothing happened."[80] Now,
the physicality of the house where Swanson stands evokes nothing but
another string of random meetings between people whom happenstance has brought together, and who will be separated without fan-
fare. Swanson's last impulse is to drive toward his grandmother's farm,
the storehouse of many of his pleasant memories, and "I went in and
she fixed me breakfast and we talked slowly about the living and the
dead."[81] The adventure books that he had read as an adolescent, an
analogue to the thousands of books that he would read as an adult
and wonder if they had imparted any of their rare wisdom to him, are

buried in the attic. He says goodbye to his grandmother, but does not kiss her. He recalls that "Perhaps she had kissed me as a child."[82]

As the circle of his journey gradually closes in an imagined kiss so many years before, a kiss that might in the present reconcile him physically with his home and the memories it evokes, Swanson finally, painfully, articulates the impulse that drives him to refashion his own narrative in the first place: a desire to return home, and a preference for the ascetic, aimless life—destined to be nothing more than a fleeting and elusive vision—that he conjures during his short stay in the wilderness. The landscape through which he attempts to redeem himself transcends even the majestic physical space that Harrison describes, and offers, in its evocation of memory in our own "false memoirs," "a clearer vision of the potential of landscape as a human necessity, quite independent of the specific real world correspondence of that landscape."[83] Swanson's future after he leaves his grandmother's home—his home—is irrelevant. He has succeeded, in part, through his immersion in place, in (re)writing his life, although that success is tempered by the knowledge that he cannot reclaim his past. Implicit in the protagonist's journey and his intense reflection is the notion that "Throughout history, people of all cultures have assumed that environment influences behavior. . . . Our actions, thoughts, and feelings are indeed shaped not just by our genes and neurochemistry, history and relationships, but also by our surroundings."[84] The individual events in the protagonist's life come into focus only when they are ordered in an apocryphal tale and in a context that itself becomes part of the ongoing story. Swanson's narrative articulates the overwhelming, and often agonizing, power of place. The "false memoir" is an eloquent statement on the immanent and inexorable pull of place—real and imagined—on the lives of the characters in Jim Harrison's fiction.

·2·

"Thoreau only pretended to loaf"

Philosophies of Conservation in Jim Harrison's *A Good Day to Die* and *Sundog*

Artists and philosophers are generally assumed to be exempt from ecological guilt. While engineers exploit nature, the poets presumably praise its beauties and the philosophers interpret its moral lessons. Whatever errors may have been committed by means of human technology, the human spiritual tradition is regarded as one that all can take pride in.

—Joseph Meeker, *The Comedy of Survival*

Resting in the autumn light we come to an old but ignored consensus: only the West's eternal wrestle for and with water stands to serve as any kind of inhibition to the growth. Even now, developers are casting eyes on the Yukon, wanting to ream it straight down to the American Southwest.

—Rick Bass, *The Lost Grizzlies*

I

The transgressions of society into a shrinking "pristine wilderness" are the focus of Jim Harrison's second novel, *A Good Day to Die (AGDTD)* (1973), a three-part narrative that predates by two years Edward Abbey's similar themes in the more recognized *Monkey Wrench Gang*.[1] Conversely, Harrison's fifth novel *Sundog: The story of an American foreman, Robert Corvus Strang, as told to Jim Harrison* (1984), a narrative in three voices, details the life of a man who builds dams and flood projects around the world. The two novels point up the contradictions inherent in a philosophy of radical environmentalism and the cult of

technology—both of which demand full compliance from their adher-
ents.[2] The unnamed narrator in *AGDTD* hesitates to destroy a small
earthen dam in Idaho just as Strang, the protagonist of *Sundog,* realizes
the dam-building technology he brings to underdeveloped countries is
often misunderstood and perhaps more often misused. Strang's culture,
unlike the anything-goes 1960s that frame *AGDTD,* is predicated on
expedience and ignorance, through which "many educated people find
it unpleasant that [electricity or food] comes from anyplace. It is a philosophical inconvenience that rivers be diverted and controlled or animals
destroyed."[3] More valuable to this study than a comparison of the two
cultures, though, is a contrasting of the two narratives that circumscribe
Harrison's growing concern for wilderness and trace an evolution in
Harrison's style that gives his characters greater depth than Abbey's styl-
ized modern-day outlaws. Harrison himself describes the characters in
Abbey's book as "plausible, sympathetic, in their sometimes comic
torments," and he concludes that "Abbey renders them as convincingly as he does the landscape with all the breathless intensity of a true
desolation angel." Still, as Scott Slovic points out, Abbey's characters
"are nonetheless caricatures, exaggerated character types," their political stance obscured by "the ubiquitous, often outrageous, use of puns
and other affectionate forms of language."[4]

The differences between the characters in Harrison's two narratives
are apparent in their motivations—the threesome in *AGDTD* are
closely aligned with Abbey's Hayduke, Smith, Doc, and Bonnie, while
Strang's sense of the value of dams has a profound effect on the narrator of that story—as well as for their markedly different understanding of human nature: the protagonists of *AGDTD* "generally fail
to reestablish meaning and purpose to their lives," and they can hardly
relate to Strang's own "literary ecology."[5] Harrison's later protagonists, however, including Strang, "succeed in restoring balance and
purpose to their lives, a fact emphasizing Harrison's changing world
vision."[6] In the decade that separates the two narratives, Harrison
shifts his focus from a prepossessing contempt for society—Abbey
without the exuberant and self-assured righteousness that accompanies the actions of his characters—to what is, in many ways, a more
realistic and mature trope that works within society's context, not
counter to it, by emphasizing re-creation and rejuvenation and giving
"full vent to all human loves and disappointments."[7]

The critical reception of *AGDTD* was mixed, although several
reviewers expressed disdain for Harrison's plotting and his attitudes

toward society in general, and women specifically. Sara Blackburn's feminist stance is typical of Harrison's most vehement critics, who regard his fiction as disturbingly and irredeemably misogynistic. Blackburn writes that the novel represents a "kind of super-machismo a-man's-a-man stuff," and that both the narrator and the author "clearly want us to see [the narrator] as somehow tragic, a heroic if lost figure upon the vast American landscape." She concludes that the narrative is "an adolescent book by a talented writer who, on the basis of it, is experienced enough to know better than to preach its me-burned-out Tarzan dogma," and she argues that "novels in this genre (soon to be outdated, I hope) always leave an aftertaste of self-pity and complacency."[8] The work did, however, have its champions. William H. Roberson defines the essence of the novel as a fleshing out of our society in the aftermath of the Vietnam War and the cultural unrest of the late sixties. Roberson contends that the characters' greatest crime is as benign as "being out of sync with the twentieth century."[9] William Crawford Woods lauds the novel as a "poet's book. Its metaphors are sharp as jagged bone," although the reviewer, like other of Harrison's critics who expect to find that the author's roots as a poet are mutually exclusive with his alter ego, the fiction writer, finds that the narrative is "more sketchpad than novel," and "Even by the looser terms of the present fiction, *A Good Day to Die* offers very little evidence that the writer knows how to find a story and then find his way through it." He concludes that the narrative is "a work of art. A bad novel, but a work of art. What a strange accomplishment!"[10]

Harrison's characters are, in fact, immediately recognizable as creations of a poet-turned-writer. That the narrator of *AGDTD* is a synthesis of expansive poetic motion, brooding philosophy, and raw experience is clear in the opening paragraphs of the narrative, a mishmash of catch-all philosophy and the understated (and too often unstated or simply abandoned, Harrison might argue) pleasures of life. The protagonist, who remains unnamed throughout, is double-anchored off Cudjoe Key, Florida. He wakes up with a woman he did not know the night before, he wants to go fishing, and he thinks as he fishes that "There is a long happy streak when half drunk: everything is possible on earth—love, sanity, enormous fish, fame."[11] The setting and characterization of the first scene are important in setting the tone for a simple story that "has a great deal of narrative urgency, propelled by characters who, once you've met them, you know it's going to be a godawful mess."[12] The frenetic action of the narrative takes place in a haze of drugs, alcohol, and sexual fantasy, themes not uncommon in the late sixties and early seventies, especially in the novels of Harrison's friends and contemporaries Thomas McGuane (*The Sporting Club* [1969]), Dan Wakefield (*Going All the Way* [1970]), and Richard Brautigan (*Trout Fishing in America* [1967]), among others.[13]

Harrison's male protagonists, the alcoholic narrator and Tim, a disaffected Vietnam vet who keeps his girlfriend in tow and at a safe distance while he solicits prostitutes, experience the alienation inherent to the social-protest novel. The narrator's alienation from the middle ground of "acceptable" society motivates the halting actions of the protagonists throughout. Although the narrative suggests a previous home life and some stability for the narrator, he spends several weeks in the Keys before he plans to head back north. His life is a struggle for balance between the reality of a society that profoundly displeases him and the release of drugs and alcohol, fishing, and women. The origin of the narrator's disdain for the damming of rivers in order to provide electricity to cities that he does not care to visit is simple enough: fishing is the only point of contact for his otherwise free-floating experiences, and the serenity of the stream and the one-on-one parrying with the trout erase for a time the myriad problems common to the tormented souls of Harrison's characters. As in much of Harrison's work, including the poetry, the water itself "so hypnotically wiped the slate clean again though only for as long as I was in the river. For a few hours, though, all problems—money, sex, alcohol, generalized craziness—disappeared in concentrating on the flow of water."[14] The narrator's dependence on the trout stream has defined his adult life, and his fear of anxiety attacks prevents him from feeling safe except in "three minimal areas of Michigan, Montana and Key West,"[15] even though he reluctantly, and without reason, agrees to travel west with Tim and Sylvia toward the manifestation of their final violent act against society.

When the narrator is not high or drunk, his credulous democratic ideas contravene the inherent knee-jerk conservatism that allows the damming of prime trout streams and prompts the three protagonists to consider demolishing a dam in the first place. Like the attitudes that have been drilled into Tim and the narrator by the heroic images (both real and imagined) that assail them daily, the aimless travelers protest for the sake of hearing their own violently obscure voices against the majority and satisfying other less righteous urges. The narrator describes "Tim's 'you'll never take me alive' attitude," and maintains that it "fit into the same code which was artificially inseminated a hundred times a year by the movies";[16] for all the braggadocio that accompanies the narrator's incessant rationalization of his actions, though, he has joined the journey to meet some real—if psychological and chemically—induced demons that only clear-running trout streams can abate. The narrative is, essentially, one of dissipation and entropy, and the three characters who make such aimless journeys to mitigate the perceived wastefulness of society are themselves the most wasteful inhabitants of that society.

The narrator and Tim form a contrast in styles that makes the narrator's fight to establish order in his own life even more imperative as the plan slowly deteriorates into chaos. The narrator unwittingly sets into motion the ill-considered and ill-fated demolition of a dam in Idaho with the drunken declaration that "They're going to dam up the Grand Canyon."[17] While the narrator incessantly and often unsuccessfully monitors his emotions as signposts to action or inaction, Tim "had neither the essential brains nor the metabolism to ever question himself. From childhood he had never slowed down, thus women were attracted to his velocity."[18] The narrator is obsessive, intelligent, and unsure. Tim is disinterested and compellingly and unpredictably violent, and he immediately forces the narrator to question his own best interests:

> I said that it had always struck me that unless you were able to become single minded about fishing and hunting you would fail. You were either obsessive and totally in control or you were nothing. [Tim] didn't appear interested in these subtleties. I suddenly thought that it would be fun to kick the shit out of someone in a few seconds, which was obviously one of his talents. I reflected on the multifoliate ways you parry when you first meet someone.[19]

The propensity for the narrator to speak without thinking, encouraged by the effects of drugs to verbally spar with Tim and then immediately regret what he has said, is apparent in his suggestion to Tim that "We probably ought to blow up the goddamn thing," to which Tim simply nods his assent.[20]

Edward Reilly connects the title of the narrative with the protagonists' proposed actions and observes that "Because of the onslaught of the twentieth century with its rapid and vast changes, both the novel's protagonists and the Nez Percé were 'disinherited.' Moreover, in alluding to the Nez Percé's heroically tragic flight and battle, Harrison underscores his protagonists' folly and their less-than-heroic lives."[21] On his return from Vietnam, Tim plays the role of the warrior, always on the warpath and always sighted on the goal, however improbable. That the protagonists are associated by the narrative's title with the heroism of the Nez Percé embeds the three symbolically and ironically in history and aligns them with the injustice perpetrated on the tribe. The protagonists and the Nez Percé both "symbolize Rilke's 'disinherited children' and the fate of the late 1960's generation, who would be dislocated by the Vietnam War."[22]

Tim, who understands the inevitability of the journey and (with the aid of pharmaceuticals) meets it head on, informs anyone within earshot that "We're going to the Grand Canyon. . . . We're going to blow up the dam out there."[23] Although the plan moves inexorably toward its climax from the time the narrator meets Tim, it is nebulous at best. Even the participants are unsure of the dam's very existence, and the narrator's conception of the canyon is based on a cartoon-like recollection of Evel Knievel's attempt at flying across the Snake River in a rocket. The significance of what he has off-handedly mentioned to Tim the night before finally occurs to the narrator and he imagines, in terms not unlike the pop and fizzle of Knievel's own ill-fated quasi-heroic attempt, "a mushroom cloud and turbulent water crashing and pouring through rubble. And men running like ants around the ruins of a huge dam. The valley would be flooded and people perish."[24] But there are no heroes in this narrative, and the narrator's inability to distinguish the reality of a luckless and drug-addled trio's recklessness from the fantasy of the stereotypically intrepid and righteous hero merely signals the myriad ways the narrator becomes "fated and doomed like a samurai or some tropical exile holding dark secrets."[25]

The stage for the trip west is set when, for the moment, the narrator convinces himself that he is involved in his own private jihad, a glorious, nearly religious quest for justice. While the narrator understands that he is weak-willed, and often acts only as a foil for Tim's aggression, Tim agrees to the plan with a visceral understanding, "lived only in terms of the act,"[26] of his own motives, which have been drilled into him by two tours in Vietnam. The narrator, whose perception of others is significantly more astute (and reliable) than his ability to act on his own behalf, posits that with Tim, "all that conscienceless vigor would soon fail him, as it does most between the mid- and late-twenties or early thirties when one first realizes one is alive and that like all other living creatures one has a beginning, a middle and a terribly certain end."[27] He muses that the relationship between

Tim and Sylvia, the most human aspect of the protagonists' journey and the only sympathetic relationship in the narrative, "was all very pitiful in a way. These two didn't seem to belong to the twentieth century though they bore so many of its characteristic scars. I've always wondered how people who don't know anything about history get by but I've realized if you are ignorant of history you're not lost in it."[28]

Sylvia, who refuses to stop loving Tim despite his ill-treatment of her, is not unlike Harrison's other heroines—strong and intelligent, possessing "innate virtues and values that could stabilize her in a world of flux," even though she "is adrift in an impersonal modern world that batters her altruistic values and her very being."[29] Because of her love for Tim, she, like Tim and the narrator, is destined from the outset to see the journey through to its tragic conclusion. The whole idea, the narrator thinks without taking action to stop it, is "so helplessly accidental; a day and a half before I was in the middle of my usual excitement over fishing and now I was within hours of leaving for the West, the ostensible reason being to blow up a dam."[30] As the trio prepare for their journey, the narrator considers his own displacement, a symptom of his larger problems, although "For once it didn't seem to matter much. I was along for the ride. Maybe we would do something interesting. If we blew up some dam it would have a sort of final interest to it like a fishing record that couldn't be taken away from you."[31]

The narrator's musing over the proliferation of machinery, like the dams that block trout from spawning or turn rainbow trout riffles into flat, slow-moving, desolate stretches of water, stirs a recollection of his body as a motor, and inculcates him in the progress of the machine at the same time that he contrasts his own notions of wilderness to the rapid and wanton expansion of technology. The narrator is envious of Tim and Sylvia, who are oblivious to the rationale behind the act, and simply keep moving as a way of not dying. Naturally, action devoid of thought creates the chaos on which Tim thrives, and the narrator again bemoans the evanescence of order, that "there was no sense of balance left in anything we were doing. All that had begun as an innocent boozy comment crossing Duval Street so many miles away had become fact and we weren't accomplishing anything but pulling our own particular emotional plugs"; he expresses distaste at his own urge to emulate Tim and Sylvia when he thinks, "I was tired of imagining actions and having them come down to merely nothing, or something as confused as what we were taking part in."[32]

Although the narrator admires Tim and Sylvia for their ability to block out distractions in their single-minded quests (Tim for the dam, and Sylvia for Tim's love), he is most bothered by Tim's fixation on the dam, not as an object that encroaches on good trout fishing, but rather as an object that exists simply to be destroyed: Tim "had become obsessed with the romantic aspects of sabotage and was always fishing around in the *Blaster's Handbook* for useful information while Sylvia tended to dwell only on her love problems and had forgotten, in fact, why we had come west in the first place."[33] Later he admits to himself that he is captivated by the romantic aspects of destruction when he imagines that Sylvia is a Nez Percé squaw. Romantically linking Sylvia with his nostalgia for the Nez Percé is another misguided attempt by the narrator to reorder his life rather than fulfill his ostensible goal of conserving nature. Both the narrator and Tim exceed the limitations of their tenuous devotion to the cause, and their delusions seal their common fate. Even the narrator, who realizes that "We were getting uncomfortably close to having to actually carry out our plans that had been made so blithely," and who imagines his picture on FBI posters at the post office, experiences a fatalistic resignation to carrying out the dam's demolition.[34]

In their discussion of possible escape routes, the memories of places where the narrator has been or would like to go recall a state of mind for the narrator that only partially explains his motivation for following through with the project. Like Carol Severin Swanson in Harrison's *Wolf,* in which the protagonist's search for a wolf becomes a symbolic search for self and an ordering of the past, the narrator can order his memories only in terms of place, and the final place is the dam in Idaho, a point in the narrator's reality that can be manipulated and destroyed so that the narrator may palpably reconnect to the physical world. That connection throughout the narrative is tenuous at best; ideally, the narrator's tormented past, which had put him in a depression "so severe . . . that I no longer noticed my wife, daughter, dog,"[35] will be destroyed along with the dam. The reverie prompts the narrator to fish in a dangerous part of the Yellowstone River, where his previous thoughts of suicide become intertwined with his fascination of place and his desire to conquer the fear of places that he articulates earlier. The scene echoes Hemingway's "Big Two-Hearted River," in which Nick Adams returns to the river to reconcile himself with some unspoken tragedy in his life: the river, however, becomes the narrator's enemy in Harrison's narrative, and when his boots fill with water, "My panic was instant and the surge of energy was incredible. . . . When it was dark I made my way back to the car and drove into town where I drank until I was comatose despite the pain of swallowing."[36] In comparing Thoreau's *Walden* to "Big Two-Hearted River," Louise Westling sees "a violence and ruin encoded in Nick's Upper Michigan landscape that is completely absent from most pastoral writing and certainly from Thoreau's Walden Pond."[37] If the story of Nick Adams is one step removed from Thoreau's pastoral toward the violent and ruinous, certainly the narrator's episode in *AGDTD* is so far from the pastoral as to be parodic of Thoreau and Hemingway, a notion that emphasizes the absurdity of the quest.

The narrator's brush with death on the river that had always acted as his symbolic umbilical cord to reality and, until now, most often rekindled his life-fires, foreshadows the tragedy and pathos (perhaps even bathos) of the narrative's conclusion. The narrator ruminates on his own mortality and suspects that "Tim wanted to slow down for the same reason I did—after our long burst of verbal energy expended in detailed planning, the future which was to be painted with a series of explosions began to appear as excessively close."[38] The narrator's honest assessment of the situation compels him to again consider his haunting past, even though he is not prepared to take responsibility for his actions: "[Tim's and Sylvia's] talk seemed to indicate a direct connection with the past and what they were now. This was startling and I felt envious. There was a shrill phenomenology in thinking about my own life in comparison—the 'we are one thing because we are not another' sort of confusion: I am only here near Bondurant, Wyoming, because I am not in the Marquesas fishing."[39] The narrator's consideration of the past becomes significantly more complex and disturbing as the journey progresses, and the imminence of the dam's destruction affects his dreams, which "orchestrat[ed] all sorts of explosions which were conducted by my dead father."[40] The simple, brutal act of destruction is motivated, finally, by the possibility of closure that his past has never afforded him; his willingness to carry out the plan speaks more to a Calvinistic predetermination for the failure of the plan than to any maleficent impulse for wanton destruction or any altruistic desire for ecological conservation.

The narrator's bravado, always mitigated by his repeated consideration of the ramifications of such an act and his wavering throughout, undermines the common critical assertion that Harrison is wholly preoccupied with the "machismo" of his characters. Rather, the motivation for their actions makes them more pathetic than sympathetic, and the narrator's "lack of courage emphasize[s] his absurd, rather than macho stance." Additionally, "Although Tim is more macho than the narrator, Harrison undercuts Tim's machismo. . . . Not only do Tim's reckless driving, fistfights, alcohol-drug binges, and living only in terms of the act symbolize his dumbbell machismo, but his machismo is especially evident when he is pointlessly killed in the dam explosion."[41] Even in his capitulation to carrying out the act, the narrator cannot help but think that

> I had so little of what I thought of as courage. It was easy enough to suppose that courage was somehow mixed up with energy and your metabolism; I knew that it was unlikely that Tim ever backed down from a fight . . . , and blowing up the dam seemed as simple to him as having a meal or going to a movie. . . . And the Nez Percé who had battled on the ground where I stood had a saying when war was near—"Take courage, this is a good day to die."[42]

The narrator concerns himself with the details of Gibbon's raid on the Nez Percé, and his well-intentioned but misguided outrage at what must have happened as he associates himself with the Nez Percé. He replays the slaughter in his own mind, when "Soldiers from Fort Fizzle killed fifty of our wives and children. It couldn't compete with Wounded Knee but then it is difficult to see atrocities racing neck and neck for the atrocity championship," and he laments the fact that his place in history will be nothing more than a flyspeck at best, or perhaps an "anti-legend."[43]

The sight of the dam shocks him from the heroic fantasy of the Nez Percé and the miseries of his own life to the reality of their plan, and strengthens the pretense of their ambition and the irony of the trio's association with the Nez Percé, "who were dedicated to preserving a way of life that was unjustly being taken from them, [while] the narrator and Tim have not been as unjustly treated as they think they have."[44] A cattle pasture surrounds the dam, and both the narrator and Tim decide that to destroy any of the cattle along with the dam would be cruel and unnecessary. The passage brings to a climax the contradictory and wholly irrational impulses that have characterized the journey, the concern for the cows in contrast to the protagonists' disregard for their own well-being.

When Tim lights the fuse on the dynamite, a catalyst for the kerosene and fertilizer, he is caught on the breast of the dam in his attempt to clear stray cattle from the blast. He and two of the cows are killed. Tim's death, along with the deaths of the two cows, offers an ironic symbol of biblical proportions in describing the rebirth of the narrator, who is figuratively purified in the blood of both his friend and the cattle, "the baptism in the blood of a beast. Quite often, indeed, the holy marriage is sanctified by the ritual killing of a totem, the ram offered in the place of Isaac."[45] Leslie Fiedler's assertion that "In the forest rather than in the brothel or bedroom, through murder rather than sex, the child enters manhood, trembles with nausea over the broken bird or lifeless rabbit rather than the spread-eagled whore" is correlative to Tim's death.[46] The narrator's clumsy and unsuccessful attempts at seducing Sylvia emphasize his childlike acquiescence to his numbness at Tim's death: "I knew that in a very direct way I was responsible [for Tim's death] but felt nothing."[47]

Any order that the narrator has hoped that he might restore to his life is destroyed along with Tim and the dam. The narrator's final tragedy is his inability to feel anything at the death of his friend, even as he finally takes responsibility for his actions. In the car's rearview mirror, the last image the narrator sees when he and Sylvia flee the scene are the "tribal stripes"[48] that Sylvia had painted on the narrator and Tim before they planted the explosives. The final irony of the narrator's connection with the Nez Percé is clear: perhaps it is a good day for Tim to die, and a bad day for the narrator to survive; the narrator is left alive to struggle with his own indecision and bad timing, and the results of his actions are as inconsequential as the metaphysical smallness that he feels as he stands on the rim of the Grand Canyon. He feels "sure that I would eventually be caught," and "An act that I had conceived of as heroic would probably go unnoticed except by a rancher who might wonder why his dam had never washed away before." He concludes, in a rare moment of brutal honesty, that "Someone should take care of [Sylvia] but if I had any qualities of kindness and mercy left, any perceptions of what I was on earth however dim and stupid, I knew it couldn't be me."[49] We are left to wonder if his disavowal of responsibility for Sylvia is by choice, or through an acceptance, finally, of his own inability to act—either on his own behalf, or anyone else's. The act which, if the narrator were to follow through with it, would become redemptive in light of the nearly comical tragedy that has befallen the trio, instead becomes a pathetic reminder of his own shortcomings.

By setting his characters up to fail, Harrison articulates the "deep ambivalence" that many contemporary writers feel for the frontier—both its mythic past and its quickly changing present: "On one hand, [many American writers] nod longingly toward some frontier American values and recognize positive traits associated with the pastoral frontier. On the other hand, they acknowledge the limitations that a nostalgic, rearward-looking frontier emphasis produced, and they recognize the problems spawned by playing what [Larry] McMurtry calls 'symbolic frontiersman.'"[50] Although he tries to convince himself that the act of destruction is heroic, the narrator sees himself in the rearview mirror as he did when he was a boy playing cowboys and Indians. The destruction of the dam, especially important in the context of Harrison's use of the Nez Percé legend, is a parody of both the Myth of the Frontier and the "last stand" narrative, a refashioning of a heroic past in order to valorize the present. The Myth of the Frontier draws "implicit comparisons between the present war and the wars of our heroic past," writes Richard Slotkin, "especially the Indian wars; centering the action in a small, isolated, ethnically diverse band, which often contains 'natives' and which fights in guerilla or commando style; building the story around a 'last stand' scenario in which heroic representatives of American civilization sacrifice themselves to delay the advance of a savage enemy."[51] In *AGDTD,* the protagonists' perceived "savage enemy" is a society that transgresses a wilderness which, according to Slotkin, has never existed in the pristine state upon which many of our romantic notions of wilderness hinge. Clearly, in this instance, the actors are their own worst enemies, and society hardly need pay them heed. The irony of the protagonists' association with Native American culture is pervasive and, in spite of Tim's melodramatic demise, nearly comic in its absurdity. Instead of becoming a hero, the narrator is rendered impotent both literally and figuratively: by Sylvia, who refuses his advances, and by his inability to decide whether he is a rebellious youth or an adult who can work his way into and through mainstream society to achieve some nebulous and ill-considered end.

As with *Wolf* before it, *AGDTD* "ends indeterminately in that both Swanson and the narrator are not sure what the future of their families and their own lives will be."[52] The narrator's life is one of rapid dissipation and decay into a seductive counterculture that, by the time Harrison published the novel, was being exposed as escapist and exhibitionist. Although the narrator asserts after the dam's destruction and his friend's death that "I felt oddly alive. Suicide wasn't the question,"[53] he faces a constant struggle with his own mortality and decides that "Suicide was a thought that consistently held vitality."[54]

II

Although Harrison's portrayal of the self-aware, philosophical, and intelligent Strang, the protagonist of *Sundog,* differs markedly from the psychotic synergy of the protagonists in *AGDTD,* the complex love-relationships between the narrative's three major characters have prompted some reviewers to question Harrison's ability to write convincing interpersonal relationships and to problematize his penchant for extolling the faults and combative attitudes of his marginal characters. Despite Harrison's assertion that Strang is a conglomeration of characters he has known and about whom he is comfortable writing, A. C. Greene concludes that in the case of *Sundog,* "Sometimes . . . even the strong stumble."[55] Michiko Kakutani, who contends that "In his previous books, Mr. Harrison has celebrated a similar macho esthetic [as that in *Sundog*]," writes that "Given Mr. Harrison's two-dimensional depiction of Strang, he is not a character capable of supporting an entire novel."[56] Richard Deveson, who admires Harrison's nature writing and acknowledges that "Nature is nearly at the center of this novel," discredits the "book's real core," "the narrator's hero-worship of Strang, and this is never properly subjected to scrutiny." Additionally, he asks, "Why is there an American need for supermen who stalk the wilderness? Why does Harrison seem at pains to avoid asking the question?"[57] An unnamed *Publisher's Weekly* reviewer anticipates Deveson's questions with the assertion that, "As his new novel makes abundantly clear, Jim Harrison understands people. . . . The writer, in his own way just as interesting a character [as Strang], is fascinated by Strang's will to live and strength in the face of great pain."[58] The protagonists, far from simply representing a search for an American Superman, "help the writer to rediscover his own strengths; they, in turn, are buoyed by his lyricism . . . in this quietly beautiful book."[59]

Significantly, Harrison's impulse to create Strang "came out of my conviction that the American literary novel as opposed to a more commercial kind of novel tends to ignore about seven-eighths of the people. The literary novel often concentrates itself upon people in New York or Los Angeles, academic and scientific communities. People don't write about the Strangs of the world because they don't know any of them."[60] In his intelligent and thorough analysis of *Sundog,* Pico Iyer combines a discussion on the ease with which Harrison moves between society and its margins with an uncommon understanding of Harrison's literary influences:

> Naturally enough, the patron saint of such a faith [as Harrison's and Strang's natural religion] is the household god of woody cabins, the guru of all craftsman, *isolatos* and pioneers, the yogi who turned common values on their heads, Thoreau. It was he, after all, who first forged a way of living at an angle to American society—and there is no more ardent angler than Jim Harrison. It is no coincidence, then, that Harrison and his characters go fishing with Thoreauvian ceremony and deliberation. For they approach rivers in much the same way as the transcendentalist meditated on his pond: to plumb silence and solitude, to take the depth of their nature and of a Nature that will never be theirs.[61]

Iyer also praises Harrison's narrative voice, "which brings to mind those writers like Henry Miller and his spiritual descendant Charles Bukowski, who boast voices so strong and compelling that they can speak in no voice except their own."[62]

In fact, the strength of Harrison's voice in *Sundog* is all the more noteworthy for its complex intertwining of three distinct narrative threads—Strang's, the narrator's, and an underlying narrative text that unifies the plot and moves the story to its conclusion—the sum of which describes a tangled ménage à trois among Strang, his ex-wife's niece Eulia, and the narrator, perhaps (or perhaps not) Harrison himself.[63] The unifying theme in the narrative is the dam-image—symbol of man's tenuous control over nature and his desire to impose order over nature—to which Strang, much like the narrator and Tim in *AGDTD,* avidly devotes his life initially through happenstance.

In order to construct a coherent narrative, the narrator of *Sundog* asserts the profoundly personal scope of his experience in the "Author's Note," in which he rearranges (in a structure not unlike that in *Wolf*) his notions of reality and underscores the poetic aspects of Harrison's fiction." The narrator writes that "I felt compelled for reasons of readability to edit out information of a highly technical nature on the building of hydroelectric dams and large Third World irrigation projects," and he observes, in contrast to the protagonists in *AGDTD,* that the wilderness is "not shrinking as fast as I previously had thought."[64] Though he asserts that "this is not my story, and I will keep my intrusions to a minimum," he only intermittently keeps that promise; [65] still, his own insights are important to the story's form in terms of both the relationships between Strang, Eulia, and the narrator, and the narrator's own understanding of the caprices of a vanishing and increasingly unpopular American idealism, here illustrated by Strang's dogged determination to continue his work as a builder of dams.

The form of the narrative parallels the themes of much eco-writing. The cumulative effect of the three different voices is to "resemble ecosystems in that they present a large and complicated panorama of experience in which the relations of humans to one another are frequently represented in the context of human relationships to nature and its intricate parts." [66] The Renaissance man Strang, unlike Tim or the narrator of *AGDTD*, is a hero after a fashion, the strongest of the three voices, and the voice, paradoxically, of nature, technology, and understanding; Harrison clearly understands that his protagonist's heroism is not typical. At the opening of the narrative Strang, who has fought epilepsy since childhood and finally must cope with the consequences of a near-fatal herbal "remedy" that he once took as a cure for the disease, is physically unable to continue the work that has defined his life. His heroism comes not only from his voice and his actions, but from their source—intricate childhood memories that predict his career as a dam foreman, his psychic strength in the face of adversity, and his unwillingness to acquiesce to the whims of his ex-wife, a symbol of the limiting aspects of a society that Strang vehemently distrusts and avoids.

At the outset, the narrator aligns himself more closely with people like Strang's ex-wife than with the Strangs of the world. He hits upon the idea of writing the narrative only when Strang's ex-father-in-law suggests that the narrator's past books are "nice enough, but you might try writing about someone who actually does something." [67] He visits the man, Marshall, and his daughter, Strang's second wife, and when he tells them that it "rarely occurs to people like myself just who actually goes into a jungle and builds an immense dam or who engineers the irrigation of thousands of acres of desert," it is a tacit admission that he is a one-dimensional, cynical, self-centered man who regards the world exclusively in terms of the past. [68] That admission at the beginning of the narrative, however, also hints at the transformation he undergoes through his relationship with Strang.

The narrator begins his search for Strang in part as a personal quest for knowledge and as a result of dissatisfaction with his previous life as a writer of features on a number of uninteresting celebrities, and he wonders if he should bother Strang, who "had lived and worked in a world that no one but its inhabitants knew."[69] In order to catalog the accumulated knowledge that Strang will give him, the narrator tapes his research, which is presented in the narrative as background information on Strang and a series of dialectical comments that reveal the author's own thoughts on the lengthy and revealing interviews. The narrator's organization of material recalls the interviews with the "famous" people who have jaded him toward society in the first place and provides a means of creating a hybrid text through a narrative structure that combines aspects of journalism and literature, between the mirror that inaccurately reflects the realities of our society and instead offers a skewed view of life in which "the roots of literary distortion are always located in the writer himself, in the deflection and refraction of the material in the filter of the self."[70]

The narrator's first tape records a biography of Strang, who was born in Engadine, Michigan, in 1935. The listing of Strang's work, which runs without interruption from 1953 to 1983, informs the narrator's later psychological analysis of Strang's unwillingness to accede to his disabling condition.[71] The tone of *Sundog* is one of admiration for Strang's accomplishments, certainly a departure from that of *AGDTD* in which the narrator calumniates dam builders as the destroyers of nature (and more important, destroyers of good fishing). In tape 2 of his observations, the narrator recalls that "A little while ago I tried to study Strang's dam handbook, along with a glossy folder Marshall gave me extolling his firm's expertise in overseeing these giant projects. I read how a dam in Brazil has taken a decade and thirty thousand men to build. Marshall told me scornfully that most people have no idea where electricity comes from."[72] The narrator contrasts the places in which Strang has worked—the true frontier—with the quasi-frontier of the places through which he travels, and implies that society has more to worry about than the damming of its rivers: "You could enter schizoid Michigan in the Detroit metropolitan area, where the old West replays itself with over six hundred murders a year, the new mythology, not the quick-draw face-off, but the squalor of anonymous slaughter."[73]

Strang represents a new kind of character for Harrison, who says that in Strang, "I wanted to create a hero who was free from dread. Dread and irony have gotten to be literary addictions. And I noticed there are people that live without it. So I created this character

Strang." [74] Indeed, one would do well to include Harrison himself in the group of writers who struggle mightily (and with varying degrees of success) against "dread and irony" in their works. Harrison's contention that he created Strang in order not to accede to dreadful and ironic impulses is perhaps the best illustration of how the author's own *Weltanschauung* transformed in the decade between the publishing of *AGDTD* and *Sundog*. Strang avoids becoming a grotesque character through his persistence and a strength of will that transcend his physical limitations, and he revels in the brutal physicality of his rehabilitation and can laugh at his own fragility when he recounts that in a previous crawl, "I covered too much ground and then had to get back. I goddamn near croaked getting back." [75]

The narrator's first impression of Strang, that his hazel eyes are cold and distant, is unfounded. Strang willingly engages him in conversation and details one of the most personal and painful events of his life when he discusses the rape of his niece Esther: "The worst suffering I see back here in the States is another matter. People here suffer terribly without knowing why. They suffer because they live without energy. . . . If you think a factory smokestack is ugly, just look at one with no smoke coming out of it. These folks have trapped themselves with the help of the government and companies." [76] The irony of Strang's remark is unmistakable in the context of the aimless and self-aggrandizing journey of the protagonists in *AGDTD*. People live without energy (a play on the word, both in the sense that they are dispassionate, and they have no electricity) or passion for life because they refuse to act as protectors of their own environment; the notion underpins the narrative's nature-life theme and contrasts Strang's life as a "sundog" with the destruction of the dam in *AGDTD*. When Strang admits that "I don't really know politics, but I'm just giving you observations," he emphasizes the journalistic quality of *Sundog*, a series of observations that the narrator records with the intention of allowing his readers to sift through and analyze them so that they may draw their own conclusions. [77]

Strang questions the narrator on his knowledge of dams and correctly assumes that he knows little (again, like the protagonists of *AGDTD*) about dam-building or the dams' benefits to society. Strang gives him books on the subject, "nearly a dead loss: Golze's *Handbook of Dam Engineering, Irrigation Principles and Practices* by Hansen, Israelsen and Stringham. The third book, D'Arcy Wentworth Thompson's *On Growth and Form* is the only one more than vaguely accessible to the layman. It is about why everything on Earth is shaped the way it is, an idea that naturally never occurred to me."[78] When the narrator enters Strang's world, he articulates for the first time the effect that knowledge has on one's perception, lamenting that the "world we think we know, the world we perceived in school, no longer exists. We think colonially. Perhaps the northern Midwest is another country."[79] The narrator admits that the books are ponderous and of little value to him; at best, he can only approximate Strang's point of view, a realization that foreshadows the indeterminate ending of *Sundog* and much of Harrison's fiction. The narrator understands that he can only assimilate the events of Strang's life into his own when he says, "I think Strang's books will mean more to me later in the same fashion that I only really read Shakespeare after I got out of college. Right now I crave the topical, the ephemeral."[80]

The narrator's incessant reaching for events out of time, the visceral and temporary security of a one-night stand or another glass of whiskey, contrasts to Strang's own sense of a well-developed past and an institutional memory that imbues him with the foresight and determination to affect society's course of events: Strang's dam-building has consumed his life from an early age, and he recalls the events of his childhood in uncommon detail, telling the narrator that "My work was my play in that it always gave me tremendous pleasure."[81] He elaborates on his life as a young evangelist on a mission to Africa, his first excursion abroad. Strang's craving for adventure was piqued when Karl, an older brother, took a page from the 1929 *Brittanica,* which informed Strang that "if you had my disease you lost the last twenty years of your life."[82] Karl gives Strang "equations to make my life livable," and the narrator responds, "'Would you mind telling me some of the rules?' I had to interrupt, in that I am a perpetual creator of rules, codes of honor, programs, dos and dont's, Calvinist self-laceration routines (without any ostensible results)."[83] Strang uses the profound chaos and pain of his early childhood to affect order—again, a much different view from the narrator of *AGDTD*—and the narrator understands as well as Strang how rare such order can be in one's life.

Still, the narrator cannot escape the notion that chaos is inevitable. The metaphor he uses to describe the process is poignant and apt: "The rearrival of the incoming tide is much more gradual and ordered [than our lives], a processional, much like the paradigm of our own early years, which appear so painfully slow when we live them. No one is ready, it seems, for the loss of control, the ineluctable character of acceleration that gathers around the later years." He envisions Strang and his family at the dinner table, his father ineffectually "trying to summon God down to the meal. Strang with his tidal insistence that life allow him to continue to work." Strang's voice, which "at times . . . gave the impression, despite his pathetic condition, that he was totally in control," as much as his actions, imbues the meetings with an order that impresses on the narrator the greatness of the man.[84] In addition, Strang is relentless in his own quest to heal himself, body and mind, by insisting that he can maintain order in his own life—and continue the work he loves—through (re)ordering a fragmented, tortured childhood.

He understands that his story is a refashioning of reality and tells the narrator, "I don't want to make this a pilgrimage backwards, because that's what humans do, they make pilgrimages back to a way they never were."[85] His recollections, then, eschew much of the ersatz philosophizing of the narrator in *AGDTD* and present the facts as he remembers them, a spilling of water over the dam without dwelling on time, a combination of Swanson, the protagonist of *Wolf,* and a mature voice that transcends Tim's visceral understanding of justice in *AGDTD*: "Just because we have invented clocks and calendars doesn't mean that's the way people keep track of their lives, do you think? One winter might be the winter you see through ice. You go out on a lake, and if it hasn't sleeted and blurred in freezing, you can wipe away the snow and look down through the ice as if it were a horizontal window." He tells the narrator that "Love and death tire a man out. You just can't answer any of these big questions, but you got to keep a weather eye out for them."[86] Strang first became interested in dam-building by listening to his father's own sermons, in which

> He railed against the gods of Mammon and Moloch who built the Hoover Dam where a boyfriend of his, and dozens of others, had died in its construction. I read about this dam in Richard Halliburton and, since I had always been so protected, I felt the appeal of doing some truly dangerous work. What boy hasn't felt the call to commit an act of daring that will lift him out of the commonplace in the eyes of others?"[87]

In a sense, Strang is a picaro intent on his own survival, a reactionary in a world governed by a natural order, embodied in religion, that he both accepts and uses to his advantage as he bridges the gap between technology and nature. Strang's nature, however, is not the roadside trout stream that holds the attention of the narrator of *AGDTD,* but

rather the elemental, essential link between man and his surroundings—with the survival of man in the balance. Joseph Meeker suggests
that "Picaresque nature is not a garden, but a wilderness. Its most
obvious features are multiplicity and diversity, for within the
picaresque world everything is tied to everything else according to
complex interdependencies which defy simplification. Pain and pleasure are equally real, as are birth and death, peace and war, hunger
and a full belly, love and hate."[88] Strang, perhaps better than any other
of Harrison's characters, understands that complexity and is willing
to work within it to regain his own physical and psychic balance.

Strang's closeness to nature, which maps out the contradictions of the
protagonist's complex adult life, differentiates his world view from the
narrowly constricted mind of the narrator of *AGDTD*. Strang asserts
that "Without question there are places in nature that own a certain
unique spirit, that are so peculiar and individual that they draw us to
them," and he recounts an unusual gathering of trout before a down-
pour in an isolated backwater, musing that "The trout might have collected in the spring like that only once in my lifetime, and the storm on
the way home allowed them to leave, I'm sure. The idea that things only
happen once used to bother me." This understanding of the ephemer-
ality and fragility of nature carries over into his assessment of the projects that don't interact harmoniously with nature, and he recalls that
"Twice I've been on a project that never should have happened. There's
no more pathetic thing than building a dam that shouldn't be there. It
usually happens for political reasons. I always demand a transfer. I can't
bear meaningless work."[89] The talk of work, so important to Strang's
essential link to nature, is clearly enervating to the sick man, although
he enjoys the narrator's company and wants to complete his life story—
quite literally—in the narrator's presence. The narrator sees a literary
work ethic in Strang's own journeys (contrasted once again to the narrator's own journalistic impulses) and the recounting of his life that is
unique "to those who work very hard. Thoreau only pretended to loaf—
every step of a walk was part of an idea. I remember reading about
Rilke's pilgrimage to see Tolstoy. He told the great count that he wanted
to be a writer. 'Then write, for God's sake,' replied Tolstoy."[90] In much
the same way, Strang teaches the narrator about geology, physics, natural history, the basics of structural engineering, and "[Strang] is an
unselfconscious visionary of technology. . . . I was pleased when he said
the Glen Canyon shouldn't have been built any more than we would
allow NASA to dye half the moon pink for research."[91]

Enthralled by Strang's life story, the narrator muses that "The trouble with television, movies, most novels, with the rarest of exceptions, is that nothing is true to the life you have experienced, or true to a life you could conceivably comprehend." Strang confides to the narrator that "I got this little theory, an utterly unimportant theory, that most people never know more than vaguely where they are, either in time or in the scheme of things. People can't read contracts or time schedules or identify countries on blank maps."[92] In the course of their conversations, Strang forces the narrator to reconsider his own views and his tapes become a way of detailing the changes that Strang affects in the narrator:

> Far out in this pine barren Strang might not quite be what I thought he was: an alpha type, a technological genius, at home in any country, the sort that does the core of the world's business, hard-driving, reality-oriented, etc. Writers by their experience are over-trained in cynicism, and cynicism along with irony is a device, a set of blinders, to keep the world in its place. Writers pretty much think they are what the total consensus of opinion says they are. . . . There is no real consensus about the Strangs of the world because there aren't many of them, they work in inaccessible and unpleasant places far off the usual world capital junket, and those like myself gifted with words (hopefully) are ignorant of their language.[93]

The narrator disavows himself of any earlier notion that Strang somehow represents the maleficent aspects of technology, in this case dam-building. In doing so, he alters the way that he perceives his characters; the narrative takes form as a litany to the literate humanist who craves the totality of the world's knowledge.

The self-educated Strang, in allowing wilderness and place to inscribe their indelible marks on him, pays fifty dollars for a world atlas before he sets out on a journey that "would have required the manic traveler a number of years."[94] Strang completes his itinerary many times over in a life that will be shortened by his own physical limitations, and although his rehabilitation is going slowly, Strang holds hope for the future through thoughts of dam-building: his ex-father-in-law Marshall sends him the plans for a project in New Guinea. The arrival of the folder and Strang's obvious interest in the prospect of returning to a "green hell" makes the narrator, as a recorder of Strang's life, feel profoundly inferior. He wants to "probe deeper for a raw nerve" in Strang's psychological makeup, and feels the resentment that "a pencil pusher feels in a country where politicians keep raising the mythological spectre of the

Frontier. Literary biographers have a special talent, too, for making writers more boring than the very least of their work," but he decides that "writers, unlike Strang, were more than willing to neglect whole continents." Strang details his further indoctrination into the small cadre of dam-building foremen when he replaces memories of an ex-lover with the technology of his trade, "a German-built MAN diesel."[95] The controlling metaphor in Strang's life is the building of structures that connect him, both physically and psychically, to the world-at-large.

In telling his story, Strang contrasts his character to the protagonists in *AGDTD* and without conceit defends his own profession with a deep understanding of human nature. He states the crux of his position and implicitly questions the narrator's position, when he tells the narrator,

> I've pretty much burned myself up, and if you looked at a succession of photos of the work I had a part in, it wouldn't mean much to anyone else. Is your true life in those books of yours? It better be. I can flip this photo over in my mind now, the bridges, the irrigation projects, dams. We no longer have much faith in that sort of thing in our country, but they do elsewhere. Those triumphs of technology and engineering are easily forgotten when the lights never go out. They are questioned the most by the people who have the most, which is not even a paradox for human beings.[96]

The scope of Strang's vision is clearly more expansive than the parochial delusions of Tim and the narrator in *AGDTD*, and we understand Strang's world better in contrast to theirs. Harrison's humanist lives in a bigger world, and he accepts technology's benefits and its drawbacks. He simply refuses the notion that one can distill the essence of life from a single vantage point, "extrapolate all of life from one place. That was Thoreau's mistake, though a very minor one. It's simply not true. The only way to extrapolate the spirit of Africa is to be in Africa." The time Strang spends in India makes him realize not only the good that the dams are doing for the people, but the depth of their poverty: "The real goad to working hard in India for some of us was the hunger you would see all around you. . . . Starvation in print remains an abstraction, something that can be ignored or dismissed with a quip. You see that in the papers right now: those who are doing well simply refuse to recognize the malnutrition in our own country."[97] While Strang realizes the good that the dams are doing to alleviate the poverty of the people of India, he adds perspective to his analysis by virtue of his having seen the issue from both sides in developed and third world nations.

The narrator, overwhelmed by Strang's stories, bemoans, "What do we do when we arrive at the present?" and he realizes that he has "made a writer's classic mistake and entered fully into the lives of my subjects to the extent that my skin was going to come off when I tried to get out. It would be any day now I sensed, and it likely wouldn't be as clean and melancholy as Strang felt when finishing a dam."[98] Strang's ex-wife Evelyn, Marshall's daughter, plans to take him to Switzerland for an experimental cure. The following morning, Evelyn arrives with news that Strang has disappeared and she blames the narrator, who can only record that "I felt quite calm." The narrator does not believe that Strang is dead. As he drives out of town, he puts himself in Strang's place, "tried to imagine what it would be like to swim down a large river at night, but couldn't quite make it. You had to see the dam or work on it your self to really understand it."[99]

The overall effect of the narrative is nothing like the distorted vision of Strang the narrator offers at the outset. Instead, the narrative becomes "a mirror with impeccably sharp resolution and high selectivity. Its image of mankind is a genuine reflection of man's deepest and most significant qualities, but not of all of them. . . . Tragic writers, like engineers, have consistently chosen to affirm those values which regard the world as mankind's property."[100] That these two novels are "tragic" is debatable, although *AGDTD* is clearly more pessimistic than the later *Sundog*. In both novels, any tragedy comes from the protagonists' misunderstanding with society—especially as Harrison so effectively conveys in both novels an awareness of the deep cleft between the real and the imagined—and the prevalent view in developed societies that the world is, in fact, "mankind's property." The protagonists' halfhearted attempt at affecting change in *AGDTD* means the death of one protagonist and the return to chaos for the other two. *Sundog,* on the other hand, presents an intricate example of the contradictory impulses that, far from limiting the scope of the "sources of imagery," instead offer in three voices the sum of a life's experience, a much more productive vision of man's intimacy and complicity with nature.

The complexity of *Sundog* cannot be overstated as a measure of Harrison's evolving and maturing vision of his fictional characters. What Harrison has accomplished by intertwining three distinctly different narratives into one overarching Narrative is nothing less than a symbiotic and seamless fusion of the three into a nearly inseparable whole. Without the narrator acting as a foil to Strang's recollection and reordering—the narrator is the catalyst for Strang's recollections, and he draws Strang out with his genuine interest in the protagonist's mind and actions—this story would never have been told and, we might assume, Strang could not have eased himself into the waiting river to fulfill a destiny that has awaited him since childhood. Without Strang, the narrator would be destined to return to the journalistic life that fuels his ennui in the first place; instead, Jim Harrison the narrator is "imagining-creating-writing Strang's continuing life rather than death. In fact, Jim Harrison has been in a significant way restored by his imaginative relationship with Strang."[101] The third narrative, the rivulet along which the plot trickles, is meaningless without the constant textual tension and interplay of the other two. Like the narrator, we are enthralled by the stories that Strang tells, and we can imagine that his disappearance, far from the gratuitous and brutal ending of *AGDTD,* is the beginning of another adventure for Strang.[102]

The narrative subtly examines the moral complexities and contradictions that characterize the player on the New Frontier, not shackled to technology and irrational paranoia, but free to explore memory and imagination as a way of conceptualizing society's advances and, within their indirect and seemingly random influences, the transgression of society past our psychological boundaries. The two very different visions Harrison presents in his novels of creation and destruction form a continuum on which we can view the author's maturing vision of the contradictions inherent in any discussion of nature and our place in it.

·3·

" . . . the Orient was totally out of the question"

Conflict, Place, and the Regional Novel in Jim Harrison's *Farmer*

Especially as practiced by Midwestern writers, realism might be said to be the democratic mode of fiction because of its concern with the depiction of middle- and lower-class characters and its attention to the "unremarkable" day-to-day details of those characters' lives. Underlying this approach is the assumption that those events, characters, and objects merit such description. Whether a way of dress, a social custom, or a local dialect, whatever is described in fiction is to some degree, by virtue of that description, elevated. The description of a flower on a dunghill elevates not only the flower but the dunghill as well.
—David Marion Holman, *A Certain Slant of Light*

We have the terms enculturation and acculturation, but nothing to describe the process of becoming placed or re-placed.
—Gary Snyder, *The Practice of the Wild: Essays*

"We have always been regions rather than states or a country, and full of a tribal intolerance for anyplace else."
—John Wesley Northridge II, from Jim Harrison's
The Road Home

Jim Harrison is a literary chameleon whose fiction explodes from an astounding number of different perspectives and at odd narrative angles—from the digressive, disjointed, and anecdotal *Wolf* to the epic *Dalva,* to his role as a prolific novella writer, he crosses a broad spectrum of narrative possibilities. It seems odd, though, for a writer who so often and readily unleashes his capacious knowledge of the world outside his own northern Michigan backyard to write a novel that has as its backdrop the parochial milieu of Joseph Lundgren's forty acres. It seems odder still, given the often indeterminate endings of his novels and novellas, that he would give away the ending of his third novel, *Farmer* (1976), in a two-page preface that begins "Imagine a late June evening in 1956 in a seacoast town—say Eureka, California, or Coos Bay, Oregon. Or a warm humid evening in Key Largo or the Sea Islands that are pine-green jewels in the Atlantic south along the coast from Savannah."[1] This effort, though, is no less expansive than any other of his works, and the foreshadowing only serves to strengthen the novel's purpose—not to evoke mystery, but rather a sense of a specific place-in-time that we might term "regional."[2]

Contrary to the opinions of some critics and writers, including Wallace Stegner, the "regional" novel is not a literature of "second-class status and a defensive support of the second-rate against persons or forces that disparage or ignore it."[3] Rather, just as authors for two decades beginning in the late fifties write the Novel of Excursion—dispossessed youth reinventing Huck Finn's own "lighting out" with cars, cigarettes, booze, and a flippant catch-all philosophy—they often just as convincingly write the novel of place: not several places held together by a unifying theme (as in Harrison's *Wolf,* for instance, in which Swanson recalls a cross-country journey in five acts), but specific places in which the centripetal forces of culture, tradition, and often ignorance hold people in place as the bigger world spins around them at a safe distance. The literature is loosely categorized as "regional," though writers and critics often have difficulty articulating the reasons for its recent critical and popular resurgence (Kent Haruf's *Plainsong* comes to mind) or, for that matter, reaching consensus on the term's definition. Critics generally agree, however, that the term is not a pejorative when it is applied to literature not limited by place, but literature which uses the characters' isolation and their unique cultural mores and customs to set their experiences apart from the larger world. The value of the "regional" novel is to give voice to viable literature of place that is vital in any strong national literary tradition.

The turning-inward described in regional literature is a response to a rapidly changing geography, economic vagaries, and a world fearful of losing its identity "in a period that has redrawn its atlases over and over again, that is constantly refiguring its surroundings; and if the process we are witnessing seems to be leading toward always greater global unity, it is also, and as blatantly, leading toward greater and greater fragmentation."[4] The discord between regionalism and materialism for Harrison is the result of the attitudes of "the people in New York [who] really don't have much interest in anything between the two dream coasts," which threatens our sense of community "not only by the machinery that drove Victorian industry and that fueled the two world wars, but also by electronic communication, which would seem to make regional loyalty an anachronism. . . . Once again, regionalism is surfacing as a counter-voice to cries of alienation and despair."[5] Gilbert Fite discusses the issue of geographic isolation in the creation of literature and art and echoes Harrison's own contention that on the Great Plains, "we're remote from the sources of power and the sources of big money. And it does have an effect on our cultural development. . . . Now if plainsmen are anything, and farmers in general, they're sort of practical. And art and literature are not very practical to a lot of people who have the real money."[6] William Stafford comes closest to defining the regionalism that Harrison draws in *Farmer* as a "process of exploration, but it's a process of exploration in which you always find something. I think there's another way to think about literature and regionalism. And that is that it's not something you decide to do: it's the recognition of a place you're already in."[7]

The themes of changing geographies, increasing access to information, and intra- and inter-personal relationships—in short, dynamics that bring us all together or are capable of wholly separating us from one another—are nothing new to Harrison, who has spent his life living in, observing, and writing about the wilderness of northern Michigan and its Upper Peninsula. Harrison's third and shortest novel both delimits the boundaries of a specific place and its people and finally allows for a transcendence of spirit from that narrowly bounded society. The protagonist feels at peace in the world he has created, but only after he reconciles his place at home against the magnetic pull of the world-at-large. In short, the novel conforms to the definitions of "regional" literature not in its limitations, but in the myriad possibilities of describing a place that, despite its shortcomings, inexorably draws one back.

The critical reception of the novel was relatively positive, and much of it centers on Harrison's ability to work within small spaces to create a story that transcends the narrow geographical and class limitations that define the characters. Christopher Lehmann-Haupt asserts that the author "has finally found a narrative pace to suit his sensibilities."[8] In his astute reading of the novel, Webster Schott is more forthcoming with praise, perceiving the outward simplicity of the narrative, the underlying complexity of human relations, and the importance of place in the situations that Harrison presents in his profound "sense of man's history. There is no stability in emotions, only needs. Continuity rises from habit, hunting game with his friend, satisfying the demands of animals and land."[9] Indeed, the dichotomy of emotion and need is the contradiction that carries the narrative to its conclusion. The story takes place exclusively, except for the preface and a short trip to Chicago that establishes the contrast between the rural and the urban, in remote northern Michigan. It is a narrative history of land and people; the two are, as in all of Harrison's fiction, defined in terms of one another.

The story is also one of desire and responsibility, the power of which is illustrated repeatedly in Joseph's dreams of water, though he "had never seen an ocean, been to war or to the Orient. He lived on his family's farm and taught at the country school a half mile down the gravel road that passed the house. He figured that some day fairly soon he would see the ocean but the Orient was totally out of the question."[10] Water is a crucial image for Joseph; his overwhelming desire to see the ocean is a powerful statement of his need to contrast his own world with what he has only read in his books. The image controls Joseph's life, and he is often powerless to stop himself when he expounds, "in a long monologue on the sea" to his students on "Darwin's *Voyage of the Beagle,* and the mysteries of the Pacific between Peru and Ecuador, and the distant Galapagos which fascinated him."[11] The same restless desire that allows Joseph to dream of other places, however, is out of place in his culture, a conflict that "is often at the heart of midwestern social realism. The result is a literature that at once glorifies the common man as the promise of America and yet depicts him as venal and narrow-minded and deplores it."[12] Joseph realizes with no little disdain for the culture that has made it so that "Some of the farm kids were so exhausted from the work they did before and after school they could scarcely stay awake for their lesson. This had led Joseph throughout his life to regard knowledge, especially knowledge that couldn't be directly applied, as a secret vice, a source of beauty and enthusiasm that, however, didn't get the chores done or make the mortgage payment."[13] Nonetheless, the dream persists, and until Joseph escapes his own closed world he will suffer the absence of competing experiences. That "the Orient was totally out of the question" is a poignant statement of the modesty—and innocence—of desire.

Joseph's innocence of desire, however, should not be construed as a naïveté toward his own situation. He understands well the intricate relationship between a particular land and its people despite its often deleterious effects on the inhabitants, a trait Barry Lopez finds disturbingly lacking in most Americans, who "profess a sincere and fierce love for the American landscape, for our rolling prairies, free-flowing rivers, and 'purple mountains' 'majesty'; but it is hard to imagine, actually, where this particular landscape is."[14] Lopez's conclusion is that ours is an increasingly "homogenized national geography, one that seems to operate independently of the land, a collection of objects rather than a continuous bolt of fabric."[15] Joseph, however, understands the special character of the land and the effect that it has on its inhabitants, and even though he feels restless enough to change the course of his own life, he balks at the possibility that the landscape should change as well and is angered by the fact that the "farm houses would be modernized and false shutters added. Sometimes white board fences would be built and the outbuildings painted a bright red. Maybe they were trying to make it resemble Kentucky or New England."[16] The marginal lives that the people make for themselves come and go in phases, and the landscape and the lives of Joseph's neighbors and his students in the local school, where he teaches literature, are nearly wholly dependent upon economic circumstances.

Despite his connection to the land, Joseph suffers the wanderlust instilled in him by his friend Orin. He recalls a night at an outdoor movie with Orin, his wife, Rosealee, and their young son Robert, that "The movie was *Mutiny on the Bounty* with Charles Laughton, and Joseph looked at the sea with eagerness."[17] Joseph is not the jaded urbanite who feels compelled to rail against the quaintness of such scenes, but one who simply desires new experiences. He had heard many stories of the outside world from Orin, a pilot killed in the Korean War when he crashed into the China Sea, and he wonders why he had not taken his friend's advice when Orin first regaled him with exotic visions so many years before:

> Orin said night after night *Joseph you got to get out of here, you're not really going to farm and there's a whole world out there.* Then as the evening progressed his brain whirled with Orin's tales of far-off places and English, French, Italian, and Spanish women. . . . The day Orin had left for the Korean War Joseph and Rosealee took him to town for the train and Orin had drawn him aside with little Robert standing there white as a sheet and said you better get out of here before your life is over just spent in these goddamn sticks.[18]

The underlying irony of the tales is that Orin's own wandering outside the relative safety of the land has cost him his life. Naturally, Orin's death dampens the urgency of Joseph's leaving; in presenting Joseph with the death of his best friend, Harrison "establishes a point central to his fiction: life is a 'death dance'" where, like the cycle of the seasons, "[t]he meaning of one's life is established in its patterns, and continuity and satisfaction come from pursuing the pattern that has been developed."[19] For a time, though, Joseph can forget about death. The felt and lingering sense of Orin's words in one as sensitive to such things as Joseph is at the core of Joseph's longing to escape—if only for a time, as Harrison hints in the preface—to another place. The getaway need not be to a specific place (Harrison posits three different spots in the opening paragraph), but not here, not northern Michigan. The temptation for Joseph to rationalize his safe, if unfulfilling, position is strong, and he recalls how he responded to his sister when she similarly implored that he "should leave this place": "So why hadn't he left and why had he let so many years slip away like smoke? But that was easy. It was Rosealee mixed with Father and Mother, then Mother alone. Also taking the seniors to Detroit or Chicago in June and seeing those places was not so much squalid as places where he just wouldn't fit in."[20] Joseph's own sheltered life parallels the lives of his students, who have experienced as much of the city as he has; undoubtedly, some of them will experience the same desire to escape that becomes the controlling narrative in Joseph's middle years.

Joseph has clearly reached a point at which any decision he makes will be fateful. The imminent loss of his mother to cancer, his dissatisfaction with teaching and the closing of the school, and his ill-considered relationship with Catherine, one of his seventeen-year-old students, "have driven him into a hole."[21] The affair is, in fact, the symptom of a profound midlife crisis that had announced its coming in subtle ways, "even before he had begun his affair with Catherine. . . . What little heart he had left for teaching was gone before the end of September."[22] The crisis is particularly debilitating for Joseph, whose constant ruminating on life, a trait perhaps unusual in a member of his closed culture, leads his friend the doctor to wonder, "What does [a nervous breakdown] mean? Often it means people are forced out of ruts by seeing certain facts of life they can't take into their systems. They're overloaded. So I give some tranquilizers which they take to make these facts less painful. . . . So if you got yourself a nervous breakdown it's about goddamn time."[23]

Even the weather, easily ignored in urban places where one simply hails a taxi or rides the subway, plays a significant part in determining the attitudes of the area's inhabitants, whose actions are not dictated artificially by clocks, meetings, and commutes, but by the cycles of nature. Though everyone in Joseph's closed community has become accustomed to the regularly occurring patterns of the seasons, they were "disgusted with winter by March and usually before, and a major April storm could bring on a fit of sheer spite in anyone. . . . And despite all the church activities, school, the dances and card parties at the Grange Hall, everyone grew morbid and nervous toward spring, about ten degrees out of kilter in fact."[24] The patterns are immutable, variable only in their intensity from one year to the next, and they offer a rhythm to life that one would have difficulty establishing in a more controlled environment. The ennui that accompanies the long winters inspires fighting at the local taverns; spring, "whether false or not, brought on laughter and a kind of easeful drowsiness, a time of general good feeling when people yawned and smelled the air with a few weeks' respite before the fields would be dry enough to plow."[25] And because of the inhabitants' isolation, the events that the area's inhabitants have learned to anticipate verge on the impossibly romantic:

> At one time from a distance you would see a man behind a single-bladed plow and a team of horses. Behind the man a boy stumbled along the uneven furrow picking up earthworms. When the boy filled a can with worms he would dump the contents of the can into a larger pail in the middle of the field . . . The father and the boy would look at the worms and try to decide if they had enough for a three-day fishing trip they planned after the spring plowing.[26]

When the events are placed into the frame of Joseph's life, they act as a foil to his own more visceral impulse to escape; the closeness of the father and the son and their communion with nature takes on an artificial feel for the protagonist, who finds himself longing for a past time in his own world that itself is a simulacrum: "imagine a time when Michigan wasn't a game farm for hunters," he thinks, "when the natural predators, the puma, wolf, coyote, and lynx still lived there. And the Indian. Not man hunting for sport and his house pets gone wild and utterly destructive."[27]

Joseph's attempts at ordering the past so he can make sense of the present and the future become the primary focus of the narrative. His sole task is to avoid an all-too-common death-like serenity associated with the lives of farmers and others far away from the frenetic centers of life. Joseph decides that he must act on his lifelong dream of visiting the ocean, and in his last year of teaching and farming he comes to grips with the underlying awkwardness that has taken control of his life. Still, if Joseph is to accomplish what he sets out to do at the beginning of the narrative, he must play by society's rules; it would be much easier for him to "exist as [a] rootless intelligence without layers of localized contexts. Just a 'self' and the 'world.'"[28] Joseph is comfortable with his life, although he feels a restlessness that cannot be assuaged by outdoor activities, which only makes him more aware that, like the seasons in northern Michigan, "life was a death dance and that he had quickly passed through the spring and summer of his life and was halfway through the fall."[29] He realizes that "He had missed much in life. He felt he should have dragged his weary leg around the earth instead of staying on the farm grieving over his dead father and his mother whose health had begun to fail."[30] As always, too, he wavers over his scandalous affair with Catherine, "whose body had graced the rug with suppleness and an implacable felinity that would trouble his sleep for years to come."[31]

Joseph's relationship with Catherine acts a catalyst to push Joseph's desire to the breaking point and forces him to make decisions about his future in the familiar culture. He is willing to give up the family homestead in response to his need to escape; he is willing to take his chances on becoming a "solitary knower," which would doom him to a life as a "boring prisoner of abstractions." To be sure, though, Joseph is not alone. The memories of the place where his family settled generations before is the backdrop for a rush of memories and a tortured replaying of his life: he sits on a rock in the front yard of the family farm and, having drunk too much, "briefly entered a state where he understood nothing. They had all been young and now they were suddenly old. Thirty years ago they played softball in this yard with their relatives from Chicago."[32] The predicament is not unusual in the fiction of place, as the "physical and emotional contact with the land" is important to the characters that inhabit a specific place, and although those characters are certainly more mobile than "their pioneering ancestors," they "lack a clear sense of their destination."[33] Indeed, up to now, Joseph identifies himself only in terms of the farm and the few people keeping him in place. The affinity that Joseph has for the farm confirms his own precarious position on the brink of a life-altering

decision, and the frenetic rush of time in a context in which such things
are counterproductive (the slow and regular procession of the seasons,
after all, is predictable in what it will bring) forces him to act. Joseph
"knew that the nature of his life wouldn't permit so simple a departure barring suicide—that the pivotal year that had begun so easily
with the grace of last October would not slip unhaltingly into the past
as so many of the years before."[34]

The contradictory impulses that Joseph feels in his affair with Catherine are not unusual in Harrison's characters, although Joseph is the only
of Harrison's characters who wrestles his demons, in both memory and
in the present, in one specific geographical location. Joseph's parochial-
ism suggests the necessity of his fighting stagnancy by almost acting on
his impulse to escape to the outside world, an action that would allow
him to reconcile his desires to an immutable culture and to find a "middle landscape, located in a middle ground somewhere 'between,' yet in
transcendent relation to, the opposing forces of civilization and
nature."[35] The crux of Joseph's anguish is his notion of place-as-anchor
and the struggle between, in both geographical and psychic terms, inside
and outside. Time and place are inseparable, and the changing of the
seasons is Joseph's only signal that forward motion is continuing at all.
The psychological confrontation with the outside world in his relationship with Catherine is symbolic of his geographical entrapment. Joseph
understands that he has recourse to connect with life in ways other than
farming and courting Rosealee, Orin's widow, although he has little
ambition to fully separate himself from place by transmuting those
impulses into action. The movement from fall to the dead of winter signals the coming of Joseph's most forgettable year:

> After their October day passed Joseph realized that he had been thinking
> about making love to [Catherine] since the first day of school. But as win-
> ter lengthened her instabilities became more obvious; she grew fretful and
> restless after the novelty of country life wore thin. . . . He could not imag-
> ine her camping by the ocean with him. She had no interest in his fishing
> or hunting; no interest in rivers and lakes and oceans.[36]

The fluctuation of Joseph's relationship with Catherine is synchronous
with the seasons and in terms that point up the cultural mores of the
place, an expression of the "community values and access to communal tragedy" that accompanies the inevitable discovery of his affair
with Catherine.[37] Joseph is too aware that the culture into which he
was raised, born of place relatively absent of outside influence, leads

to a specific predetermined and, for him, unacceptable conclusion. In a reversal of traditional gender roles, Catherine, the worldly temptress, tells her teacher, the mark, that "'I just loved that Keats poem you read yesterday.' She knew Keats was Joseph's favorite."[38] The student seduces the master by using his love of poetry to undermine any control he has over the relationship. That she focuses on Keats is significant not only for Joseph's weakness for poetry, but also the implication that by having an affair with one of his students he must work within the contradictions of such an awkward relationship, a clear demonstration of Keats's "negative capability." That contradiction is important not only in the relationship at hand, but in refining a definition of "regional literature" to include the "ambivalence, the dialectic to and fro which seems peculiar to our age."[39]

Joseph establishes an economy of ennui that pits his relationship with Rosealee against an ephemeral, and largely symbolic, series of sexual encounters with Catherine, which is nothing like Joseph has ever experienced. For that reason alone she becomes primary in his life. Although he muses that "on very rare occasions life will offer up something as full and wonderful as anything the imagination can muster," his desire for Catherine unnerves him and prompts him to consider that "he needed at least a month to break it off." [40] In the swirling vortex of Catherine's influence, Joseph's life becomes the unreality of the books through which he has educated himself and through which he has gained most of his knowledge of the outside world:

> [The relationship with Catherine] was so much like the novels and he wanted to totally enter the reality of it before he came to his senses. . . . Outside of the novels he read, the word "lover" had always been mysterious to him. He felt that Rosealee and he were not really lovers but in the more mundane category labeled "going to get married. . . ." But now he had managed to become a living, breathing, sweating lover without really trying. It simply had happened upon him on an otherwise average October day and now in the first week of June it had become much less than a mixed blessing.[41]

When Catherine tells Joseph that she needs to speak with him, he was "giddy through the afternoon over the idea she might be pregnant. . . . Oh, my God, he thought, with the guilty urge to head for a far place, some island in the ocean. Zanzibar would be ideal, at least the *National Geographic* rendition."[42] Joseph's fantasizing about his escape from Catherine (she is, in fact, not pregnant) again underscores his own romantic notions of what lies outside his limited scope and provides access to the regional aspect of the narrative in sharp contrast to Harrison's otherwise worldly vision: while Joseph admits that he has never seen the ocean, he gets his idea of Zanzibar from a magazine, and he is rendered impotent by the thought of having impregnated Catherine; Strang travels the world building dams; Swanson details the stages of his life as he travels from place to place; and Dalva recalls her life from her time in California, Arizona, Nebraska, and abroad.

Joseph's isolation—from the ocean, from the Orient, from Rosealee and Catherine and his dead friend Orin—is further emphasized when a game warden tells Joseph that "he had seen a coyote in the country. Coyotes were assumed to have totally disappeared, moving north where they were safe from the irate farmers who blamed them for all sorts of impossible predations." Joseph plans to see the animal, and in his preparation he "remembered that he and Orin had once called a fox upwind of their hiding place by using a predator call."[43] Joseph phones Rosealee, who still has a trunk of Orin's belongings, and asks her to bring the call to school the next day. That Joseph can live with the memory of Orin is significant, as Rosealee does not shun her past and will always remember Orin fondly. For Joseph to think of Rosealee often in terms of his dead friend privileges the past and influences the future toward which he so blindly progresses. Only the town doctor, a friend and confidante of Joseph's, understands the situation fully: "Oh fuck the ghost of Orin. That's what's wrong with you in part. Orin is dead. Dead meat . . . , like you and I will be someday not all that distant from us. Rosealee is alive. She's three miles up the road and she is probably wondering why she gave her life over to a goddamn lunatic."[44]

Joseph's attempts at seeing the coyote, like his several previous half-hearted attempts at changing his life, are failures. His isolation, heightened by a handful of ill-considered failures to break with his society, is accompanied by a profound alienation from the community that refuses to support the school where he and Rosealee teach. Joseph is, after all, not like the parents of the children he teaches, even though he is very much a part of their culture. Perhaps most hurtful to Joseph is the fact that, despite his resentment toward the townspeople for their provincial and ignorant attitudes,

they all knew Joseph was somehow one of them, no matter how strange and removed his behavior. They knew his parents and sisters, the dimen-

sions of the family farm, who his relations were, how the family fared during the Depression and the war. Most of all they knew that Joseph was only
accidentally a schoolteacher, that were it not for his withered leg he would
be an average, unsuccessful farmer like his father: someone who tended to
fish and hunt when he should have worked his land a bit harder.[45]

Joseph's inability to accept the attitudes of the people around whom
he has grown up stems from his self-education, although the fact that
he has no formal education beyond high school places him in the unen-
viable position of being treated like one of the town's own.

He has jeopardized even that tenuous position in the town, though,
in his affair with Catherine. For a time, the cultural mores Joseph has
transgressed in his relationship with Catherine are protected by the
doctor, the titular wise man of the township who brings with him a
knowledge of the "old ways," and who berates Joseph for an affair
that is bound to become public knowledge. The doctor's admonition
carries some weight with Joseph, as his attitudes toward hunting and
fishing have greatly influenced the protagonist. Later the doctor reiterates his warning: "You know why you like Catherine other than her
obvious body there on the couch? It's because she is not even a person
yet. You've given her nothing and even if you had there would be nothing there in return. And it's because she hasn't anything to return yet
except her body. . . . The life is draining out of you. You're a strong
person and when a strong person fucks up they do so with a
vengeance."[46] Still, Joseph is stubborn enough to ignore such simple
remedies as the doctor offers him, and he spends a considerable
amount of time contriving reasons that he cannot marry Rosealee, the
one palpable anchor, along with the place itself, that defines the
boundaries of Joseph's life.

Both Joseph's memories of Orin and Rosealee's commitment to her
son symbolize the closed world in which Joseph is trapped. Joseph's
current relationship with Robert is a complex intermingling of his
dead friend's memory and a constant reminder that Orin's departure
from the womb of northern Michigan ultimately caused his own
death. Joseph is irritated by the boy, even "though he saw Robert daily
in school. It was incomprehensible to Joseph that Robert so closely
resembled his father physically, yet so utterly lacked Orin's boldness
and humor." Robert is void of the personality traits that set Orin apart
from his friends and which, the narrator implies, prematurely ended
his life. Unlike most of his friends, "Orin hated farming even [in his
childhood]. He only wanted to hunt and read about airplanes. When

Orin was only eight his father had bought him a ride from some barn-stormers at the fair and that had changed Orin's life and finally killed him." When Joseph visits Rosealee, her house "always hopelessly reminded him of Orin. The house was large and solid, much better than the house he lived in."[47]

The memory of Orin forces Joseph to constantly reassess his own position in the community, and he uses his favorite poet, Keats, to offer perspective on Orin's death and his subsequent relationships with Catherine and Rosealee: "Does Keats know Fanny in death? I know Catherine is a secret conniver and ultimately no good but who said a woman, a girl, has to be good for you to like her and want her . . . ? I want to see a shark. I always wanted to see Keats's grave but I'd rather see a shark and the ocean. I'm tired of looking at photos of the ocean." Joseph's lack of worldliness and his frustration at never having traveled to the places that interest him most prompt him to consider that he "had come to be suspicious of mere literacy when it was so ubiquitously devoted to idiocies, livestock reports, comics, and the sports page." His romantic attitudes are ill-matched to the provincialism that surrounds him, and he is bemused by the work of his two best students—ironically, Robert and Catherine—when they insist on writing analyses of poetry based on "arch posturings" in which the "world was full of lonely, bored individuals."[48] Joseph is amused by the cynicism of his students (here contrasted to the intimacy that he shares with both outside the classroom), although the implication that his own life is hardly more fulfilling is not wasted on him.

The death of Joseph's mother and the awful decision engendered by her illness—Joseph and the doctor facilitate the dying woman's last wish to die with dignity—awaken in him the knowledge of what it means to have grown up in northern Michigan and to take control of one's own life.[49] He is determined to center his life on the world with which he is familiar, to make himself less vulnerable to a "pitiless world," and he pledges to become accountable for his actions, even if he loses Rosealee in the process. A dream of water, a direct precursor to the death of Joseph's mother, is the key to Joseph's reconciling himself with Rosealee. Joseph begins to closely monitor the content of his dreams, and he suffers from a fever that changes his perception in a way that his surroundings cannot. He is at peace with the life he is leading, and for the first time in the crisis he reconciles his life in northern Michigan with the lives about which he has read and one day hopes to experience. The fever had "sharpened his interest in Rosealee.

He frequently dreamed of her anyway but his sickness had cast the dreams in a pleasanter more sexual light. Conversely his thoughts of Catherine turned sour and he wondered how he could have been so stupid as to get involved with her." When he is well again, Joseph "almost regretted that his fever had passed. The fever was helping him sort his problems. Sickness often creates a space to live in, freeing the mind from the habitual if only for a day or two. Ordinary stresses disappear and when one returns to usual routines everything seems a bit more clear though sadly the clarity quickly passes." The same fever that brings a new, if brief, clarity of experience and judgment also causes Joseph to make "a tentative decision to begin farming again. He knew it might dissipate but his resolve increased with good memories of the years immediately before the Depression."[50]

In a scene that evokes the imagery Willa Cather made famous in *My Antonia,* the quintessential Midwestern novel of place, Joseph's renewed clarity of purpose upon his spiritual return home from a year-long crisis contrasts to Swanson's own unfulfilling journey in *Wolf:* "About a mile from home Joseph stopped in front of the last deserted farm before the land became acceptably fertile again. . . . The sun was huge and red and sinking into the state forest. Joseph smiled remembering that when he was very young he believed the sun sank in the field out behind the barn." With the dreams and his fever-vision still fresh in his mind, Joseph listens to the doctor's ultimatum to either marry Rosalee or not and "do something other than walking around this place pissing your life away brooding." The doctor's ability to succinctly articulate Joseph's dilemma, that "the source of most unhappiness was that nearly everyone wanted to be someplace or someone else," underpins the narrative's conclusion. Joseph affirms, finally, what we already know from the preface: "There's nothing to decide. I always intended to marry her. In a way there's no choice. There's not much choice in what I'm going to do anyway because I have to make a living. . . . Nothing he said surprised him though he hadn't voiced it before. . . . I taught and that's over and I know how to farm and that's fine."[51] The doctor's wisdom allows Joseph to make the fateful, inevitable decision. Finally, he is content to live out his life with Rosealee at his side, and the two of them will travel together to the ocean. Even though he will leave briefly, Joseph has acquiesced fully to the culture that created him. The warmth has, as it inevitably must in such a cyclical existence, returned to Joseph's life.

Joseph recognizes the advantages of living in a place where people look out for each other, and when he enters a conversation with a group of his sister's friends, actors who clearly represent the worldliness of Chicago, the world-outside, he is drawn "into telling some extravagantly obscene stories of country life, many of them originating with the doctor who knew everyone's business."[52] He also admits to himself that his relationship with Catherine has come to an end. Joseph slips into a waking dream and ponders the connection between his own love for literature and his permanent place in northern Michigan. He considers the theatricality of the actors that Arlice, his sister, has brought to the room and recalls "how once when he was reading to his class he was so carried away everyone was enthused. Carried away where?"[53]

The last passage of the narrative prefigures the preface and brings the story full circle: "Joseph stands against the grape arbor watching Rosealee in her flower-print dress and bare feet trot the horse around the barnyard. She slows the horse by the grape arbor and he takes the halter and she smiles at him, the miniature violets on her cotton dress."[54] Joseph has not had to alienate himself absolutely from the place with which he is so familiar, as he had thought for a long year that he must. Instead, he accepts the strangeness of the new place readily because he is with Rosealee, and because he understands that to travel away from his home is not necessarily to repudiate it. The preface, read as the conclusion of the narrative rather than the opening, reaffirms the sincerity and innocent acceptance with which Joseph has lived his life: "They become nervous again deciding what to leave for a tip. The man peers into a change purse but then opts for a dollar bill and the woman raises her eyes and smiles. After all, they are on vacation."[55] The dream-like quality of the understated finale (the final passage or the preface read as conclusion—after all, they are one and the same) echoes the cycle of seasons that dictates the lives of the inhabitants of Joseph's culture; with its evocation of the permanence of nature and the resilience of the Midwestern spirit, the finale gives the novel a closure that is unique in the body of Harrison's fiction. That the novel conforms to certain definitions of "regional" literature, then, is hardly arguable. Equally important is an understanding of Harrison's versatility in offering such a marked contrast to his two previous works, *Wolf* and *A Good Day to Die,* in its triumphant avowal of the power of place—not the place that forces its appeal on us through its novelty, but the familiar place that renews itself and heals us through its simply stated everydayness, the dichotomy of life and death that delves deep into our existence and, finally, so readily affirms life.

·4·

" . . . to eat well and not die from it"

The Dubious Art of Consumption in Jim Harrison's *Warlock*

Your fathers ate the manna in the wilderness. / This is the bread which comes down from heaven, that one may eat of it and not die.

—John 6:49–50

To write of the pleasure of eating is to observe the conventions of the gourmet's text: words that would signal intimate caresses of the palate, the throat's convulsive satisfaction. This written enjoyment is framed by unseen recipes for dizzying nausea, soul-shaking retching, voluptuous heaving, overpowering and involuntary expulsions of abhorrent fare.

—David Bevan, *Literary Gastronomy*

I

The most common images in Jim Harrison's fiction—food and drink and its preparation and consumption—create thematic continuity and often act as metaphors and catalysts for the larger events in his narratives. The imagery is so pervasive that Harrison's thoroughgoing attention to consumption can be read as a backdrop against which his characters live out their lives always in search of the perfect meal. The author's use of food imagery in his fiction is no doubt derived from his own love of food and eating, his reputation as a gastronome, and the intimate connection the author draws in his essay "Consciousness Dining" between writing and the preparation and consumption of food where, "Curiously, in both writing and cooking you're a dead duck if you don't love the process. When you short-circuit or jump

73

start the process in either, you end up with an imitation of your own or someone else's best effects."[1] Harrison has written extensively on the subject, most notably in his *Esquire* column "The Raw and the Cooked" (which ran monthly for more than two years in the early 1990s), and many of the essays collected in *Just before Dark* (1991) detail the gastronomic exploits of Harrison, writer Guy de la Valdéne, artist Russell Chatham, author and fellow Michigan State University alumnus Thomas McGuane, and other sportsmen and world-class gourmands who worship at the altar of food, therapeutic for the body and the spirit and symbolic of a society's health or an individual's state of mind.[2]

While Harrison's observations on food can take on a playful quality, his skillful weaving of food imagery with the abstract, philosophical aspects of his narratives gives the preparation and consumption of food and drink an importance not normally associated with American literature. David Bevan, who understands that a European sensibility of love for food and drink is a rarity in American literature, writes that critics have often focused their attention in gastro-alimentary discourse on French literature, and "the filiation ingestion/expression in all its avatars is obviously far more extensive [than in American literature], and never more so than at a time and in a world increasingly contaminated by the residual effects of synthetic products and toxic sprays."[3] The world that Bevan describes is the world that Harrison's characters inhabit.

Nowhere in Harrison's fiction is the discourse unique to food and drink, and critical of a culture's ignorance of "the residual effects" of its habits, as significant to his artistic vision as in *Warlock* (1981), part detective-fiction spoof and part serious novel, about which J. D. Reed writes, "If Henry Miller, S. J. Perelman and Walt Whitman had holed up in a Michigan roadhouse to concoct a mystery yarn, the resulting melange of comic erotica, snappish humor and hirsute lyricism might resemble this send-up of the 'tecs.'"[4] The evolution of the protagonist through a series of improbable, life-altering events is accompanied by detailed descriptions of meals that denote success (or, more likely, defeat) for the protagonist, "Warlock" (the protagonist's name is Johnny Lundgren; he took the name "Warlock" "thirty years ago as a cub scout when he was inducted into the sacred order of the Webelos"), in his repeated attempts at reconciling with his wife and regaining his fragile psychic and physical balance.[5] The final result, entirely consistent with Harrison's working within the contradictions inherent in the complex societies he constructs, is neither heroic nor tragic—but often disarmingly ambivalent: though he is able to right himself after a period of near-breakdown and finally re-establishes his relationship with his wife, Warlock never quite fulfills the promise of the American Dream.

Harrison's undermining of the American Dream, replete with Reagan-era corporate executives, wildly successful entrepreneurs, sabotage and intrigue, and an abundance of sex and drugs, is as humorous as it is unnerving. The story is undeniably, darkly comic, a trait that not only gives the novel its quirky appeal, but places Harrison in the realm of writers who are skillful enough—and brazen enough—to risk combining farce with "serious literature." The novel works on both farcical and serious planes, as it "rests on the premise that beneath the slick and sophisticated surface of American life the old nature gods still exercise their capricious power." And although "this fauns-in-the-shopping-mall territory has been explored before . . . the landscape is a rich one, and to it Jim Harrison has brought a fresh and original eye."[6]

Thomas Maher Gilligan compares Harrison's hit-and-run multi-pronged critiques of American culture to Kurt Vonnegut's fiction. Harrison, like Vonnegut, "allows the small touches, the sharp but shallow thrusts, to set the tone of the novel and indicate how we are to view the larger issues. We may find that ultimately the larger issues are not simply humorous and irreverent, but if we do not view, first, their humor and irreverence we may never understand what they really are."[7] Paul Stuewe and a host of other reviewers, though, are less enthusiastic in their assessments of the novel. Stuewe, for instance, contends that *Warlock* "attempts to bring comedy, tragedy and irony into a simple moral tale of good and evil but succeeds only in making a pretentious mess out of some not terribly promising material," and William H. Roberson finds that the story is "marred only by the flawed pacing of the work. [Harrison] takes too long to establish his story and then too quickly concludes it."[8]

In the frontispiece to the paperback edition of the novel, Harrison answers the more disparaging remarks of his critics when he writes that *Warlock* "is an attempt at a comic novel not ruled by Irony, who drags her tired ass, making us snicker cynically rather than laugh out loud."[9] The novel "aims to draw its energies from more primary colors, say from the dance that is *A Midsummer Night's Dream* to those two archfools Don Quixote and Walter Mitty, with the definite modification of a venal Quixote and a gluttonous, horny Mitty," and although Harrison claims to avoid irony at all cost, the statement is accompanied by a certain heavy-handed manipulation of the characters' actions that leaves the reader guessing as to the author's "intent" in the narrative. [10] Harrison's narrative intrusions—the preface itself is a good example—alert us to the self-referential and playful nature of the story that follows. As in his first novel, *Wolf,* Harrison plays fast and loose with the conventions of literature; his caveat for the reader of this novel is similar in tone to Twain's own at the beginning of the *Adventures of Huckleberry Finn* (to wit, "persons attempt to find a plot in it will be shot").[11] The narrative's structure and content closely mirror Mikhail Bakhtin's notion of the "carnivalization of literature" (Harrison, a student of Russian literature, certainly knows Bakhtin's work) in which hierarchical strictures are obliterated, along with "all the forms of terror, reverence, piety, and etiquette connected with it—that is, everything resulting from socio-hierarchical inequality or any other form of inequality among people." Finally, "Carnival is the place for working out, in a concretely sensuous, half-real and half-play-acted form, *a new mode of interrelationship between individuals,* counterposed to the all-powerful socio-hierarchical relationships of noncarnival life."[12] Harrison divides Warlock's Quixotic quest into three parts, each of which details the protagonist's increasing psychic fragmentation, his lack of motivation (and lack of discretion, brought on by the banality of day-to-day existence), and his uncanny knack for the failed relationship—all elements that dispel the notion that the narrative is devoid of irony.

Warlock also fancies himself a connoisseur of fine food and drink, one role among many that the protagonist fills with little success. Anticipating Warlock's predicament, famed French gourmand Jean-Anthelme Brillat-Savarin warns nearly two centuries ago that "when gourmandise becomes gluttony, voracity, or debauchery, it loses its name and its advantages, escapes from our jurisdiction, and falls into that of the moralist, to be treated with advice, or of the physician, who will cure it by his remedies."[13] Food and drink inform all aspects of Warlock's quest, and neither Brillat-Savarin's moralist nor his physician can offer a remedy for the ills that Warlock brings upon himself. Not surprisingly, Warlock's quest for acceptance from those around him and for a positive self-image is at the root of the narrative, as "One of the central concerns of Harrison's fiction is the angst of the middle-aged American male as he struggles with the questions of who he is and what his life means. His characters are seekers;

they quest for that intangible element that will bring stability and completeness to their lives."[14] That quest is both facilitated through, and exacerbated by, the food and drink that Warlock prepares and consumes—the single touchstone of the "real" for Harrison's protagonist.[15]

II

. . . I have had a most rare vision. I have had a dream, past the wit of man to say what dream it was: man is but an ass, if he go about to expound this dream.
—William Shakespeare, *A Midsummer-Night's Dream,* 4.1

Both Harrison and his wife . . . are accomplished cooks, as are Chatham and de la Valdéne, and this is also, it must be said, a fattening time. An enormous portion of each day is devoted to planning, shopping for, preparing, discussing, and finally eating one breathtaking meal after another, at the end of which preliminary discussions and preparations for the next meal begin almost immediately.
—Jim Fergus, interview with Jim Harrison
(October 1986); published in *Paris Review* (1988)

During a disturbing dream, Warlock has, at age forty-two, "just figured out he's going to die someday."[16] At the kitchen table the following morning, he meditates on a mediocre meal that he had made the night before. His attempts at creating original meals are sincere, however, as Warlock "revered the words of an old Jewish professor who said the downfall of a nation could be detected in the misuse of language by its public officials, and the disintegration of its eating habits."[17] Warlock's inability to follow the recipe for the dish, a haphazard and excessive comingling of spices that taints its flavor, accurately reflects his life at the narrative's opening and echoes Harrison's own views on the role of food in centering our lives: "Much earlier in this century, an Austrian journalist, Karl Kraus, pointed out that if you actually perceived the true reality behind the news, you would run, screaming, into the streets. I have run screaming into the streets dozens of times but have always managed to return home for dinner—and usually an hour early so that I can help in the preparation."[18]

Harrison's portrayal of Warlock is sympathetic: Warlock's puerile romanticism manifests itself in his aimless drifting, the quintessential

American Dream always just out of his reach—a beautiful wife, a high-paying job as a corporate executive (from which he is released), a playful imagination, a gourmand's sensibility, and no sense of what the future holds for him except death. Further, Warlock's indiscretion in his cooking—"He had absentmindedly added a half dozen cloves of garlic late in the cooking and had been forced to admit to Diana that the taste was a tad raw"[19]—mirrors his indecision about the direction his life should take and the emotional separation that characterizes his life with Diana. Their lives together consist primarily of chance sexual encounters, seemingly Warlock's only passion other than food and drink, consummated directly before or after the preparation and consumption of a meal. Warlock's first action after he sees himself in a dream lying dead on the kitchen floor is to fantasize about his wife's body, enticing, edible; he forgets the dream by making sexual advances toward Diana, who deflects Warlock's attempts at making love to her even after his offer to "make you a dinner you won't forget. Fish, game, veal, pork? Throw a dart at the culinary map, baby, and it'll be on the table."[20] Warlock's intense interest in cooking and his use of the proffered meal as an enticement for sex is a fascination that parallels Warlock's reification of his wife as a sexual object or something more fundamental, "as suppression of the distance between a mouth and its desire, a need made possible by the sensitive, felt difference between two lips which can never be completely erased. This is the temporary fix, the insertion of any object which, in its density, texture, opacity and palpable substance, takes the place of an irreducible, originary lack."[21] Warlock is rarely without food or drink, which takes the place of his wife when she is not sexually available; in the extramarital affairs detailed later in the narrative, food and drink accompany the seduction process and the protagonist often remembers not specific events, but rather only meals eaten. Not surprisingly, taste is the most important of the five senses, and Warlock often disregards the other four to privilege his own appetites.

The dinner-table scene with Diana establishes Warlock's addictive nature, which is based on the commodification of food and sex and a primary need—and its subsequent fulfillment throughout the narrative—for immediate gratification. Warlock's offer of dinner in return for sex is not sufficient enticement for Diana, and he fails in his attempt at bridging the physical and emotional gap between them. Any connection would eliminate the elemental lack Warlock feels in his relationship with her; for Diana to acquiesce, however, would require a relinquishing of the spontaneous impulse she believes should characterize a healthy sexual relationship. By commodifying the act in terms of food, Warlock has exposed his essential desire and its lack in his life: food, whether as nourishment or as currency, has become a controlling image, and the protagonist's subsequent actions focus on his attempts at subduing his desires and directing those desires toward a leveling in both his personal and social lives.

The first act of ingestion in the narrative is significant for the juxtaposition of the one who partakes, Warlock, and those who do not, Diana and the Lundgren's dog, Hudley, who, when offered the meal, "after one tentative lap, rejected the hasenpfeffer. Hudley had never refused food before, not even an experimental leaf of lettuce, or a cracker with Tabasco for punishment."[22] Warlock's desire for food holds him captive in a disordered here-and-now; he is unable to seriously consider the future, or to make sense of his past. Only when he leaves the table does he begin to understand the controlling images of food and their pervasive effects on the other aspects of his life: "So much for cuisine, back to the future, he thought. Plans. Take a shower. Examine moments and how they might be radicalized. A mere fruit fly alters the taste of a glass of wine. Specific plans. I have the unemployment office." The reverie breaks down when Warlock's only conclusion is to aimlessly wonder, "What's for dinner?"[23]

Warlock's "vertiginous plunge from forty-five thousand a year as a foundation executive to the dole" takes on added significance in light of another unsuccessful dinner. As he stares into the sink at a mass of frozen squid, his confused contemplation at his inability to create a satisfying meal brings on a nagging sense of predetermination. He knows that to acquiesce to visions of the past, as he does throughout the narrative, and to allow those visions to distort his perception of the present, is to experience death which, "when it came, came all at once, like a soap bubble bursting."[24] Just as there is more to preparing oyster stuffing than Warlock at first comprehends, food imagery exposes the underlying complexities of his life, the reconciliation of his present, his past, and an uncertain future; only when food imagery provides a bridge into the past does the past become comprehensible. Warlock's failure to fulfill his role as gourmand is an articulation of a concept that Harrison, after Gerald Vizenor, uses as the basis for his essay "The Panic Hole," "a place where you go physically or mentally or both when the life is being squeezed out of you or when you think it is, which is the same thing. A panic hole is a place where you flee to get back the present as a wild season rather than a ruse." The notion of the "panic hole," in this instance Warlock's attempt at establishing order in the present by grounding himself in the preparation of food, is key to our understanding of Warlock's quest and the power of memory in his search for balance.[25]

Warlock recalls an affair in New York City twenty years before and can describe in detail the dinner that the two lovers shared, a pasta meal that included garlic, "a spice never known in his parents' house and for that matter rarely used in the heartland in those days."[26] The novelty of the sexual encounter corresponds to the novelty of the food they have eaten and signals a break for the twenty-two-year-old adventurer from the inhibitions of his Midwestern upbringing. In recalling his emotional attachment to the woman, Warlock equates his feelings for her only in terms of their meal together. The woman, an unnamed thirty-five-year-old Korean War widow, initiates Warlock into the intricate relationship between sex and consumption, a connection that parallels the Victorian predilection toward "the cojoining of women and food. . . . In cookery lay the enchantment of Circe, the mystery of Cleopatra and the witchery of Medea. The pent-up, hermetically-sealed, stove-heated dens of life immurement were transmuted in men's imaginations into lairs of potent magic, from which issued loaves and fishes."[27] Harrison's use of such a well-worn association points up the comic aspect of Warlock's predicament—the hedonic impulse that necessitates the "commingling" of food and sex—and Warlock's addictive slavishness to his base instincts—the satiation of hunger, thirst, and sexual desire. Significantly, the meal the widow serves leaves him unfulfilled, at least until he can appease his appetite in sexual encounter. In this case, the inadequacy of the food as a precursor to sex mirrors Harrison's focus on the fragmentary, contradictory events that characterize Warlock's pursuit of psychic balance. Warlock's slack-jawed reverie affirms the notion that, as one ages, it is not unusual to attempt to "capture symbolically through food, the rewarding and nurturing experiences of earlier life." In addition, and more important to his present relationship with Diana, "Food and drink relieve frustration by substituting for desired love or affection."[28]

The morsels of food available to Warlock—in this case only popcorn and an empty Chablis bottle—are a metaphor for the absence of direction in his life; day-old popcorn and an empty wine bottle certainly suggest that he is far from achieving the success that he half-heartedly desires. Warlock believes that, were it available, the food that he craves, nourishment for the sea-changes he resolves to make, would be a symbolic ingestion of the "power" that has eluded him and the marital peace lacking in his relationship with Diana, "[feeding] the dream of power and peace with which the atomized individual engulfs the world and all its separate things."[29]

Warlock's contemplation of his situation reaches its absurd pinnacle when he prepares turkey legs and a rutabaga. Again, the protagonist finds himself unable to define his nebulous future outside the realm of food and its preparation. Warlock "hollowed out and peeled [the rutabaga], albeit clumsily, and filled [it] with gravy as one might fill a Halloween pumpkin without eyes, nose and mouth. He put the rutabaga in the oven with a warm sense of inventiveness. . . . He owned the future whose face could be made by the touch of his fingertips."[30] The comic possibilities of the novel and Harrison's serio-comic social commentary intersect in Warlock's resolution to change his life, a culmination of the "novel's spectacle of human weakness and failure" in which "Lundgren watches too much television and eats too much, especially his own exotic, highly seasoned dishes."[31] Warlock makes the decision to change in terms similar to an alcoholic's "moment of clarity" or the born-again Christian's "calling": "Life drew certain lines, it wasn't some big glob of mashed potatoes. His clear view of change, of the perimeters of the future, owned a strong enough religious impulse to lead him inevitably to rule making. He took a law tablet and ballpoint pen from the briefcase."[32] The fact that Warlock is bound to fail in his attempts at fulfilling the four directives that he outlines for himself becomes evident in the deceptive simplicity of the statements and the protagonist's addictive nature. The reader is privy to a joke that Warlock has not quite figured out:

- Number One. EAT SPARINGLY. . . .
- Number Two. AVOID ADULTERY. . . .
- Number Three. DO YOUR BEST IN EVERYTHING. . . .
- Number Four. GET IN FIRST RATE SHAPE.[33]

Not surprisingly, Warlock defines his life-changes in terms of food, which "becomes a manifestation of personality."[34] Much of the narrative's comedy arises from Warlock overstating his desire to change and a perceived need for change based on nothing more than a dream and an impending midlife crisis.

The dream that prompts Warlock to make such overarching and ambitious statements for his future reflects his own increasing dissatisfaction with life, in no small part because of his wife's success and contentment in her own career as a nurse. The eating, drinking, and adultery have become substitutes for his wife, and his obsession becomes so profound that Diana suggests that he see a psychiatrist. Still, Warlock steadfastly refuses to admit that he has little control over his life, although his eating habits clearly describe someone who, as Diana astutely points out, has lost control, direction, and ambition.[35] The dishes Warlock concocts often contain ingredients not commonly combined, and the result is unpredictable and only marginally edible. The oxtail soup (which Warlock was eating when Diana confronted him about his depression) provides a context within which Diana may express her concern over Warlock's state of mind: "You've been dawdling for months. You're not happy [in Northern Michigan] and maybe we should move back downstate where there are more opportunities. . . . You go to the grocery store and cook dinner. That's it." The discussion over dinner of Warlock's antipathy in his relationship with Diana and others leads to Diana dumping the soup on Warlock and retreating to "her secret room," where Warlock has never disturbed her. The argument culminates in the protagonist's single act of aggression against his wife when "he delivered a karate kick with all his weight, exploding the secret door off its hinges. There was a scream. He didn't look in."[36]

The argument leads to Warlock's first of many transgressions, an affair with a woman named Patty after "two quick doubles" at Dick's Pour House. Warlock himself becomes edible as his genitalia provide a comic food metaphor: Patty wonders that Warlock "smell[s] like vegetable soup," and Warlock relates the argument with Diana before she performs oral sex on him. After he finds some satisfaction in being "eaten" and providing ostensible satiety to Patty with himself as food, Warlock mends his relationship with Diana, without a second thought for Patty, as he realizes for the first time as he kisses her knee that "this is Diana's knee—she is not me, nor I her." Warlock's newfound "understanding" of his relationship with Diana, in the context of his being consumed by someone previously outside the scope of his obsession, allows him to actively search for work, a small step toward fulfilling his four mandates. The clarity of purpose and the determination to recast his identity that arise after his argument with Diana, soon vanish—a cycle that repeats itself several times in the narrative. But for all Warlock's resolve to direct his own life, "life changed with as little reason as it had previously refused to change," and Warlock "somehow knew that he needed the wilderness even though what he thought of as wilderness included a twinge of fright for him."[37]

Warlock's journey into the wilderness begins with a stop at the home of an old friend, Clete Griscombe, the embodiment of Brillat-Savarin's "moralist" who understands the power of food and folk wisdom. Clete's fare is simply prepared and the very act of eating becomes a ritual; Warlock's journey into the wilderness, initiated by a meal of trout and whiskey, emphasizes Clete's own pragmatism as a purveyor of the common sense that Warlock so sorely lacks. His unambiguous assertion that Warlock is a "drag-ass" is preferable to Warlock's incessant philosophizing and tortured recollection.[38] Clete is not alone in his assessment of Warlock's inability to act: as he heads into the wilderness, Warlock recalls Diana's teasing "about his penchant for sitting in a corner and 'thinking things over.'" Warlock's meeting with Clete and the subsequent affirmation of his banal notion that "we don't live forever" places Warlock on the verge of the wilderness, both physically and metaphorically. With Clete's words still fresh in his mind, Warlock stands at his refrigerator and asserts himself as a man's man ready to take on the wilderness by "pick[ing] at the ample amount of rare meat . . . , washing it down with a cold Stroh's. He felt the solid, adventurous clarity of a trapper setting off into the mountains, an unknown vastness, for another season."[39] Joining work, which "inevitably embeds us in nature, including what we consider wild and pristine places," and the solitude of the road is analogous to Warlock's association of "manly" meals with his newfound desire to renew his life in the wilderness, which offers him a chance to become as assertive, productive, and content as he imagines himself to be.[40] Warlock's eating habits, which become less complex and more atavistic as he prepares to trek into the wilderness, are a natural precursor to subsequent action, signaling the "Carniverousness [that] generally goes with ferocity and with the disposition to fight and slash and kill . . . Humanization becomes inseparable from spiritedness or aggressiveness, rooted in (or, at least, correlative with) meat eating."[41] For Warlock, it seems, the higher on the food chain he eats, the more likely he is to take decisive action to remedy his life.

Warlock's discussion with Clete allows him to alter, if only for a time, the way he perceives his future. The ride home from Clete's recalls Warlock's flight to New York with a trustee on the board of his previous employer. The meeting, which culminates in the trustee's evaluation of Warlock based in large part on their food talk, relies wholly on food metaphors and food knowledge for its context. The recollection foreshadows his relationship with Dr. Rabun, the man who hires Warlock and betrays him with Diana. In fact, in his meeting with Rabun, the doctor admits that "I called Vergil Schmidt. We're old acquaintances, both thirty-second degree Masons. He spoke very highly of you." The protagonist's relationship with Rabun (Brillat-Savarin's "physician") parallels their eating habits during their initial dinner-meeting, which features a plethora of rich food and the finest wines.[42] The exquisite meal opens Warlock to the possibilities of the table and foreshadows his continuing struggles with an addictive personality later, when he is removed from Diana and familiar surroundings. The image of Warlock-as-hedonist emphasizes the protagonist's ravenous appetite for the pleasures of food and food's continuing appeal to Warlock as an aphrodisiac, a connection that is clear in the two much different connotations of the word: "In our culture at least, sexual climax has the reputation of providing one of the most intense pleasures. The Greek word, though, derives from the pleasures of eating."[43] Additionally, the hedonist acts "so as to maximize anticipated pleasure. Whether it is good or bad is of no consequence."[44]

Warlock treads a fine line between the glutton whose rapacity for food eventually decreases his own sexual appetites and the well-balanced individual who monitors his impulses and can keep them in check—the sure road to success, it seems. Rabun's own modest eating habits should forewarn Warlock, whose weight has risen to 200 pounds and who is a prime candidate for gout.[45] Rabun now plays ascetic to Warlock's glutton, and emphasizes the relationship between food and sex so important for the protagonist. Rabun's alertness, his business savvy, and his clarity of purpose (in fact, Rabun knows a great deal about Warlock's past life before they ever meet) are all seemingly related to his ability to control his consumption of food and drink, and Harrison implies the correlation between the two: "While Warlock had his blackberry torte, demitasse, and Hine cognac, Rabun studied the memo, his pen poised over it like a bird of prey."[46] The sated Warlock becomes Rabun's employee as a detective, a job for which Warlock is eminently unprepared and which can only exacerbate his relationship with Diana, his recollections of the past, and his late-blooming intimation of mortality.

III

There is an imagination below the earth that abounds in animal forms, that revels and makes music.
                    —James Hillman, *The Dream and the Underworld*

A gourmet who thinks of calories is like a tart who looks at her watch.
                                                        —James Beard

Warlock's first assignment as Rabun's lackey is to patrol a plot of land that Rabun believes is being illegally logged. The protagonist imagines his escape into the wilderness primarily in terms of the "chunks of deer meat" he will eat.[47] The vision recalls Kass's notion of the atavism fueled by the consumption of meat, which readies man for survival in the wilderness by any means necessary. The purity of Warlock's vision, however, is mitigated by his recollection that Diana has "packed him a large cellophane sack full of dried fruit and nuts after he had announced at breakfast that the trip would be a fine shot at losing a few pounds. . . . They drove on with the memory of the roasting meat causing him discomfort."[48] The push and pull of wilderness and civilization—a relationship with his wife and the welcome loneliness of wilderness, identity and nonidentity—is repeatedly defined by food and its consumption.

Warlock's brash statement that he would lose weight on the trip, his first directive, is undermined by the reality of his situation: he is either unable or unwilling to "EAT SPARINGLY." When Warlock eats a handful of the dried fruit and nuts, he experiences "a sense of instantly losing weight, however short-lived. A few minutes later he swerved into the parking lot of a small restaurant called the Rathskeller. There were no trucks in the parking lot, a good sign, he thought. And only one car, which made it iffy." Despite his inclination, Warlock gluts himself on heavy food and falls back into his previous pattern of waking reverie. The sleep Warlock fights as he heads into the wilderness brings with it another dream, a vision of Diana and then his mother, in an echo of Faulkner's Vardaman in *As I Lay Dying*, with a fish: "The brief dream came roaring in, the antipodes of promise and grace. Mom was a trout with a woman's face flopping on a riverbank, and Dad pushed him into haunted basements. . . . No one was out there, not even a religion. He sat down cross-legged, utterly giving up. His eyes were still open but he wasn't seeing anything, not past, present, future."[49] The chain of events leading to Warlock's most disturbing dream is initiated by his traveling unprepared into the "wilderness" and by his excessive appetites. Warlock's eating habits are a metaphor for his gluttony of imagination, his excessive and torturous dwelling on the past, and his relationship with Diana, all of which threaten to wantonly consume him as indiscriminately as he consumes the food and drink that feed only unproductive memories and bizarre dreams. When illness forces him to stay home from a Thanksgiving feast, Warlock's alienation from his family and friends is a prelude to an even more profound alienation from nearly everyone he meets.

Warlock's anxiety at having to "hightail it out of town" after he rashly threatens two men prompts him to "stop at a party store and buy a pint of schnapps to tamp down the steaks which were acting up." He muses that "Fear was bad for digestion. A fear diet would be big on rice and poached fish. Soda crackers and soup. Nothing heavy." Warlock broods incessantly on his life, an accretion of the fears that manifest themselves throughout the narrative and are always accompanied by unsatisfying meals. Typically, after associating fear with indigestion, Warlock's thoughts drift to the abstract, prompted by "a deep swig of schnapps."[50] Alcohol is important in Warlock's life, because "It lets loose powerful animalistic forces latent in the soul; forces that wash out our ability to make distinctions; that work to overthrow our customs and restraints; that conduce to violence; that seek, as it were, to dissolve all form and formality into the primordial watery chaos."[51] The protagonist's alcohol-induced wandering, one of many such events in the narrative, takes him to Sault St. Marie, where he meets Aurora, an Armenian grade school teacher who passes herself off as a Chippewa. On the way to Warlock's motel, "she insisted on stopping for a takeout pizza, with everything. Pizza was perhaps his least favorite food, he thought, hoping it wasn't a bad omen." His sexual encounter with Aurora forces him into a new experience that prompts him to dull the vision with a "largish glass of whiskey from his travel bottle," the result of which is that "He envisioned [Aurora] scrubbing her buckskin clothes by a river while being watched by deer and raccoons. There was a miniscule gobbet of tomato sauce on her neck embedded with a speck of oregano, a red jewel of sorts. He reached for her."[52] Food, and in this case drink, act as the catalysts for Warlock's advances toward Aurora as he carries consumption to absurd degrees. He is unable to approach Aurora without the aid of whiskey, and his lack of inhibition prompts him to leave a $100 bill in her wallet. He creates the stereotypical Indian squaw as an exotic illusion of a naïve partner, willing and edible, covered in tomato-sauce jewels.

A confrontation with Aurora the next morning, near the middle of the narrative, brings on the first anxiety attack of Warlock's life, which begins "with the usual sense of displacement, the eternal question of 'what am I doing here?' The spark for the displacement was a liquor advertisement in a magazine, quoting Robert Service's 'The Men That Don't Fit In.'"[53] He is crushed by the mocking irony of the image, the fine line between the intrepid wilderness adventurer and society's outcast. The anxiety attack impels an unbearable homesickness, and the meals Warlock has consumed since his departure—primarily in communal settings where Warlock is the single outcast—leave him unable to simulate the domesticity of cooking for Diana. The anxiety attack, brought about by the lack of a stabilizing influence in his life, brings to the surface the fears that preclude him from living a "normal" life. He realizes that "he was at the awesome crossroads where the hero must continue the quest or turn his back on it," and he muses that "Reality was amazing: one minute he was having a nervous breakdown, and the next moment he broke through the soup of despondency with a clean hammerlock on the future. Had that sacred summer solstice night in the forest imbued him with new powers, he wondered? It was possible."[54]

Warlock accedes, finally, to Diana's request to see a psychiatrist. The result of his sessions is only that "he received a few interesting recipes, some good travel talk, the suggestion that there were some infantile characteristics in his psychological makeup." In an attempt at reconciling with Diana, Warlock stops "for a takeout pizza at Little Richard's, Diana's favorite infantile dish. . . . Perhaps he could use this dish to win back her favor. Rare, indeed, is a woman or man so sullied that they can't be rebaptized with a few drinks, a pizza, and a shower."[55] The encounter with Aurora is improbably repeated when she agrees to see Warlock the following night. With relative ease, Warlock further alienates himself from Aurora, a vegetarian, by forcing her to eat a piece of bloody steak. That Warlock is an avowed carnivore and sometimes-defender of wilderness and the environment casts him as the alpha male, the relationship's aggressor who craves control and considers it his privilege to eat red meat (bloody, and a lot of it). His forcing the meat into Aurora's mouth is a rape scene without the threat of sexual violence, an abject attempt on the part of the protagonist to wield the power that he so sorely lacks in every other aspect of his life.

Warlock's sullen drive home follows the predictable pattern of abstract reverie and recall and concentrates on Diana's deep understanding of his psychic stagnation, which hinges upon his inability (or unwillingness) to change: "You're going mad from self-pity, self-concern, self-indulgence. You begin every fucking sentence with 'I' or 'my.' You

say 'I'm hungry,' 'My stomach is upset,' 'I'm horny.'"[56] Warlock's earlier death-dream has revealed (at a rather late age which, coupled with
the fact that he prefers a name given him thirty years before in a cub
scout initiation, hints at Warlock's psychological makeup) the inevitability of death, a notion that irrationally controls the protagonist's everyday life. The dream, which haunts him in one form or another throughout the course of his transformation, emphasizes the importance of
food, "the basely material vulgarity of those who indulge in [its] immediate satisfactions," not only as a contextual grounding for his memories, but as a symbol for Warlock's inexorable slamming toward self-
destruction at a pace that only rarely bothers him.[57]

Warlock's second meeting with Rabun, who "somehow knew about
his diet" (and, through Diana, much more intimate details), gives the
doctor an opportunity to torment the dieting Warlock. Rabun presents
him with "an elaborate cuisine minceur dinner,"[58] an exquisitely prepared meal in excruciatingly small portions, which allows the doctor
to further manipulate him. Although Warlock's weakness for food is
transparent, he tries to accept what Vergil Schmidt has told him earlier and what Rabun has corroborated—that quality takes precedent
over quantity, that "when appreciated by the discerning tastes of the
diners, the virtues of the meal itself transform and elevate the souls of
the diners. The aesthetic experience mysteriously provides both bod-
ily and spiritual satisfaction."[59] Even in his attempt to exercise moderation, though, Warlock finds himself unable to balance his alcohol
consumption with the relatively small quantity of food he has ingested,
and he makes a fool of himself to his cuckold. Warlock's ignorance of
the relationship between Rabun and Diana, and his overestimation of
his own progress toward the goals he has set for himself, is clear in his
conversation with Rabun. The doctor, by exposing himself as a gourmand and chef who can indulge his appetites and tame them at the
same time, proves himself to be more cultured, and in a world more
impressed by restraint than by the attitudes that Warlock has assumed
in his table habits, more worthy of Diana's affections. Food and drink
alone cannot save Warlock from himself.

IV

O the animal masks of the Ostend Carnival: bloated vicuna faces,
misshapen birds with the tails of birds of paradise, cranes with sky-

blue bills gabbling nonsense, clay-footed architects, obtuse sciolists
with moldy skulls, heartless vivisectionists, odd insects, hard shells
giving shelter to soft beasts. . . .

—James Ensor, "Speech at the Ensor Exhibition
at the Jeu du Paume," in *James Ensor*

Warlock's final assignment for Rabun offers a quick, untidy, and ultimately unsatisfying conclusion to the narrative: Warlock discovers
that Rabun has sent him to Florida under false pretense so that he can
spend more time with Diana, who sees Rabun as a creative genius, the
"Linus Pauling" of sexual-enhancement prostheses. While Warlock
has reached a better understanding of the nature of his existence, "that
reality was shot through with large empty spaces, spaces in which
nothing whatsoever occurred."[60] His innocence of Rabun's complex
scheme finally leads him back to his starting point, through a series of
incidents that resemble his earlier struggle with the unpleasant idea of
his own death and into his search for Rabun's estranged wife, his son,
and a woman who has allegedly injured herself at a fitness club owned
by the doctor. When Warlock discovers, seemingly by accident, the
paraplegic woman who has sued Rabun, he involves himself in an
episode that quickly leads to the narrative's climax. The "cripple"
Laura Fardel seduces the willing Warlock, who is frantic to connect
with someone—anyone—even though he often thinks of Diana. He
makes an easy target for Mrs. Fardel who, with her husband, contrives
to extort money from Rabun.

In his absence from Diana, Warlock continues to give in to his
immoderate impulses. In an attempt to connect with the bartender
where Warlock is drinking alone, he further alienates those around
him, reverting to much the same character he was at the outset of his
journeys. That alienation once again forces him back into the reveries
he has experienced throughout his quest, and he muses that "So much
had happened since the dream, now five months back, that he seriously wondered if some secret power had been given him that summer
solstice night in the forest. Had that knoll been the burial ground of
ancient warriors and had his sleeping body osmotically sucked up their
forgotten powers? Something definitely had happened."[61] The visions,
and Warlock's assessment of their meaning, reach the saturation point
and, instead of leading him toward resolution, become nothing more
than a pulsing background of white noise signaling the seriousness of
Warlock's condition.

Harrison uses absurd images and situations to heighten the humor of Warlock's plight and to expose the farcical underpinnings of his creation: a beautiful handicapped woman who knows a little too much about Warlock and who has indiscriminate sex with him; videotapes and blackmail and death threats; gay bars and identity crises. The Florida landscape is littered with characters who prefigure Carl Hiaasen or recall Harry Crews's own bizarre creations thrown together to perform one final variety act before they disappear with the falling sun, and the memory of the whole melange leaves nothing more than a bittersweet saccharin aftertaste in Warlock's mouth; nor do those memories lead him any closer to the "truth" he seeks.

As a result of his sexual exploits with Laura Fardel, Warlock receives what he believes to be a Mafia death threat in the form of "a very dead pompano with a white rose stuck in its mouth." The fish ironically recalls the two earlier dreams in which fish were significant and the trout Warlock ate with Clete to begin his journey into the wilderness. Warlock places a frantic call to his director-friend Garth, who explains that "you are the dead fish and the rose is an obvious symbol of the funereal spirit in the culture of that ancient land. . . . I'm being honest. I'm throwing the raw meat on the floor. This world's for the meat eaters, baby."[62] Garth's statement, which recalls Kass's own argument on the nature of such people and their place high on the hierarchical ladder of power, makes Warlock the unsuspecting and uncomfortable prey. Also, for the first time, Warlock realizes the extent to which he has alienated himself from his wife.

The death threat and Warlock's fatalistic attitude prompt him, for the first time in the narrative, to change his physical identity after months of unsuccessfully trying to alter his lifestyle. The physical change, he discovers, is relatively uncomplicated and has a more immediate effect on those he meets. Warlock stares at himself in the mirror and wonders if he had "gone too far. . . . But what was too far when you were saving your life?" The physical change forces Warlock into an uncomfortable situation in a roadside barbecue shack where his appearance alienates him from the other patrons because they confuse him for a gay man. He deflects the gravity of the situation by employing his well-worn bravado, but the scene leaves him contemplative, as he "had been nominally involved in the civil rights movement and began to see gays as blacks in the early sixties."[63] By recalling his "nominal" interest in civil rights, Warlock exposes himself again, despite the humor of the scene, as a self-centered and eminently unchangeable man who assumes numerous identities to little effect. The protagonist seemingly has accomplished the converse of his original stated intentions by distancing himself, physically and psychically, from his wife and from the four-step process that figures so prominently (and, despite Harrison's assertion otherwise in the preface, I suggest, ironically) in the narrative. The tragi-comic shortcomings of the protagonist are profound. The last events of the narrative, in which Rabun's family exacts its revenge on the doctor and Warlock realizes that he has been duped by him, seem almost tangential to the low point of Warlock's life.

The narrative comes full circle from the protagonist's dream of death in his own kitchen when Warlock discusses with Diana the death of two men who "had suffered heart attacks cutting up branches. . . . 'About your age. Overweight, violent men, no doubt paranoid drinkers, killers of birds and fish and deer.'" Warlock is an American Everyman who selfishly seeks his pleasures at the cost of his most important relationships; Diana's description provides a fittingly succinct summary of Warlock's problems. Warlock attempts one last time to adhere to the four steps whose fulfillment has thus far proven elusive: in his newfound moderation he gets his weight down to 177 pounds, and on his forays into the wilderness his "feet were light, his legs like steel springs as he ran through the wet forest. Perhaps deer watched with envy. Or not."[64]

The story of Warlock is not a Manichean tract on the nature of good and evil, nor is it a serious attempt at writing detective fiction with its intricate plotting and denouement. The conclusion of the novel has, perhaps understandably, come under fire as a hastily written finale to an otherwise clever delimiting of the power and pervasiveness of food in our lives. Any formal foibles notwithstanding, though, most important to an examination of Harrison's work is the novel's centering on the notion that food and drink—as nourishment, as symbol, as a context for recollection and contemplation—perform a number of significant tasks in our lives. A study of food and drink and its preparation in literature opens up to us the possibility of examining our own habits, our addictions, our desires, our means of moderating in order to reach an elusive "balance."[65] In Harrison's work, that balance is only alluded to, an ideal as ambitious as Warlock's own culinary vision and often as elusive. The novel's serio-comic tension expresses a symptom of a collective national hangover: as with the protagonist's plight, whose own darkly humorous life echoes the lives of so many of Harrison's characters, the result is never tidy. Warlock "does battle with the earth herself, whose vast, globy body has never been known to smile," an act which neither elevates nor diminishes him, but rather offers him a context within which to view the absurdities of life.[66] In "Sporting Food," one of his many essays on the vagaries of eating well and not dying from it, Harrison whimsically opines that "many of our failures in politics, art, and domestic life come from our failure to eat vividly."[67] Such a statement might be confused for exaggeration or flippancy in writers who lack Harrison's ability to mold such a collection of simple, astute observations—in this case the preparation and consumption of food and drink—into a truism that so accurately defines American culture.

"To what degree are these people dead?"

The Weight of History and Care of the Soul in Jim Harrison's *Dalva* and *The Road Home*

O History, as Carl Becker remarked, how many truths are committed in thy name! But there is no cynicism in this observation as long as it means that the course of events, like a moving train, provides new positions from which to survey the track left behind. Later events must inevitably focus our attention on earlier ones. Similarly, all inquiry is guided by developing concepts that have their own history.
—Cushing Strout, *The Veracious Imagination*

Just as revisionists cling to the traditional rhetoric of the American literary tradition they are critiquing, Americanists have always viewed the past as something to be both abandoned and revered. Plagued by this ambivalence, American Literary Scholarship has been consumed with the self-justifying task of connecting works of literary art to an exclusively American social context while largely ignoring the larger contextual field. They have danced around text and context in a typically Romantic oscillation that identifies the continuing entrapment of contemporary criticism in unresolved and unresolvable traditional terms.
—Peter Carafiol, *The American Ideal*

The girl of beautiful face / still goes on gathering olives, / with the grey arm of the wind / encircling her waist.
—Federico Garcia Lorca, "Song"

In his assessment of American fiction up to the 1970s, Henry Claridge writes that "It is an accepted part of the 'conventional wisdom' about the American novel that it has largely eschewed history and society in

preference for existential and metaphysical speculation."[1] The assertion, it seems, is well-founded: Philip Roth comments that the overwhelming and increasing number of history-changing events that are
a result of a networked "global community" (which has become expo-
nentially more complex since Roth considered the subject four decades
ago) can only lead to further chaos and fragmentation. The novelist,
hiding in his fiction, might safely ignore the historical aspects of his
craft, and who could blame him? He had "his hands full in trying to
understand, describe, and then make credible much of American reality. It asserts, it sickens, it infuriates, and finally it is even a kind of
embarrassment to one's meagre imagination. The actuality is contin-
ually outdoing our talents, and the culture tosses up figures almost
daily that are the envy of any novelist."[2]

In breaking with those self-imposed limitations on the simultaneous consideration of literature and history, Jim Harrison recounts, in
a notion that he terms "soul history," the profound effects of the past
on the present.[3] The notion synthesizes the Jungian concept of a collective unconscious and an accreted Calvinistic guilt for past actions
that holds us all accountable for those events; our present, far removed
from some of the most blatant appropriations of our culture on America's native cultures, and ultimately on each other, echoes with the dis-
quietude of the past. Harrison defines "soul history" in his essay
"Poetry as Survival": "Our nation has a soul history, not as immediately verifiable as the artifacts of the Smithsonian, whose presence we
sense in public affairs right down to [Ronald Reagan's] use of the word
'preservation,' or his cinema-tainted reference to oil-rich Indians."[4]

Soul history insists on our culpability for the past even as we
reshape and deny that past, and it allows us to study contemporary
American history as distinctly different from, although always part of,
the history that the Eurocentric majority has appropriated in perpetuating the myth of the American Dream, a term that has come to con-
note two dissimilar notions: first, the fervor with which we have dec-
imated our natural resources and continue to ignore (at the least; at
the worst, persecute) our marginalized peoples; second, the mythos of
the individual who lives apart from history and forges a place among
the demigods of American lore. The first focuses on our commodification of freedom, while the second fixes squarely on the corruption
of the Dream in its original, and purest, sense by exhorting Americans
to retain their individual spirit at all cost. Literature, in some ways an
odd synthesis of Jungian psychology and the American Dream, can,

above all other forms of expression, serve as a litmus test for a society's ability to accurately assess its own goals, in no small part "Because literature is a repository of both a society's ideologies and its psychological conflicts, [and] it has the capacity to reveal aspects of a culture's collective psyche."[5]

The notion that writers of fiction who use history as a contextual grounding should be wary of that history is nothing new. Marc Chenetier writes in his study of history in contemporary American fiction that "Oscar Wilde, lamenting that 'lying [should] have fallen into disrepute,' already considered Herodotus as 'the father of lies' and held that our duty towards history was to rewrite it. The works of Michel Foucault have given the last push, shifting the status of History from positivistic to 'Western myth.'"[6] Chenetier's treatise, which he appropriately subtitles "The Constrained Nightmare," traces an American obsession with history that has its most inauspicious beginnings in Columbus's plunge into the wilderness and continues into the late nineteenth century until the height of the Industrial Revolution and the extermination of our native peoples.[7] That history—the history of appropriation—is the focus of Harrison's *Dalva* (1988) and its prequel/sequel *The Road Home* (1998), both of which detail, in different ways and with different ends in mind, intricate interpersonal relationships and the forms of oppression and obsession that are magnified by the weight of history and instrumental to the well-being of the individual soul.

I

Dalva, the one-eighth Native American ancestor of the chronicler of history John Wesley Northridge, searches for her son, whom she gave up for adoption when she gave birth out of wedlock at sixteen.[8] Northridge, a missionary and adventurer who "had been always treated with some suspicion for being on the wrong side of the 'Indian Question,'" keeps diaries of his journeys and his close contact with the Native Americans.[9] In Dalva's present, Michael, a Stanford historian—whom Dalva's mother Naomi describes as a man who can "shape all history into a continual reign of terror. I have never met a man less in touch with the 'dailiness of life,' so relentlessly blind to his immediate surroundings"—attempts to salvage his career by reconstructing a history based on the diaries.[10] While Dalva's narrative is ostensibly being told for her son, who finds her at the end of the novel and who is a newfound friend of Dalva's mother, the overarching theme of the narrative is the way in which history, and the histories of people long since dead, come to life and change the present; or, as Michael wonders when he walks into the family cemetery, "To what degree are these people dead?"[11]

The narrative is presented in three different narrative voices—Dalva's, Michael's, and Northridge's—which combine Harrison's poetic sensibility with an unblinking eye for the less palatable events of history. Harrison's narrative technique, with its constant digressions and its scrupulous attention to the details of history, creates the impression of suspended time and implies the complex and difficult task of reconstructing a family's history. The novel shifts from Northridge's own entanglement in the "Indian Question" to Michael's personal dilemmas to Dalva's force of spirit; from first-person accounts of the Civil War and its aftermath to Michael's unoriginal notion that "this is the first time in history that we get to know all of the world's bad news at once."[12] For Harrison, the sources of history can come from any place at any time. In that sense, history is not unlike fiction and, to be sure, the two are inseparable.

The author claims that the inspiration for Dalva is "an embarrassment because I actually dreamed her, and I have better training and education than to put much stock in that sort of thing."[13] Dalva's character, Harrison says, is a conglomeration of the women he has met—the kinds of women who are too often ignored in fiction—and her voice and spirit propel Dalva past her relationship with Michael and toward a meeting with her son that allows her to reconcile her own life with her family's past: "Dalva—and I think that's probably the attraction of a lot of women to Dalva—I had known a lot of inordinately strong women in my life but I had very rarely seen them in fiction, even women's fiction where there's of course a great deal of whining just like the contemporary male middle-class novel—as I call it nifty guys at loose ends."[14] In his essay "First Person Female," Harrison writes,

> Why did I think I might be able to write in the voice of a woman? Anyone who knows a novelist or poet very well has probably figured out that they are not dealing with a true intellectual. Intellectuals have a compulsion to be right and this urge is inimical to what John Keats called "negative capability," the capacity a poem or novel has to keep afloat a thousand contradictory people and questions in order to create the parallel universe of

art. Rationality, to borrow from Foucault, may be an inferior level of discourse. This is a very high-minded thing for me to say, keeping in view the recent moment when my wonderful mother, who is 84 and of 100 percent Swedish derivation, said, "You've made quite a living out of your fibs."[15]

James McClintock takes Harrison's affinity for Dalva one step further than a mere dream connection, asserting that Dalva is, in a Jungian sense (through James Hillman), Harrison's "twin sister," who allows the author to overcome "despair so that he can continue to write truthfully and insightfully."[16] Although McClintock personalizes the depression that Harrison has felt intermittently in his own life, the example works equally well when applied to Harrison's profound sense of regret and confusion at the vagaries of American history that he articulates in the novels. McClintock's notion of "soul-making" (again, drawn from Hillman), closely aligned here with Harrison's definition of soul history, though on an individual level, describes a "movement towards wholeness. . . . The depressions that afflict *Dalva*'s characters and distract them from meaningful relations with others are not to be taken as entirely negative. They are necessary for engaging the anima or animus."[17]

Despite Harrison's expression of his anima through a woman's point of view—certainly a courageous act given the critical reception of much of his work to this point—the novel has been both praised and vilified for its themes and structure. While Michiko Kakutani finds that several of the events in the narrative "have a contrived, sensationalistic air about them," she also realizes that Harrison's "storytelling instincts are nearly flawless." In discussing his ability to render place in the novel, Kakutani asserts that, "Unlike many nature writers, he adamantly refuses to sentimentalize the landscape, but instead takes it on its own terms, delineating—in tough, but rhapsodic language—both the physical beauty and danger of those empty spaces." John Clute, on the other hand, writes that *Dalva* is a "failed novel" because, apparently, the protagonist is too vital: "as a lover [Dalva] is flamboyant and generous; on horseback she is superb; she cooks well and knows wine; she drives like a man. She is rich."[18] If Dalva is all the things that Clute claims (and she is), she is also much more: like Melville's Ishmael (she states early in the narrative, "My name is Dalva"), she is the controller of her narrative, the only one suited to adequately reconstruct her tale.[19] She has at her command the memories of her childhood in Nebraska, her dead lover and the father of her son, her grandfather and great-grandfather—histories that have come down to her through firsthand experience, journals, and the family's orality. The narrative is a story-within-a-story, each successive paragraph a further accretion of the Northridge family's soul history, which finally divulges information about the family and allows the protagonist to find her lost son in a staid and simple reunion. The narrative exposes the ineluctable complexity of attempting, as Michael does, to capture the essence of history from experience filtered through time and the pages of a brittle journal, rather than from events related by the principals.

For Dalva, who recalls that "Everyone in the history of my family was a letter writer, a diary keeper. It's as if they thought they'd disappear if they didn't put themselves on paper," the practice of writing and reading diaries orders her thoughts, and it allows her to generate new perspectives on her own life by synthesizing past events and her felt sense of where they will take her. [20] The writing is also an identity-forming exercise. Dalva's role as the keeper of the family's history requires a vision and balance that none of the other characters exhibits; in protecting the integrity of her family's history, she makes space for new experiences by writing out the old ones, a process that makes linear time irrelevant for her. Michael observes that "Dalva is punctual on a nominal level but never seems to know the date or year of anything within the nearest decade. She says she sees events, the past itself, in terms of 'clumps' of years, which is a blithe evasion indeed. I told her that the study of history can't afford such messiness."[21] Michael is caught up in the histories of others, and he is unable to purge himself of past experience—a failed marriage, an average career, a drinking problem. His mind is cluttered, fragmented; he is easily distracted and malleable in all the wrong directions. Dalva and Michael have only the journals of Northridge in common; at the same time the journals revitalize Dalva in her search for her son and her own history, they act as a catalyst for Michael's descent into the madness of his solitude and an inescapable past.

Michael's tenuous grasp on the importance of the events detailed in the journals contrasts to Northridge's own understanding of the social context in his role as a spokesman for Native Americans. Even though the clan's patriarch has been dead for nearly a century at the outset of the novel, he is the vital link between the White man and the Indian, the history of the Sioux in the Midwest and Northridge's own prosperous Nebraska descendants.[22] In short, he represents the "soul" in

Harrison's notion of an American "soul history," and he describes the distinct possibility of losing one's soul in his own Dantean journey across Georgia in June 1865: "I do not know the day, and none in my vermin-ridden pack of men knows the day. We are together for safety. Mother has always abjured me to look daily after the condition of my soul, but yesterday I saw a man shot for a dead dog another man wanted for supper. In the land of dog eaters no one has a soul."[23]

Dalva's reticence in exposing her family's history to outside scrutiny acts as a filter to Michael's subsequent attempts at writing a history of the Sioux in the Reconstruction. Michael, then, can only hope to construct history (not re-construct history, and the distinction is crucial, as reconstruction implies the continuity of soul history), a series of facts devoid of motive or passion, even though he has in his possession a firsthand account of the events of Northridge's life. Michael's dilemma is an important part of writing history. While his first inclination is to distill from Northridge's journals the "facts" of his experiences with the Sioux and, more important, "how the first John Wesley Northridge [Dalva's father was the second] looked at the Sioux,"[24] he finds himself unwittingly drawn into Northridge's narrative as a subjective, excited observer of emotional events, not a chronicler of history.

Dalva correctly assumes that in Michael's dealings with the journals, he will "put a dress of [his] own designing on [the journals]." Also, "history in [Michael's] terms was utterly self-serving and no one had a right to know what he was looking for. Everyone was dead, and everything that followed in political terms was the equivalent of spitting on the memory of the dead. I said, You seem to think that if you don't tell someone, nothing has happened. I won't allow you to paw over these people for historical novelty." When Michael replies that Dalva believes herself to be "the keeper of the Grail and no one deserves to know what and why the Grail is," Dalva takes issue with Michael's motivation for commodifying events without fully understanding their implications in the present: "What you call history avoids any valuable concern for people. The essence is the mythology that allows us to conquer the native populations—actually over a hundred small civilizations—and then to make sure that their destiny becomes one of humiliation, a day-by-day shame and defeat, and what's more, we can feel right about it because they are drunken Indians."[25]

Still, Michael divides his time between studying the diaries in earnest and exploring his own relationship with Dalva. The two activities are not as dissimilar as they may at first appear. While Northridge (whom Michael finds interesting "because of his consciousness and his conscience, just as Schindler alone is fascinating while millions of Germans who didn't give a fuck are lost to history"[26]) describes his advocacy of the Sioux, the treachery of the government, and his subsequent marriage to a Sioux woman, Michael's love for Dalva and her independence provides a contemporary analogue in all its contemporary variations: Michael is trapped by his own ambition as a man utterly removed from a sense of the humanness of history and half a life wasted by alcohol and drugs, and Dalva is the unattainable ideal of Native American spirit and grace. Michael's perusal of Northridge's diaries juxtaposes the recording of history for professional gain with the keeping of the family's history for its own sake, known only to a few family members and close friends. Michael discusses the project with Naomi, Dalva's mother, and tries to convince her that his motives for studying the diaries are not grounded in greed, but in an altruism that uncovering the government's treatment of the Sioux would provide: "On our ride from town, I had told Naomi that the *soul of history* could not be approached with the cautious servility of the scholar. She said that sounded fine but wasn't sure what I meant. What it really meant was that I wanted her to think well of my high calling, but I certainly couldn't say that directly" (emphasis mine).[27]

Michael continues his attempts at ingratiating himself to the family, though the land—"a haven to which Dalva returns to heal her personal world-hurts"—that alienates Michael in his experience on the plains of Nebraska, both in his reading and in his relationship with Dalva, is essential in describing the history of the Sioux and the Northridge family and the consequences of the destruction of both the land and its people.[28] Without reconciling himself to the place, he is destined to fail. While Dalva sees the Native Americans' closeness to the land as characteristic of their existence, and she bemoans the loss of pristine nature, Michael adopts the Myth of the Frontier and claims that government agencies adequately justified their appropriation of land that "belonged" to the Native American for centuries before Columbus's arrival in the "New World." The Native Americans' unwillingness to embrace change "was another confirmation that Indians were backward failures in the evolutionary process, and must disappear along with the buffalo and the forest from whom they could scarcely be distinguished."[29] Michael, whose perspective of history is carved out of an indelibly Eurocentric indebtedness to his conquering white forebears, is "disturbed" by many of the places that he visits, including spots sacred to Dalva and Duane. Despite the years that have elapsed since their short affair, Duane's spirit is still very much with Dalva, who writes in her journal in *The Road Home* that he "has drifted far backward in time but is not the less vivid for being so long dead. I wonder if anyone can stand back from earth and get a clear look for more than a few moments at a time."[30]

Although Michael seems at times to stumble over his own notions of what history should be and how he will present it to an academic audience, in large part because of his fatalistic attitude toward himself and his relationship with Dalva, he is an astute observer of his own actions. He realizes early in his journal-reading that his immersion in history is drawing him into and making him a part of the history, "which is far easier to manage in a carrel in a research library" than in the company of his lover, Northridge's great-granddaughter and a woman who is a "spiritual heir" of the people whose history he is attempting to construct. Michael claims that "we are not in the business to lick the wounds of history but to describe them. . . . [I]t behooves the scholar to immerse himself in the analyses of the problem, rather than the problem itself."[31] After several failures at objectively reporting his conclusions, though, he admits that he is trapped too close to the events themselves on an alien and largely unforgiving landscape:

> My attempts to keep a distance from my material were losing ground. There is a reason why scholars work in libraries. A number of studies of the Holocaust have clearly illustrated that it constituted the most repellent series of events in human history. I doubt, though, if any of the writers and scholars of the studies had set up shop in Buchenwald, Belsen, or Treblinka to compose. Here, I was too much in the thick of it.[32]

Michael vacillates between his unprofessional (and, for him, unfamiliar) desire to become part of the history of the journals and his need to fulfill a professional obligation that keeps him tenuously employed while he walks the tightrope between academic accolades and neurosis; what precludes him from understanding the spirit of the journals, though, is the absence in him of a sense of soul history. Still, his work with the journals unsettles him and he relishes the mysterious feeling that was "normally beyond my ken. It was the very rare feeling that life was indeed larger and much more awesome than I presumed it to be."[33]

He finds himself drawn still further into the research, which touches on myth-making, when he interviews the old ranch hand Lundquist

on the history of Dalva's family and muses that "By experience I know
these rural types insist on beginning at the virtual dawn of creation."
Lundquist relates to Michael "the murder of his own grandfather during the Sioux uprising near New Ulm, Minnesota, in 1862. Lundquist
had decided, for reasons he didn't care to explain, that all Indians were
members of a 'lost tribe of Israel,' and our mistreatment of them would
bring our eventual doom. I attempted to divert him from this gibber-
ish back to actuality, with mixed luck." Michael's insincere hearing of
Lundquist's story, passed down to the ranch hand through generations
of oral re-creations of history, is ironic in light of Harrison's own dis-
mal view of our sense of American history, the shame of that history,
and Michael's own predicament in the narrative. By dismissing
Lundquist's oral narrative—"It's not that we're in a genetic slump but
that literacy, the educative system, barely scratches the surface of the
ordinary consciousness," he says about his meeting with the old
man—Michael aligns himself with the world of academia, for Harrison certainly not the "last best place." Lundquist's assertion that
"Indians were ignored because they were bothersome. They were
bothersome because they were a different kind of 'animal' compared
to us, wolves as opposed to foxes, horses compared to cows" is amus-
ing only insofar as Michael places himself above the folk wisdom of
Lundquist, one more bumpkin whom Michael will never bathe "in
logic and right reason."[34] Michael refuses to acquiesce to Lundquist's
view of the past, although his realization that he can no longer be
objective in his research opens avenues for his greater understanding
of what Dalva must feel when she views the destruction of the landscape from airplanes or when she recalls the past that she holds close,
apart from Michael's prying.

Michael's slowly changing conception of history, even though his
voice occupies fully one-third of the narrative, is important solely
because it contrasts Michael and Dalva and fully inculcates Dalva in
her own family's history. Her sense of the importance of past events,
because she has, in many ways, lived them (or at the very least lived
with them), is from the outset more in tune with their implications for
the present than Michael's own limited analysis. For that, Dalva suffers the pain of soul history, for which she is finally rewarded with the
return of her son. This is, after all, Dalva's story, and once Michael's
section, "Michael's Notebook," is closed, the history that is in danger
of becoming an academic commodity is applied at the personal level:
Dalva's love for the doomed Duane, Shakespearean in its intensity and

its tragic conclusion, his life destined to end in tragedy; the loss of Rachel, Duane's mother, who has borne a son by Dalva's father; the relationship between Dalva and her mother Naomi; and Dalva's love for her grandfather, whose knowledge of family history underpins the narrative and forms a second link from Northridge to the present. Though the narrative offers a sense of closure with the return of Nelse, "When Dalva's journals record the past . . . they reveal the painfully tragic details clouding both her past and present life. She recalls her father and grandfather, but her central focus is her ill-starred love for Duane Stone Horse."[35]

Dalva's own history begins with an explication of her purpose in writing, not as a journal that would facilitate her own creativity, but as a family history recorded for her son, "in case I never get to see him, and in case something should happen to me, what I have written would tell him about his mother."[36] The writing is cathartic for Dalva, and she underscores her relationships with men, whom "you can only meet . . . at the level of [their] intentions," all of which, with the exception of her short relationship with Duane, either threaten to destroy her identity or reinforce her independence. Her sense of history differs markedly from Michael's initial belief that history can be appropriated for personal gain. Instead, Dalva insists that "I'm not one to live or subsist on memory, treating it as most do, the past and the future as an encapsulated space or nodule we walked into, and then out of, rather than a continuum of the life we have already lived and will live."[37]

For Dalva, history determines the ways her family views itself; although her sister Ruth, like Dalva, is only one-eighth Sioux, "she had assumed certain Sioux qualities as she grew older, a kind of stillness that she forced to surround her."[38] Ruth has marginalized herself from society, the domain of the white, empowered male. The history that controls her life is the history of the Sioux and her great-grandfather's interaction with mythic figures, and she lives within that history as surely as Michael struggles, except in rare moments that he often regrets, to live outside it as an objective observer. To give oneself over to the history of the family is paramount, though forfeiting the soul to the events of the past rather than keeping them in abeyance comes at a price. Even more so than Ruth in her fight to reconcile her past with the present and the future, Dalva is a heroic figure in a society that aggrandizes a paucity of character. Although Harrison has created strong female characters in past narratives, "each work marks the progression in his ability to portray heroines. As critics and reviewers

have noted, however, his consummate portrait is Dalva. While combining the hearth goddess virtues of Harrison's other heroines, she per-
sonifies his idea that women should have the same prerogatives as a
man. Dalva emerges, therefore, as a stronger and more independent
heroine."[39] Though Harrison's is necessarily a "trespass vision," a
man writing from a woman's perspective, his willingness and ability
to struggle with the unknown make Dalva a boundless character.

In fact, Dalva is the one character who has the courage to wonder
if she might use history itself as a springboard to escape history when
she writes, "Is the story always how we tried to continue our lives as
if we had once lived in Eden? Eden is the childhood still in the garden,
or at least the part of it we try to keep there. Maybe childhood is a
myth of survival for us."[40] To live in the past and to treat it "as an
encapsulated space or nodule," is destructive: for Ruth, history is a barrier upon which she can view the high-water mark of her own limitations; for Michael, history empowers (here again distinct from the
understanding of "soul history" which is central to the narrative),
especially for those who have exclusive access to it and can control its
dispensation. Not surprisingly, neither Ruth nor Michael can transcend history; rather, that task is left to Dalva, who is closest to the
soul history of her family and in conflict with a nation that largely
ignores the implications of its actions.

Through her work with abused children, Dalva maintains order in
her own life by grounding herself in the present, as others in her family have: "All of us work. My mother has an involved theory of work
that she claims comes from my father, uncles, grandparents, and on
into the past: people have an instinct to be useful and can't handle the
relentless *everydayness* of life unless they work hard."[41] She avoids
being haunted by the concreteness of Northridge's journals, which
detail so vividly the final answer to the "Indian Question"; rather, the
"everydayness" of events threatens her in a way that Northridge's
journals cannot. When Dalva confronts a young boy's abuser, "The
eyes startled me because they belonged to someone long dead whom
I had loved. I tried to move away but his eyes slowed me and he
grabbed my wrist."[42] By recalling Duane's eyes in the eyes of the
abuser, Dalva eliminates any possibility of tidy recollections: history
is where it finds her, even in the eyes of a child molester.

Dalva's unwillingness to dwell on her father's death (the event gets
two sentences in her recollection) is reinforced by the structure of the
narrative, which takes on the form of distinct points-in-time separated

by space and silence, which Dalva fills in matter-of-factly with statements such as, "Here is how it happened to me, how I had my child early in my sixteenth year," and "His name was Duane, though he was half Sioux and he gave me many versions of his Sioux name depending on how he felt that day." More than once, she ends passages simply with "Enough!" The narrative page itself contains empty physical space, silences that reinforce the separation of the individual events in Dalva's consciousness, "a process of reduction or exclusion fundamental to the sentient self, a process that ends always by placing the self outside of Being."[43] Dalva's recollections of her own childhood are redolent with the effects of history on one girl, nearly thirty years before, unknowingly mapping out a course of events that encompasses the death of her father, the desertion of a lover, and her own tenuous existence in the desert of Arizona. She manipulates the spatial and temporal events of the past, an innate ability that precludes her from wandering through history, as Michael does, with the baggage of his own memories slowing his reconciliation with the past and the present and denying him the hope of a meaningful future.

Her concept of the holiness of places and her ability to sensually recall specific events leads her to a conclusion that evades Michael: "I had the odd sensation that I was understanding the earth. This is all very simple-minded and I mention it only because I still do much the same thing when troubled."[44] Dalva's easy dismissal of her understanding of history in terms of the earth does not mitigate its profound effect on her life. She is selfish in her needs because she must be in order to survive. The stories that Dalva relates undermine the uses of history that Michael would present in his "findings" on Northridge's journals: the stories acontextualize past events and downplay the importance of such events in the characters' present lives. Michael dwells incessantly on the events in his own life, and they render him unable to live his life except in terms of Northridge's journals, the Holy Grail of Michael's professional life and a constant reminder of his chaotic personal life. The same journals become, for Dalva, a manifestation of soul history that brings her to reconciliation and, finally, allows her to transcend the weight of history.

II

In *The Road Home*, the prequel/sequel to *Dalva*, Harrison reiterates the connectedness of family and nature and sharpens his vision of soul history to the point that it becomes, in Hillman's terms, a "soul-making" endeavor that begins when Dalva first meets her son and her life takes on "a richness, texture, clarity, and meaning unavailable to her before living with and through her depression."[45] In *Dalva,* the history of the family is recorded in a thick Native American context; in *The Road Home,* disparate voices lead, as they must in Harrison's work (certainly an argument for the necessity of *The Road Home* as a companion, almost an annotation, to the earlier book), to an intricate study of the individual. Harrison exhibits a profound sense of the ways that history informs all action in the present and how the inexorable movement of time annihilates the present in making it past; he is never at a loss for words in decrying society's venality or the absurd ironies that define American culture. On another level, though, *The Road Home* is the story that had to be written in order for Harrison to remain true to his vision: one that, poignantly punctuated by Dalva's last days and her suicide, praises the warts-and-all "dailiness of life" as the most accurate vision—finally, the only viable portrait— of our existence.

Although Harrison published *The Beast God Forgot to Invent* two years after *The Road Home,* this book is widely regarded as the most mature vision of a writer who has, like Dalva herself, come tantalizingly close to understanding the world around him. With the publication of *The Road Home* critics seem finally to have accepted Harrison's far-ranging sensibility. Thomas McNamee appreciates the randomness of the characters' recollections, writing that the narratives "plunge into the past, leap decades forward in time, then snap back to the present like a whip crack as [Harrison] assembles what at first seem unrelated fragments into a comprehensive and harmonious composition."[46] Wendy Smith praises the courage and skill of a writer who takes on themes that "In the hands of a lesser writer . . . might seem tacked on or smug. . . . Harrison aims high, pondering the meaning and the cost of American civilization through the story of a single family vividly rendered. He doesn't succeed in everything he attempts to do, but we could use more writers who attempt so much."[47] She also astutely points out that the narrative is much more narrowly focused on the characters' inner worlds, art in particular, than on outside events. Finally, the language that we all use to communicate our deepest desires and fears "has its limits, especially in extreme situations," which precludes delving any deeper into the human psyche and makes Dalva's death all the more appropriate as a stopping point.[48]

The story is delivered by five narrators—Dalva's grandfather John Wesley Northridge II; Nelse; Naomi; Paul, Dalva's uncle; and Dalva—who cover more than three decades in meticulous detail. Even more than in *Dalva,* whose controlling symbol is Northridge's "Indian" journals, *The Road Home* is an accretion of different points of view punctuated by seemingly disparate stories that move from the study of a broad soul history of the Northridge clan to the more intimate care of the individual soul that culminates in Dalva's bittersweet death. The book's first narrator, John Wesley Northridge II, the son of the family's journal keeper, muses that "It is easy to forget that in the main we die only seven times more slowly than our dogs," and "I had also noted in others that life largely passes while they are making grand plans for it."[49] His recollections, especially his melancholy acceptance of the vagaries of time, form a crucial link between the history of the family's patriarch, Dalva's great-grandfather, and the family's future, Nelse Carlson, who has fallen in love with J. M., a married exotic dancer and college student he meets in Nebraska. Northridge's story is one of nearly unbearable love and loss, a theme that runs throughout the narrative with Nelse's own attempts at wooing J. M. and Dalva's further recollection of her short-lived affair with Duane Stone Horse and his suicide off the Florida Keys.

Northridge, who in his youth was a passionate artist and devotee of Keats (like Harrison himself), first loved Willow, a young Native American girl, but was forced to stop pursuing her by her family and, Harrison implies with no little disgust, the moral code of the day. In an echo of the controlling theme of *Dalva,* Northridge II writes that the Native American spirit that is presumed to have been crushed a century ago is alive and well. In a confrontation with Willow's family, Northridge learns that "These were not Methodist Indians but warriors with a lineage that owed nothing to the white man. We did not live upon the same earth that they did and we flatter ourselves when we think we understand them. To pity these men is to pity the gods." His own notions of high art—"At that moment the word 'art' meant as much to me as the name 'Jesus' does to a cloistered nun"—contrast to the more visceral relationship that Willow's family has to the land. In his awakening sexuality, Northridge realizes that the romantic notions of the artist are simulacra of the real world, that "It is largely misunderstood that the first forays of a young man or young woman into the world of arts and literature, the making of them, are utterly comic and full of misadventures, rather than most of the dour and

melancholy renditions that are made public."[50] Still, he cannot dispel
all of his romantic notions and "a Keatsian fever" that affects him
throughout his life. His subsequent love affairs, especially one with
Adele, the sister of the woman who would eventually be his wife, are
life-altering experiences that haunt him until his death. Near the end
of his life, Northridge recalls telling his father, the diarist, that "*John
Keats was the greatest man in the world*," and he asserts that "I rather
like Keats's notion of 'negative capability' where one cherishes and
nurtures the thousands of contradictory ideas in one's head, rather
than trying to reduce them to functional piths and gists." He also
attempts to write poetry for Willow, an endeavor which fails miser-
ably and "which mainly served to increase my respect for Keats."[51]

Harrison's obsession with language becomes more pronounced,
and the characters more introspective, as the narrative progresses:
Northridge II, maddened by his inability to express his essence in his
journals—the same journals kept by his father before him, and soon
by his granddaughter and grandson—bemoans that "The language my
brain kept muttering to itself was supposedly the glue that bound it all
together. Only it didn't. . . . I was struck by the immutable presence of
the nameless." Perhaps silence has always been an alternative means
of communicating for Northridge II: he recalls sitting with his Native
American mother, Small Bird, "on the banks of the Niobrara for hours
on a summer morning simply watching and listening to the nature of
nature, or whatever one calls all that happens without immediate
human intervention, and not speak a word to each other but I would
be left with the feeling we had communicated perfectly."[52] The power
of highly personal written communication (the journals themselves,
which are important for pointing up the occasional failure of language) and unspoken communication and their link to the natural
world that is so important in the lives of the Northridge family manifests itself as a shorthand through which the family communicates to
each other and to the initiated who read the journals: the rules and
uses of language are "tied to custom but if this mutability demonstrates agreements within conventions determined by time and place,
it demonstrates as well the instability of concepts such as truth, knowledge, understanding and meaning. It encourages specific activity in its
dividedness, particularities and fallibility against the hegemonic claims
of tradition, canonicity and institutional authority."[53] On his deathbed,
Northridge II writes the last entry in his journal and "Rachel chants
for me in Lakota as my mother had done for my father. I am charmed

at this continuity though I have difficulty staying awake and my dreams are full of birds. . . . I sleep again and hear those billions of birds again. Christ, what a grand noise." Even his granddaughter's understated goodbye, "I'm sorry you're dying,"[54] is a fitting conclusion to his life.

The importance of dreams for the Northridge family, as Harrison also suggests in the companion novel, is in their ability, independent of language, to order the world-at-large by mediating experience and bringing us closer to an understanding of death which, in the case of Dalva's suicide and her hope to be reunited with loved ones who have preceded her in death, brings the family's saga to closure. Clearly, contemporary American society has little real understanding of death and only grudgingly accedes to the use of death metaphors in its literature. Indeed, as Hillman asserts, "Our culture is singular for its ignorance of death. . . . We have no ancestor cult, although we are pathetically nostalgic. We keep no relics, though collect antiques. We rarely see dead human beings, though watch a hundred imitations each week on the television tube. The animals we eat are put away out of sight. We have no myths of the *nekyia,* yet our popular heroes in films and music are shady underworld characters."[55] Still, Dalva's death at the end of the narrative is, in one sense, a metaphor that denotes not silence and an unspeakable void, but rather legacy and the cycles of nature whose inevitability is too often a fearful presence.

Hillman also makes a distinction between two kinds of soul: the "psyche-soul," which presents itself in dreams, and the "life-soul," present during our conscious, waking hours. Although, according to Hillman, the "two-soul theory seems to draw a hard-and-fast line between psyche and life," he concedes that "there is an operation, which we call dreaming, that makes the heroic ego a more subtle body, enabling it to become a free soul. . . . The dream is the most near and regular place where we can experience the subtle play between kinds of soul." He sees the intermingling of the two not necessarily as a bridge, but as a process through which the two souls can interact.[56] The Northridges transfer this knowledge from generation to generation, either in written or unvoiced communication, and dream, soul, and death are combined in the process of creating the "individualized soul" that prepares us, ultimately, for our "individual death."[57] Paul recalls his father's death-dream; in the course of the five stories that make up the novel, every character dreams and comments on those dreams. In an echo of *Dalva* and an invocation of history and the collective world of dreams that we share, Northridge II's mother, with her characteristic astuteness, cuts to the heart of the "Indian Question" when she suggests to him that "The saddest thing about Native dispossession is that the people weren't able to live out the cues from their dreams."[58]

Harrison's manipulation of dreams and the use of nonlinear narrative time (the book is, after all, a prequel/sequel to *Dalva,* a tricky notion in itself) in Northridge II's journals at the beginning of *The Road Home* are significant: with the death of Northridge II, which occurs chronologically long before Dalva is given the guardianship of Northridge's "Indian" journals, the family's generational bonds in the five different voices presented in *The Road Home* are broken. To be sure, the residual effect of such a close connection to the "Indian Question" through Northridge and his son remains: every member of the family knows the details of history, and Nelse, for one, rails incessantly on the injustice that he sees around him in his extensive travels; Dalva, Paul, and Naomi, who own the three concluding narratives, have similar reactions.[59] Still, the four narratives that follow are not beholden to the soul history of the family, but rather lend themselves to a closer study of the individual lives of the characters.

Nelse, in fact, has much of his great-grandfather's passion for life, and Nelse's own journal parallels Northridge II's on enough points to imply that the two were similar as young men. Harrison, who is chronologically much closer to Northridge II than Nelse, admits that he had difficulty recapturing "that free-floating anger you have at 30— that rage at everything. I talked to guys that age off and on—they didn't know why I was asking. But what I finally did was reread *Wolf,* my first novel, which I wrote at about that age. I said, 'My god, is this guy pissed off. Nelse has a more restrained voice than Swanson but it's bubbling underneath.'"[60] The romantic impulse that tortured Northridge II throughout his life is equally strong and tormenting in Nelse, a headstrong naturalist whose own search for identity inculcates him in the "soul-making" process.[61] In having spent much of the last decade experiencing the country, Nelse's singlemindedness finally forces him to wonder at his ability to "ignore the dimensions of other humans."[62] Though he does not engage himself with his great-great-grandfather's journals the way Dalva does, he feels the burden of his heritage, and "his deepening knowledge of the never-ending waste of Indian greatness darkens the novel's tone shade by shade, edging toward the anguish and compassion that are the irrecusable estate of his bloodline."[63] Still, he understands the nature of being well enough to assert that "I have no control of the world beyond my own skin," and the "bottom line was manifestly simple like the billions of galaxies which, no matter how inconceivably vast, had an existence with origins as mysterious as our own. If it all was based so resolutely on chance it seemed by far the best course to seize what chances were offered."[64]

Like his great-grandfather, Nelse questions language and takes stock in his dreams "of the Omaha Indians well north of the city. I don't even like to tell a piece of paper about them." In an echo of Northridge II's death, Nelse finds that language has its limitations. Like the other members of his family, though, Nelse is a hyperliterate journalist to whom jotting down the names of birds and geologic formations is as natural as speaking (perhaps even more so; he recalls chanting out "the whole expanded Linnaean hierarchy which I memorized while listening to the Rolling Stones").[65] Ironically, though, he did not learn the trait from his genetic family, but his adoptive father, "who instigated my journal writing in the first place so I wouldn't simply 'drift,'" though he "didn't care much for my social commentary when he read the first few years' worth. . . . He said I was too full of cynical 'nay-saying' and I shouldn't write about people as if I were Jane Goodall writing about chimps." Again, Nelse's notions of language are intertwined with his distaste for society.[66]

Through his connection with Northridge II and Dalva, Nelse is the one character in the novel who will perpetuate the family's legacy, and he admits that "My anthropology tells me in a pukey little whisper that I'm feeling a late mating urge, that my nine years of wandering around and looking things over were a ritual I had devised to frame reality, that the search for secret places was basically a primitive religious impulse."[67] Because of his role as future patriarch, his increasing awareness of his family's history is of vital importance to the narrative's thread. Like Northridge II, Nelse is impetuous and at first cares little for his role. Instead, he is much more concerned with experiencing the world, regardless of its practicality (itself a loaded term, and one that assumes the complicity of the individual with society): "I can't see the virtue in studying the natural world, just that everybody should do it. It's the only world you're going to get as far as we know. You read up a bit then look at it closely. Why are people adverse to it? I'm not sure but suspect it's because it's not immediately functional in the economy."[68]

The fact that Nelse so vehemently fights the constraints of society is acceptable because of the legacy that has been passed down to him, though the story is as old as Oedipus: "Communal action is rarely story's domain. The wrong in most narrative cannot be righted by the community. Instead, the task falls to an individual. . . . Story centers on the very action society restricts: that of the loner. But whereas the villain acts entirely in his own interest, the hero acts on his behalf of the group even when he appears to oppose it, and even when the meaning of his actions is not apparent to him."[69] As much as he fights the notion that he will become what he has always loathed, Nelse is destined, in a sense, to fulfill his obligations to society, even if he will never accept the venality and absurdity of that society. The maturation of the soul is as inevitable as death (in fact, part of the soul's maturation process is to experience death), Harrison implies, and a chorus of voices lead him through the process; how successful he is in appreciating and understanding the care of the soul, though, is dependent upon a lifelong attention to history, dreams, life itself.

For Nelse, those voices come from the family that he so desperately seeks in order to confirm his identity: in searching for his mother, Nelse establishes a relationship with his grandmother, Naomi, under the pretense of doing a phenological survey of her property along the Niobrara River in Nebraska. Between Nelse's search for his mother and Dalva's own narrative, the voices of Naomi and Paul serve both to reinforce and call into question the history of the family: even though the family is close in one sense, the stories that each of the narrators tells necessarily deviate from one another, naturally focusing on events that are more or less important in the lives of those characters than in the lives of their family members. The voices of Paul and Naomi, who become lovers after the death of Northridge III, Naomi's husband and Paul's brother, have the same matter-of-fact aphoristic quality that Harrison gives Joseph in *Farmer*. Naomi has reconciled herself to living out her life as she sees fit, a sixty-five-year-old schoolteacher who realizes, like Northridge II before her, that "There are somewhat comic realizations in the aging process that you thought you understood previously but it was very much a surface understanding. Primary among these is that it all happens just once." Her ability to "live within her skin," take what life offers her, is much more profound than Nelse's, her attitude that of an "older woman looking at the moon and stars, ordinary as the earth they shine down upon. If that's not enough I have no more to offer, and to whom am I offering?"[70]

The voices of the older generation are juxtaposed to Nelse's, and Harrison implies that both Naomi and Paul will act as stabilizing influences for the young man after Dalva's death, an identity-affirming relationship that stresses the importance of living with contradiction: "Today, many of us are no longer acknowledged by others. We are at best recognized intermittently and so become intermittent ourselves. Subject to constant change, most relationships are no longer dependable. . . . We are not all alike. If *you* are okay, there must be something wrong with me."[71] The false binary that society implies in its relationship with the individual (the traditional symbiotic relationship that was, at least in part, negotiable, has in effect become a zero-sum game) is one that the Northridge family, even in its fierce independence, sees as absurd. The necessity of nurturing the individual, then, is clear.

When Nelse loses his journal, he is symbolically divested of the responsibility of recording his own and the family's history, leaving him free to pursue his love for J. M. For the first time, he realizes that "All I really seem to have is consciousness." Nelse's happiness with J. M. becomes important to Naomi, when she recalls that "I warned Nelse this summer over his beloved J. M. that such passion for most of us occurs only once in this life and seems quite unlikely if there is a next." That notion is echoed in the narratives of both Paul and Naomi when they bemoan the fact that Naomi had married Paul's brother, Northridge III. Naomi, who had carried on an irregular affair with Paul over the intervening years, wonders, "Why didn't I marry my husband's brother, Paul?" Paul, too, asks, "Why couldn't I find a Naomi for myself? The answer is there is just one of each of us, both the question and the answer repeated numberless times over the years."[72] By grouping them with Nelse and J. M. at the end of the novel, when Dalva brings the family together to tell them that she wants to die with dignity, Harrison suggests that the two young lovers will make the same soul connection that Paul and Naomi have made after so many years. At the end of Nelse's narrative, when he first meets his mother, the story comes full circle. Nelse realizes that "What was left of [Naomi's] whole family was down there around the picnic table. I couldn't say it was my family but it was a start when we went down to join them." Of the five family members who tell their stories in *The Road Home,* perhaps only Paul fully understands the continuum upon which life exists, neither wholly inside nor outside the self, positing that "the mind instinctively creates a safe middle way for memory?" He also understands, echoing again the inadequacy of language—his uncertainty punctuated by a question mark, even though the statement is not really a question—and the limits that language imposes upon our observations, that "Phenomena are far more interesting than my reductive conclusions."[73]

Written as complement to Dalva's reunion with Nelse, her final days, when she has "the naïve but rather poignant feeling that I should memorize the earth,"[74] flesh out the details of the earlier novel and articulate a philosophy of life that Harrison has spent more than forty years discovering and refining:

> It occurred to me that my time might become foreshortened at a rate that was less than bearable, and that I shouldn't be counting possible years, but months, and singular days themselves might be a better idea. The fact that this was also applicable to perfectly healthy people did not miss my thoughts. I supposed that most of us drifted, floated, even happily bobbed along and it was not within our capabilities to have a clear view of when and where the river emptied into the ocean.[75]

Dalva's death seems to be secondary to the legacy that she leaves for her son and her remaining family, both in the future and in the immediate present, when it occurs to her that "once the death sentence is given and there are no possible appeals it is then up to you to comfort others. You have accepted the sentence but others whom you love have not yet been able to internalize the fact and it keeps re-occurring to them with fresh energy." Certainly with death imminent, she recognizes the place "where the river empties into the ocean," and in retelling the story of Michael and the Northridge journals, she realizes that "You can't greedily suck out of another culture what you failed to find in your own heart. You may recognize it in another culture but only if it already exists in the core of your own soul." Harrison suggests that there is hope for society: one crucial aspect for the care of the soul, defined by the romantic notion that underpins the characters' sensibilities and all of Harrison's fiction, is to eschew the venality and greed of society and to understand that the "human beings who pillage and made war as we did . . . also had a great deal of soul life that was not totally wiped out by clutter and greed." Dalva's strongest statement of that sensibility comes when Nelse tells his mother that she "should have been married to John Keats, and how could I continue such romanticism when there was an actual world of evidence to the contrary." Dalva's response is a delicate "Fuck the world."[76]

Harrison's accomplishment, aside from the Faulknerian articulation of a family's history, is the movement from an emphasis on a jaundiced portrait of society to a poignant and life-affirming articulation of the individual, from soul history to a personal history that has as its center the care of the soul. Implicit in any study of the individual is a focusing on death not in the abstract, but as a palpable and meaningful end to life:

> To be vital, the imagination must come to terms with death. The central problem from the beginning of *Dalva* and in Harrison's own life, as he points out in his autobiographical essays, is how to acknowledge death, even embrace it in some sense, without being incapacitated. Dalva, despairing because she is still in the arms of her father and her lover, must learn to return the embrace.[77]

Dalva does learn to return the embrace. Harrison's mature vision is a complex contextual grounding for the work that will follow.

The soul history that is so important in shaping the lives of Dalva and her family has served its purpose. Although it is not negated in the five narratives that comprise *The Road Home*, it has been transmuted into something even more important, more personal, to the characters. Though they understand perhaps too well the weight of history, they realize that to live their lives always with that history in mind—opposed to keeping it in the soul, where it belongs—is to demean the memory of what has come before, the notion that "There can be a wonderful substratum of thinking going on beneath the banal tonnage of human behavior. . . . The mind by itself must discipline itself to open wide enough to allow the soul to clap its hands and sing. The dark comic aspect is in our resistance to the nature of our minds, pretending we have no more freedom than a train on its predestined tracks." Dalva, whose only traveling companion on her final journey is "an anthology of American poetry about which I now had doubts," has, in a grander sense even than Northridge II or Nelse, transcended the limitations of the written word—the history that has come down to her through her great-grandfather, her grandfather, her mother, her uncle. Instead, her story becomes an unbearably personal one: "I was dealing with quite enough consciousness of my own, and anyone else's at this point seemed senselessly invasive."[78] Dalva's death, much as the lives and deaths of all of Harrison's characters, offers a bittersweet closure to a life and places before the reader the unanswerable and unutterable epistemological concerns implicit in all of Harrison's fiction: How is the soul embodied in a life spent always searching, paradoxically, for ways to live—and die—with as much dignity as we can muster?

·6·

"They headed west"

Postmodernism, Twain, and a Reassessment of the American Myth and the American Dream in Jim Harrison's Brown Dog Series

Man wird mich schwer davon überzeugen, daß die Geschichte des verlorenen Sohnes nicht die Legende dessen ist, der nicht geliebt wer-den wollen. . . . Das Geheimnis seines noch nie gewesenen Lebens bre-itete sich vor ihm aus. Unwillkürlich verließ er den Fusspfad unlief weiter feldein, die Arme ausgestreckt, als könnte er in dieser Breite mehrere Richtungen auf einmal bewältigen. Und dann warf er sich irgendwo hinter eine Hecke, un niemand legte Wert auf ihn.[1]
—Rilke, "The Prodigal Son," from
The Notebooks of Malte Laurids Brigge

Our desire to distill truth from fiction, the purity of the individual will from the corrupting influence of the institution, is essential in delin-eating the postmodern aspects of Jim Harrison's fiction. Jean-François Lyotard sees the conflict between the reality and the dream, so vital as a catalyst for the actions of Harrison's characters, as consistent with the postmodern tendency, in its most general terms, toward the con-fusion of reality and imagination through the play of language and context that organize a "metanarrative." That story is based not on optimism (here, such a thing would roughly equate to the survival of the Frontier Myth), but on "great codes which in their abstraction nec-essarily deny the specificity of the local and traduce it in the interests of a global homogeneity, a universal history."[2] That conflict between the individual and society implicit in the creation of a "global homogeneity" is closely aligned with the notion of an inherently corrupt and corrupting society that underpins Harrison's three Brown Dog novellas, *Brown Dog* (from *The Woman Lit by Fireflies* [1990]), *The Seven-Ounce Man* (from *Julip* [1994]), and *Westward Ho* (from *The Beast God Forgot to Invent* [2000]).[3]

Brown Dog, the quintessential American backwoods picaro, is a character who unflaggingly articulates his "impressions of the contending values within the culture," and embodies "values other than those of the contending factions or parties."[4] The novellas in *The Beast God Forgot to Invent* cement "Harrison's reputation as versatile, astute, and fearless commentator on American culture, specifically, and the foibles of humanity in general. In the collection, the author takes on some common (for Harrison) enemies: Hollywood, mass culture, pretense, the federal government, workshop writers and their teachers—in short, any institution or profession that deigns to impose artificial order on a world whose exquisite chaos, to Harrison's mind, should rather be lauded and lived in."[5] In his reading of *The Seven-Ounce Man,* Jerry Leath Mills writes that Brown Dog "presents resilience, tolerance of risk and zest for life in such direct and stripped-down terms that we almost forgive him his recklessness."[6] Jonis Agee asserts that Brown Dog "possesses enough wit to laugh at himself, to remain open and curious about the convolutions of human endeavor. By refusing to be locked into a single pattern, ritual or myth—including that offered by the American Indian family friend who gives him a cabin and work—Brown Dog remains true to himself."[7] Alexander Harrison posits that *The Seven-Ounce Man* is "dark, hilarious and poignant," although he overstates the optimism of the novella's ending: "[W]hen Brown Dog ends up heading west with a Canadian Mohawk on the run from the government, there is a sense of wonder and possibility."[8] Judith Freeman implies the protagonist's lack of identity when she writes, "[i]n *Brown Dog,* we hear another kind of voice, the voice of the Man of Nature and Appetite, the hard-drinking, womanizing B.D., or Brown Dog—not quite Indian, not quite white, a failed Bible student who has found a corpse while scavenging shipwrecks."[9]

To be sure, the novellas are irreverent and darkly and profoundly humorous. The culture of disintegration, though, is the culture that Harrison writes: we pride ourselves as a nation (Harrison relates with no little irony, despite his paradoxical contention in the novel *Warlock* that irony serves no particularly constructive purpose in literature) on our individuality and our ability to piece together a future from the remnants of our collective past. Thomas Docherty and John Barth state similar views on the effect of the postmodern on our reckoning of the past, the present, and the future: Docherty posits that we "are condemned to live in a present, and [to adopt] a specific—some have said 'schizophrenic'—mood as a result of acknowledging that this present is characterised by struggle or contradiction and incoherence."[10] In his essay "The Literature of Exhaustion," Barth understands the paradoxical necessity for a society that could lose its identity at any moment to remain "always-already" on the brink of apocalypse: "The commonality, alas, will *always* lose their way and their souls: it's the chosen remnant, the virtuoso, the Thesean *hero,* who, confronted with Baroque reality, Baroque history, the Baroque state of his art, need *not* rehearse its possibilities to exhaustion. . . . He need only be aware of their existence or possibility."[11]

The postmodern (anti-)hero, from Barth's own Todd Andrews in *The Floating Opera* to Paul Auster's Benjamin Sachs (whose story is told by his friend Peter Aaron) in *Leviathan,* generally performs the role of the virtuoso, giving voice to the author at the same time the author breathes life into his faltering hero in a complex self-referential metanarrative. The landscapes inhabited by these characters, who literally cannot wait for the future—and who, because of their restlessness and recklessness alienate themselves from society—are stark and resound with the meaningless words and actions of their constituents: Barth's protagonist plans his own suicide in meticulous detail; Auster's Aaron rushes against the arrival of the authorities as he unfolds the bizarre and convoluted tale of his relationship to Sachs, a friend who incinerates himself on a desolate Wisconsin roadside. The heroic virtuosi of the postmodern text act in the margins of "conventional" society, often in obtuse, inconsistent ways. Their actions are not predictable (Barth's protagonist insists on being "consistent with my policy of incomplete consistency")[12]; nor do their actions always lead to rational, or traditionally "satisfactory" endings. Their lives are merely eclectic representations, pastiches, of past lives.

An American fascination with the notion that our lives are inexorably intertwined with history and should embody the (often nebulous) principles of some fateful mission on its last leg, that, as David Mogen writes, our "fate is ultimately an emblem of the last pure experience of

A 1969 publicity photo for *Five Blind Men*, an anthology of poetry by (l. to r.) Dan Gerber, J. D. Reed, George Quasha, Jim Harrison, and Charles Simic. The volume was published by the Sumac Press, jointly operated by Gerber and Harrison. *Sumac*, the literary journal that Harrison and Gerber co-edited, was conceived by the two in 1967 and had a run of nine issues that extended from late 1968 to the fall of 1971. In its brief life, the journal contained work—both poetry and prose—from some of the world's most important established and up-and-coming writers. Thomas McGuane joined the editorial staff in 1969 as fiction editor. (Courtesy of Dan Gerber)

Jim Harrison, 31, in 1969. Harrison—already an established poet who had garnered numerous grants to continue his critically acclaimed work—would publish his first novel, *Wolf: A False Memoir*, within 18 months. Friend Thomas McGuane suggested that Harrison attempt the longer form during the latter's convalescence from a hunting accident. (This photo was taken, Dan Gerber points out, "after Jim had savaged his back and contracted a near-fatal infection while in the hospital which caused him to lose a great deal of weight.") (Courtesy of Dan Gerber)

Harrison in August 1972, shortly before the publication of *A Good Day to Die*. The novel, which details the decision of a rag-tag group of quasi-environmentalists to destroy a dam that symbolizes the hand of man on pristine nature, predated Edward Abbey's similar eco-novel *The Monkey Wrench Gang* by two years. Like the author himself, Harrison's narrator in *A Good Day to Die* sustains himself through his connection to the land, particularly enjoying and being renewed by the country's great fishing spots. (Photo credit: Guy de la Valdéne)

Harrison and McGuane, August 1972. In reference to the two Michigan writers, critic Jonathan Yardley wrote in December 1971 in the *New York Times Book Review* that they "possess extraordinary talent, but they are also extravagantly free-male, male-animal. That may be a refreshing alternative to a plastic society, but by the same token it manufactures a fraternity of he-men who use women in the fashion of town pumps and romanticize about an ecologically balanced utopia where, fishing pole in hand and Rover by his side, a man can be a man—while the rest of the world staggers on in its admittedly lamentable, but inescapably real, way." Yardley's perception of Harrison's fiction as misogynistic—or at the very least anti-feminist—stuck with Harrison until the publication of *Dalva* (1988) and *The Woman Lit by Fireflies* (1990), both of which were written from a woman's point of view. (Photo credit: Guy de la Valdéne)

Jim Harrison in front of the statue of Russian writer Alexander Pushkin, Leningrad, November 1971. Harrison's wanderlust and an appetite for the best in world literature opened him to new influences. He would publish *Letters to Yesenin*—a collection of poems influenced by the brief life and tragic death of Sergei Yesenin, the young Russian poet who hanged himself in St. Petersburg, Russia, in 1925—fewer than two years after his trip with writer Dan Gerber to the Soviet Union. Harrison's experiences in Russia prompted him to write the following: "So this is a song of Yesenin's noose which came / to nothing, but did a good job as we say back home / where there's nothing but snow. But I stood under / your balcony in St. Petersburg, yes St. Petersburg! / a crazed tourist with so much nothing in my heart / it wanted to implode."

Many of the themes that Harrison tackles in the collection—particularly suicide and a profound restlessness with the life that he was leading—would manifest themselves in the fiction of this period as well. (Courtesy of Dan Gerber)

Harrison in Key West, Florida, mid-1970s. Harrison, McGuane, Guy de la Valdéne, Jimmy Buffett, and a host of other of Harrison's friends and hedonic compatriots enjoyed some of the world's best tarpon fishing during the 1970s and early 1980s. Fictionalized accounts of the events of those years are related throughout Harrison's work (as well as McGuane's), from *A Good Day to Die* (1973) to *Julip* (1994). (Photo credit: Guy de la Valdéne)

Portraits of the artist, Fremont and Lake Leelanau, Michigan, between 1968 and 1972. (Courtesy of Dan Gerber)

Harrison and friend and fellow writer Peter Matthiessen, May 1991, at the Crescent H Ranch near Wilson, Wyoming, for a gathering of writers arranged by Terry Tempest Williams.

Harrison gleaned much of his interest in and appreciation for the practice of Zen from Matthiessen (an ordained Zen priest), whose own closeness to nature and to the art of writing in such works as *Far Tortuga*, *Nine-Headed Dragon River*, and *Zen Journals*, has undoubtedly influenced Harrison. Matthiessen's attention to Native American history, especially his account of the events leading to the arrest and conviction of Leonard Peltier for his alleged role in the deaths of two federal agents in 1975, appeared five years before Harrison's *Dalva*. (Courtesy of Dan Gerber)

Early in 1997 in East Lansing, Michigan, Harrison and Gerber celebrate the publication of the *Sumac Reader*, a collection of work from the original run of *Sumac* edited by Joseph Bednarik (Photo credit: Rollie McKenna. Photo courtesy of Dan Gerber).

Harrison reading, signing books, and chatting with McGuane in Key West, Florida, January 1996. Harrison had returned to his old haunts for the Key West Literary Seminar, "American Writers and the Natural World." The seminar, a rare event for the typically conference-shy Harrison, featured Annie Dillard, Gretel Ehrlich, Linda Hogan, McGuane, Doug Peacock, Frederick Turner, and Terry Tempest Williams, among others. Although Harrison's fiction was finding a wider critical and popular audience (in the five years before the event, he had published *The Woman Lit by Fireflies* and *Julip* [1994], two collections of novellas with strong female protagonists), he chose to read poetry—his first love—on this particular occasion. (Photo credits: Douglas Seifert)

Harrison and Guy de la Valdéne, authors, sportsmen, and longtime friends, hunting quail at de la Valdéne's Dogwood Farm in Havana, Florida, January 1995. (Photo credit: Douglas Seifert)

the American Dream," pervades the realist literature of the nineteenth century and carries over well into the postmodern literature of the twentieth century.[13] In the second half of the twentieth century, this ideal has fallen prey to cynicism and kitsch: when the myth is stripped from our perception of frontier reality, only the nostalgia for the myth remains. The myths that we perpetuate in our literature eventually crumble around us, and the (re)presentation of our cultural conflicts calls into question our myths and dreams until they lose their evocative powers.[14] Today, the American Dream in both fiction and reality often fails in a flurry of violence and irredeemable death. The idealism inherent in the American sensibility, in Mogen's view, undermines both the Myth and the Dream, ultimately denying their realization in contemporary American literature. According to Mogen, the varied and rich traditions of the "The American Myth" and "The American Dream" "often evoke a vaporous and unexamined conviction of special destiny." In fact, the terms themselves—"Myth" and "Dream"—are problematic: "Myth suggests falsehood and illusion, commonly held misconceptions, stories perpetuating the mystique of entrenched power structures"; likewise, the word "dream" "suggests unrealized ideal . . . , perhaps even a potentially destructive habit of escapism."[15]

Such an ironic reading of the Myth and the Dream, concepts that have in many ways defined Americans since Plymouth Rock, provides us with a contextual framework through which we can analyze the dual failure of the "American Dream" and the "American Myth" in *Brown Dog, The Seven-Ounce Man,* and *Westward Ho.* Each of these texts conveys "the overwhelming sense not merely of the relativity of ideas, but of the sheer quantity and incoherence of information, [in] a culture of inextricable cross-currents and energies."[16] Harrison is writing a culture in which the archetypes that have come down to us as constitutive of an American Myth are no longer tenable. Still, Brown Dog, in the third installment of his saga, is able (unwittingly) to affect the change that he so sorely needs: "Brown Dog's reward for navigating his improbable mission is the responsibility of helping to raise the children of his ex-love Rose, and, most importantly, the opportunity to immerse himself once more in his beloved Michigan wilderness."[17]

Harrison's texts themselves are grounded in the deepest tradition of American literature—which includes, of course, an intimate acquaintance with the style of Mark Twain—and the author's narrative strategy allows him to borrow from the traditional narrative as he constructs a text that relies on a cultural milieu unique to his Upper

Peninsula characters, "a kind of American that never gets into fiction. It's people like Brown Dog."[18] Frederic Jameson writes that the use of the pastiche in the postmodern text is, "like parody, the imitation of a peculiar or unique, idiosyncratic style, the wearing of a linguistic mask, speech in a dead language. But it is a neutral practice of such mimicry, without any of parody's ulterior motives, amputated of the satiric impulse, devoid of laughter and of any conviction that alongside the abnormal tongue you have momentarily borrowed, some healthy linguistic normality still exists."[19]

With the advent of the postmodern (such a thing, naturally, is relatively indeterminate: Jameson would locate it in the early 1960s, the historian Arnold Toynbee in the years between the two World Wars), the literature of idealism has given way to a literature of irony relatively devoid of parody, in which the protagonist who finds himself at odds with society can paradoxically only establish his identity by alienating himself from society and forfeiting an identity nurtured solely by society's expectations.[20] The worth of Harrison's protagonists can be measured only against the more "normal" characters that inhabit America's small towns and backwoods. And while the author's novellas exhibit a great deal of self-aware humor, Harrison's stylistic debt to Twain fulfills Jameson's notion of the pastiche in the postmodern. Harrison's first two texts present an overarching irony that constitutes a reaction to the "happy endings" of narratives that espouse a pursuit of a mythical end for their protagonists, and the author's narrative strategies point up the hypocrisy of a society that chooses to ignore an ever-shrinking psychic and physical frontier. Brown Dog becomes, through his actions and his voice, a postmodern Huckleberry Finn.

Brown Dog is, in a sense, a trickster figure, a "comic and communal sign with no hope or tragic promises. . . . The trickster is as aggressive as those who imagine the narrative, but the trickster bears no evil or malice in narrative voices. . . . The trickster is a chance, a comic holotrope in a postmodern language game that uncovers the distinctions and ironies between narrative voices."[21] Significantly, "the comic spirit keeps us pure in mind by requiring that we regard ourselves skeptically."[22] The comedy of the stories, though, masks the subtext, a skepticism for a society that manifests itself in a refashioning of our oldest, most deeply ingrained myths. The protagonist recalls Barth's invocation of the Thesean hero in Borges, although his role as a failing hero accentuates his inability to grasp and follow the threads that a number of Ariadne-figures leave for him in the texts. Delmore Burns (formerly Delmore Short Bear), a wealthy Indian chief who has bridged the gap between white and Native American societies, acts as Brown Dog's benefactor, attempting to steer his charge away from a number of ill-fated sexual escapades and still other legal transgressions. Both *Brown Dog* and *The Seven-Ounce Man,* informed by the tradition of "light[ing] out for the Territory," paint an ironic, cynical portrait of the fate of the marginalized individual in American literature and in our society.[23] Harrison's bleak forecast for both the individual and the society manifests itself in Brown Dog's flight from a society that is itself morally ambiguous only to find that that society defines him; but unlike Twain's visionary protagonist Huckleberry Finn, or Thoreau's more introspective view of the freedom of man, Brown Dog may "head west," but he cannot escape the influence of a society whose sole purpose is to co-opt what little physical and psychic frontier space remains.

Harrison, whose artistic vision often limns the appropriation of individual freedom by the Establishment, is quite comfortable writing an epitaph for the culture of disintegration. The self-referentiality of his texts is a trope for his characters' constant search for identity, a puzzle whose pieces are constantly in flux. Harrison's own personality mirrors the controlled freneticism of his narratives. As Jim Fergus points out, a dialogue with the author is "somehow akin to watching his dogs work the cover for birds. They race off on tangents, describing broad loops and arcs, or tight circles, always returning in a controlled, if circuitous, pattern that is at once instinct, training, ritual, and play."[24] Harrison's fidelity to the object, that which is directly observed and recorded, places him outside the realm of the purely postmodern and phenomenologically privileges his work by grounding his characters in a recognizably "normal" context, unlike Auster, for instance, whose narratives rely almost entirely on coincidence and self-referential play between characters and plot threads for their effect. In a statement on the "double function" of Harrison's work, Kay Bonetti sees Harrison as

> one of our most original writers, a poetic experimentalist who brings to his novels his gifts for compression and precision of language. Because of this and his subject matter he and his work are too often misunderstood, especially by critics who lump him with writers like James Dickey and his best friend Tom McGuane, and dismiss him as macho, primarily by mixing Harrison up with his characters and their opinions. In any case, at his

best Jim Harrison without doubt fulfills the demand for postmodern fiction laid down by John Barth in the "Literature of Replenishment." [Harrison's] work offers challenges for those professional devotees of high art who want to examine it, but he also offers interesting characters and good stories for those who don't.[25]

Harrison's fiction harnesses the entropy of time and meaning-making in the postmodern text by using the linear narrative form (the plot-driven "realistic" text) for its superficial structure and colloquial English, a wealth of idiomatic expressions, and vernacular dialogue that are obvious manifestations of Twain's influence.

The saga of *Brown Dog* begins with an ambiguous invocation to time that informs the protagonist's narrative throughout: "*Just before Dark* at the bottom of the sea I found the Indian. It was the inland sea called Lake Superior" (emphasis mine).[26] Similarly, the opening paragraph of *The Seven-Ounce Man* makes use of seasonal changes to convey the passage of time. In setting scene, time becomes important when Harrison writes only that "It was the darkest and coldest summer of the century in the Upper Peninsula, or so everyone said."[27] Harrison's characters are intertwined with the seasons, subject to the "finiteness" of time that is so often important in the construction of the myth-text that calls into question the viability of the myth.[28] In this case, paradoxically, time's arrow is hardly that, operating on a very narrowly defined closed loop (the four seasons) and also working its way through an infinite number of cycles, both concepts defined by circular rather than nonlinear images. The technique provides an ironic subtext for the conversational tones of these passages, tones reminiscent of Twain's own use of the colloquial voice to introduce Huckleberry Finn to the world to negate, at least on the surface, the importance of passing time: "Well, three or four months run along, and it was well into the winter, now. I had been to school most all the time, and could spell, and read, and write just a little, and could say the multiplication table up to six times seven is thirty-five, and I don't reckon I could ever get any further than that if I was to live forever."[29]

The texts diverge significantly, however, in their different uses of narrative time. Huck Finn places his own story in relation to the earlier *Tom Sawyer* as he writes, "Now the way that the book winds up, is this: Tom and me found the money that the robbers hid in the cave, and it made us rich."[30] Twain's story contains very few digressions and comprises an essentially linear narrative in which the passage of time is readily apparent and predictable, and he employs a dramatic unity that holds it together, even though the text is representative of the disorder of Huck's society; the reason that we see the narrative as disordered at all is that "the disorder is presented through a narrator who is incapable of perceiving order under the surface of the things and events he reports."[31] Harrison's protagonist, however, faces the converse problem: because he is intimately familiar with time in terms of the changing seasons, his own sense of disorder comes not from within, but from without—the society that forces Brown Dog to offer obeisance to its too-ordered mandates. Brown Dog is quite capable of "perceiving order," but he is incapable of working within the context that society demands. When he is the messenger, society rarely cares to hear the news.

The oscillation of time through Harrison's use of narrative regression and his placement of characters outside the mainstream creates an atemporality that is the cornerstone of any postmodern reading of Harrison's texts, a reading that culminates in a number "of insignificant and serious little stories that sometimes let themselves be collected together to constitute big stories and sometimes disperse into digressive elements."[32] Each of the characters' actions takes on its own significance apart from any of the narrative's preceding or subsequent actions; they are, in fact, important only because those actions often lack context and undermine the commonplace—the events that we have been programmed to expect in certain situations. Such a singularization of events necessarily precludes identity-making; without a coherent linear accretion of events, one is forced "always already" to live in a present quasi-historical construct whose outward veneer of order belies its instability.[33]

Brown Dog's short-lived affair with Rose, his childhood love, is one of the most important images in the narratives in molding our understanding of the postmodern elements of the texts. The union illustrates the protagonist's uncanny ability to disregard (or to learn from) past events at will; the warping of time that accompanies any random remembrances, placed merely as points-in-time on the circle of Time, removes him historically from the text. His perfunctory lovemaking with Rose also characterizes the difficulty that Brown Dog has in reconciling himself either to leaving society or adapting to it. Throughout the absurd act, Rose watches television, switching channels until she falls asleep. Brown Dog "pumped away in unison to her burgeoning snores, his orgasm seemingly timed to when Leno changed to Letterman and her eyes popped open. . . . It rarely is, but it can be a blessed event when a dream dies. The bigger the dream, the bigger the vacuum when the dream slips off into the void."[34] The relationship is consistent with the television in the background, a comic scene that suggests the meaninglessness of both the act and the mindless acquiescence of society (here embodied by Rose) to mass media.

After he leaves Rose in her alcoholic slumber, Brown Dog recalls a memory that "happened thirty years back but could have been only a moment ago." This telescoping of time, a signature of the protagonist's mind, further characterizes the protagonist's actions and adds a poignant dimension, set against the backdrop of a forgetful climax to the relationship, to the text's snapshot images. Brown Dog's dream of making love to Rose ends the next night when the protagonist discovers that all of Rose's "loves" are coupled with some exchange of money: "'We could do it once more but it would have to be the last time," Rose tells him. "I also got to send thirty bucks to Fred up in Amasa so he can get his carburetor fixed. Or else he can't come to see me."[35] Brown Dog's accession to Rose's demands, giving her money so Fred (her only "love") can visit and perpetuate the automatic act of sex, neatly circumscribes the cycle of self-defeat inherent in Brown Dog's predicament.

While Brown Dog is a more pessimistic and overdetermined pawn of society than Huck Finn, both texts' protagonists tend to ignore the significance of the events around them and refuse to bargain with society on its terms. In short, Huck believes that six times seven is thirty-five, and his belief in that "fact" will not alter his life significantly. Rather, the narrative crux of Twain's story lies in the presentation of one boy's escape from symbolic and real captivity into a world that, should he choose it, offers a promise of the "American Dream." Conversely, in a society that slouches toward its own historical and moral disintegration, Brown Dog's life will be significantly changed by his illegal possession of the chief's body, a totem that comes to him as a random event foreshadowing a future incompatible with society's expectations. While Twain's protagonist exhibits a naïveté that allows him to "light out for the Territory" with the optimism of the American Dream to buttress that escape, Brown Dog struggles in a society where his failure to conform defines the last vestiges of the American Dream gone awry. All that he can do to come to terms with his own identity is to not conform, a decision that leaves him penniless and alone in a society that values not at all the quaint "individuality" that it finds so endearing in Huck.[36]

Brown Dog's own first-person narrative in *The Seven-Ounce Man* further illustrates his relegation to society's margins. The most important thought that comes to him during the lengthy personal narrative is his recollection of a near-fatal meeting with an Indian girl at a pow-wow. Nearly all of the philosophically important thoughts present in the narrative rely on an omniscient narrator for their effect. Unlike Huck Finn, whose actions take him away from an abusive situation and accrete, finally, to reflect his growing identity apart from society, Brown Dog *does* little to establish his own identity. After the accident that he so nonchalantly describes, Brown Dog's life does not change significantly. In fact, we understand implicitly, through Brown Dog's own random thoughts, that the means no longer have an end for Brown Dog; he exists, rather, with little thought for the future.

Although Brown Dog seems to understand the ethical underpinnings of his society (though he rarely acknowledges them), his capacity for adaptation to that society is seriously limited. Those limitations manifest themselves not as a result of a careless abstraction of society by Harrison and Twain, but rather through two divergent views of the society that is set before them. Huck is ostensibly educated well enough to compose his own narrative, although he remains naïve to the intricate workings of that society; Brown Dog, no doubt in part for his infatuation with Shelley, a representative of the enemy camp (academia), allows her to transcribe his thoughts and actions. We accept that Huck writes his own narrative because we are able to suspend disbelief for the duration of the narrative.[37] Brown Dog, however, giving in to society for a moment at the promise of sexual gratification, forfeits his narrative freedom when he ironically admits that "These aren't my exact words. A fine young woman named Shelley, who is also acting as my legal guardian and semi-probation officer, is helping me get this all down on paper. . . . The main reason she is helping me write this is so I can stop lying to myself and others, which from my way of thinking will cut the interesting heart right out of my life."[38]

The layering of the narrative through Shelley's mediation obscures Brown Dog's own narrative and further distances him (and the reader) from his true identity; the extent to which Brown Dog has alienated himself from society is clear when he recalls with pride that "he kept his driver's license current though in fact the renewal form constituted the only mail he ever received, not being a member of any organization or even owning a social security number."[39] The filtering of the narrative through a "hostile" narrator signifies the postmodern text, where "The convention of realism does not pluralize the syntaxes of perception, only individual acts of perception; postmodern narrative pluralizes the very syntaxes of perception in order to bring back into a reader's present awareness all the 'action' involved in following the perpetual play of its differential sequences."[40] The essential difference in perception between Huck and Brown Dog, then, is that while Huck's perception oscillates in the very act of perceiving, his perception is immediate; Brown Dog's perception, on the other hand, comes to us mediated by the perceptions of others, in particular, an academic who uses Brown Dog for her own professional gain. The manifold points of view uncovered and re-covered in the text "remain open, perpetual, always renewed by new readings, new readers, new acts of attention."[41] And while the same is true of many texts, the continuously shifting narrative points-of-view—in the context of an ironic American Dream and its dissipation—act as a foil to Brown Dog's identity-making, the crux of Harrison's narrative.

Brown Dog himself seems to be aware of his precarious placement at the nexus of a societal identity (the popular and collective identity) and his own non-identity outside the constraints of society, which fosters an "untypical fragile feeling in his mind, a fluttery sense that forbade him from getting his true bearings."[42] When, at the beginning of *Westward Ho,* he travels to Los Angeles "with the single purpose being to retrieve his bearskin and head back to the country, wherever that might be," "the fact of the matter is that he felt utterly dislocated, a rapacious modern disease. The only familiar part of his surroundings was when he raised his hands from the bed, stared at them, and said 'hands.'"[43] His sheepish admission that he has allowed Shelley to "shrink his head" establishes a conflict between both Brown Dog and society, and within himself: we know that he is in trouble with the law; we know that Shelley will not allow him to write his own story without her intrusion; and, in the end, we know that Shelley has turned traitor. Shelley's perception of Brown Dog constitutes the ultimate ironic expression in the narrative, as she conveys the party line in terms of Brown Dog's transgressions against society, a narrative strategy that "automatically constitutes an offense to common reason and understanding—an offense not necessarily intended by the ironist but somehow involuntarily connected with his claim and almost regularly taken as such by the public."[44] Brown Dog's acquiescence to Shelley contrasts to the youthful ebullience of the escaping Huck Finn, as well as Twain's own caveat, in which the author writes, "Persons attempting to find a motive in this narrative will be prosecuted; persons attempting to find a moral in it will be banished; persons attempting to find a plot in it will be shot."[45] At times, Brown Dog has little control over what is written about him, while Huck writes his story in a context in which the American Myth and the American Dream are still tenable.[46]

The ironic narrative is reprised in *The Seven-Ounce Man* where, as in *Brown Dog*, Harrison adopts several different points of view to the novella's three sections, the most important written in Brown Dog's own voice, which comes through without mediation; Brown Dog's voice, liberated for a time in a first-person narrative, is evocative of Twain's colloquialism. Aptly titled "The Mind of the Maker," the section opens with a bang: "GAAGAAGFHIRMH! I found this on my notepad I kept for Shelley. It is the word the [Chippewas] use for raven. Claude told me so. . . . Delmore is hard on my case and loaned me this cabin which is only fourteen by fourteen. . . . I am paying about four hundred dollars a month for this midget cabin with an outhouse."[47] Later, he recalls that Delmore had explained that "all that language was comprised of was agreed-upon sounds. And now he was listening to this batshit writer talk about his incapability of repeating meals within the same year. He wondered idly what his anthropologist lover, Shelley, would have had to say about it?"[48]

Even though Brown Dog has a voice in *The Seven-Ounce Man,* his identity is compromised by the decisions he makes and the ways in which he is written about. The first and third sections of the text, the narrative sections that surround Brown Dog's own voice and ultimately undermine his construction of reality, reveal Brown Dog's search for identity and the unlikelihood of his ever finding it. When the protagonist meets Gretchen, a social worker assigned to his case, the meeting ends in the typical adolescent sexual fantasy for Brown Dog; he invalidates both her genuine, if overweening, concern for him, and maintains his own subversive stance toward society. The fact that Brown Dog later finds out that Gretchen is a lesbian calls into question the nature of identity, as well as Brown Dog's own assumptions. Unable to fully grasp the implications of Gretchen's lesbianism, he can only reply, "'You don't say. Well, there's more than one way to skin a cat, that's for sure.' . . . His mind had quickly become a whirl of intrigue and pleasure, also he was flattered that this fine young woman had confided in him. She was a bit of an outsider just like himself."[49] Brown Dog's confusion about his own identity is exacerbated by Gretchen's inexplicable sexual orientation. He is forced to reassess the world as he knows it and to deal with questions of his own identity in terms of his ancestral origins (when he buries the chief that he finds floating in Lake Superior in the opening lines of *Brown Dog,* he says "'Goodbye, Dad'"[50]; the fact is that he has no idea who his father is). Much of Brown Dog's attitude relies on Harrison's own contention that "As Rimbaud said, which I believed very much when I was nineteen and which I've now come back to, for our purposes as artists, everything we are taught is false—everything."[51] Clearly, Twain is not so suspicious. His character builds identity as a means of relating to society, and "From the very beginning, Huck's quest to 'light out' into the new will be determined by his attachment to the old."[52] Conversely, Brown Dog's lack of identity situates him as a postmodern character.

The protagonist's inability to accept Gretchen's confession for what it is—a simple matter of a refused sexual advance—locates Brown Dog in a widening circle of unrecognition that culminates in his return to the burial mounds with a group of radical Native Americans with whom he has nothing in common. Before the raid on the mounds, Marten, one of the leaders of the group, calls Brown Dog "a pussy-crazed backwoods rooster."[53] Marten's scathing assessment of the protagonist is as close to the "truth" of Brown Dog's identity as anyone will come. For reasons known only to himself, Brown Dog joins the raid, an action so blatantly against what Delmore Burns has warned him of that he is forced, in a final irony, to "head west" with a man whom he does not particularly like; his escape is not an action indicative of the spirit of the American Dream, but a reaction to his self-imposed ostracism from society.

Harrison's pastiche of Twain, Brown Dog's "lighting out" with Marten, twists Twain's narrative into the implicit social criticism Mogen finds so important in a discussion of the traditional myth-narrative. While both *Huckleberry Finn* and *Brown Dog* criticize society, Twain's protagonist fantasizes with the reader about escape; Brown Dog, on the other hand, replays Huck's action ("Heading west"; "lighting out for the Territory") with no little comic irony in order to mitigate the seriousness of his own situation. While Huck is escaping *into* a tenable adult life, Brown Dog is escaping *from* an adult life as an outcast and a petty criminal who cuts a comic figure. Brown Dog would rather not interact at all with society. In *Huckleberry Finn,* however, "The coincidence of narrative and reality, while pleasurable, still bespeaks the symbiotic relationship between Huck's adventures as a social exile and the society from which he is supposedly fleeing. Huck requires the shore society in order to play out his fantasy of escape."[54] Indeed, Huck writes that "Next morning I said it was getting slow and dull, and I wanted to get a stirring up, some way. I said I reckoned I would slip over the river and find out what was going on."[55]

Brown Dog still represents the myth of the American Dreamer, but under the smudged, ironic lens of a cynicism that mocks the dream. Such a stance does not constitute "bad faith" on Harrison's part, but rather an understanding that the rules of the game have changed and the luster of the picaro has tarnished. Brown Dog, even when he manages to escape for a time, finds himself caught in the backwash of another pocket of social corruption, the concentric circles of which are widened by the promise of ascension into the "responsible" world of academia, the realm of "high-capitalism," which tempts Shelley to excavate the Indian burial mounds. On Brown Dog's foray to Los Angeles, he soon realizes that the city—civilization—"resembles the history of American politics, or the structure of American society itself. The connection between Brentwood and Boyle Heights is as fragile as that between Congress and the citizenry though the emotional makeup of both resembled the passion and power of the *Jerry Springer Show*."[56] As Reilly points out, Brown Dog records the "insensitivity and greed of contemporary anthropologists who destroy artifacts and burial mounds. Moreover, just as the U.S. government condoned the atrocities Northridge recorded [discussed at length in Harrison's novels *Dalva* and *The Road Home* and in chapter 5 of this study], Shelley's lawyer and a state police detective condone her actions."[57] Shelley's disregard for the history and culture of a people is consistent with the postmodern emergence of consumer or multinational capitalism and the relegation of our history to a series of easily digested pop-culture images. The result, Frederic Jameson writes, is that "What the past has to tell us is therefore little more than a matter of idle curiosity, and indeed our interest in it—fantastic genealogies, alternate histories!—come to look like an in-group hobby or adoptive tourism, like the encyclopedic specialization in the late show or Pynchon's interest in Malta."[58] Lyotard puts it more succinctly: "Eclecticism is the degree zero of contemporary general culture. . . . [K]nowledge is a matter for TV games."[59]

One need not read far in these novellas to find the obliteration of tradition. Brown Dog's own disregard for the sanctity of the burial

mounds and his disingenuous, maudlin response—the same presump-
tuous and opportunistic co-option of the Native American culture and
language that surrounds the characters—to their molestation by his
lover "Shelley Thurman" is nothing more than an artless non sequitur
that Brown Dog assumes will ingratiate him to the Native American
radicals.[60] He assumes he can achieve identity by becoming part of a
political protest group with which he has nothing in common. Additionally, he uses a Chippewa pejorative (*wagutz*) in order to describe
Shelley. Just as his earlier thoughts will never truly be his own because
Shelley has mediated them, his speech is not his own because he insists
on being a poseur for the group that fights to protect the burial
mounds. The inherent difficulty in identity-making in the texts goes
even deeper: Brown Dog's mentor Delmore Short Bear, by changing his
name to Delmore Burns in order to succeed in the "white man's" society, gives up his claim to the history of his people, and confuses the
search for identity that forms such an integral part of the narrative.

The regression that forms Delmore's story gives the narrative an intricate, chaotic dimension by recalling the bizarre turn of events that leads
to Brown Dog inheriting Delmore's bearskin rug, the totem of power in
the narrative and his sole reason for tracking Lone Marten to Los Angeles. By entrusting the rug to Brown Dog, Delmore ostensibly gives him
powers that would allow him, finally, to confront society; of course, the
powers do not exist. Even if they did, Brown Dog would not be worthy
to use them because he cannot understand them. The protagonist's most
insightful response to the power of nature is "there was the mildly trou-
bling thought that bears can help you if you stay out in their world, but
not in your own."[61] By losing the bearskin to Lone Marten, Brown Dog
has proven himself unworthy of Delmore's trust.

The bearskin rug is a metaphor for Brown Dog's displacement from
his society. Before he redeems himself in part by bringing the rug back
from Los Angeles, Brown Dog is even less able of assuming the man-
tle of the American myth-figure than he is of making good use of a
powerless totem. His manner of living always in the present, without
the buoy of tradition (now euphemistically "institutional memory," a
phrase that dampens the individual spirit perhaps more than any other
we have created), precludes his participation in the traditional American myth, whose myth-figures are defined in terms of their actions:
"The soul often breaks down into disintegration. What true myth concerns itself with is not the disintegration product. True myth concerns
itself centrally with the onward adventure of the integral soul. . . .

When this man breaks from his static isolation, and makes a new move, then look out, something will be happening."[62] Brown Dog is the "disintegration product" of the breakdown of his own soul and, we are led to believe, "onward adventure" is no more tenable an abstraction than the myth that springs from it. The rug is a miasma in the text of disintegration; Brown Dog's "integral soul," if it ever existed, has been silted over by the sediment of a lifestyle that falls well outside the parameters of a society that chooses its myth-figures based on their willingness to accede to society, not on their individual spirit or their initiative. Brown Dog can never understand, let alone make ready, the "bear medicine" that Delmore felt in taking the bear's life.

Harrison's portrayal of Brown Dog as the unraveling of the American Dream, in his inability to reconcile his views with those of society—especially evident in the first two novellas—deconstructs the myth of the Myth and knells the death of the American myth-figure, not because Brown Dog is amoral and perverse (which he is, in fact, in the context of the society with which he is at odds), but because the society with which he associates does not deserve, and cannot perpetuate, the ideal of a mythic hero. Brown Dog, then, is not necessarily the agent of his own undoing as myth-figure. Harrison implies, rather, that we should blame a society that has no need for such individuals.

Such a capacious claim can hardly be overstated in the context of Harrison's fiction. The author is relentless in circumscribing Brown Dog as the corruption of a mythic figure. Brown Dog's actions, not the least irreverent of which is a sexual conquest on sacred Indian burial mounds, are the antithesis of Huck's discovery of a now-outdated and naïve American idealism when he protects Jim. Brown Dog's nonchalance toward the sacredness of the mounds and his treatment of the emotionally shaken Tarah, a friend of Shelley's, point up an essential difference between Huck and Brown Dog in the evolution of the American frontier archetype: Brown Dog cannot muster the same sense of responsibility for his actions that Huck the boy feels in his relationship with Jim. Consequently, he cannot escape the materialism that his society forces upon him (contrasted to the spiritual and emotional captivity that Huck Finn feels): "Where Brown Dog hurt the most . . . was in the double pocket of love and money. The truth was that he was out of both, the pockets utterly empty, and there didn't seem to be a philosophical or theological palliative for the condition. The presence of one somewhat consoles the absence of the other, and when one possesses neither, the soul is left sucking a very bad egg indeed."[63]

Huck Finn, on the other hand, analyzes his role as a white boy on the lam with a runaway slave and comes to the conclusion, in a scene that defines the nineteenth-century American notion of individual freedom, that he will do what he can to ensure that Jim remains free. Even though he believes he is doing the "wrong" thing, Huck composes a letter to Miss Watson telling her that he is with Jim; in one of the most memorable scenes in American literature, Huck decides, "'All right, then, I'll go to hell'—and tore it up."[64] Huck's innocence and his inability to justify wrongdoing contrast the destruction of the letter to Brown Dog's own revelation and subsequent rationalization of his actions in the back of an ice truck. *Huckleberry Finn* embodies the infinite; Harrison's texts dwell on the finite, the three short narratives leaving off where they began in Michigan a decade before. Brown Dog's inability to internalize his own quest for identity, a fact that manifests itself in his constant acting-upon rather than acting-within, correlates to Huck's maturation at the moment when he renounces the strictures of society that would have him turn traitor to his best friend. Brown Dog's epiphanies fade as quickly as his libido after intercourse with Tarah or any of his convenient partners; Huck's realization is neither easy nor convenient.

Harrison's pervasive use of digression without providing a coherent context upon which Brown Dog can order his life points to elements of the postmodern in his texts and amputates the narrative structure from the strictly linear narrative of Twain or the philosophical meanderings of Thoreau in the creation of an American hero. On one level, the difference between the narratives of Harrison and his predecessors is characterized by the shift between the epistemological, the ways in which we gain knowledge and understanding, and the ontological, the narrative's "concern with the making of autonomous worlds."[65] That difference in narrative structure, and ultimately in the semantic underpinnings of the texts, allows Harrison to articulate a vision rooted in the greatest traditions of American literature at the same time that it relies on an uncompromising eye for the uniqueness of every detail: "Nearly everyone goes through life with the same potential perceptions and baggage, whether it's marriage, children, education, or unhappy childhoods, whatever . . . ," says Harrison. But he adds, "This old Chippewa I know—he's about seventy-five years old—said to me, 'Did you know that there are people who don't know that every tree is different from every other tree?' This amazed him."[66] Twain's vision, on the other hand, does not stress the importance of difference in perception as much as it asks us to "suspend disbelief" for a time, especially in the much-criticized last eleven chapters of the text.

David Mogen explains these two radically different visions of the American Dream and the sovereignty of the individual in terms of the cultural and moral decay of the society that has spawned these visions: "Our national mythology based on frontier experience is the vehicle with which we examine the ironies and contradictory values expressed in that curious phrase, 'The American Dream'—which, after all, has been the implicit subject of many of our best writers since our diverse ancestors arrived on their many different errands into the wilderness."[67] A myth of individualism means nothing, then, when it is not in conflict with some aspect of the society which it describes. But when the intended myth-figure breaks the rules implicit in the attainment of the American Dream, he fails in his quest for myth-status and, in Brown Dog's case, he fails in his escape. Harrison chooses to invoke, not without irony, the conflict between the rights of Native Americans and white society, and he places Brown Dog, ignorant of his heritage, in the middle of a battle that has no winners. Brown Dog is eminently unsuited to act in such an intermediary role, and much of the comedy (and, to Harrison's credit, there is much comedy in these novellas despite their serious undertones) undermines the very notion of myth-making in the first place, or at the very least calls for a serious reassessment of our myth-making processes (see chapter 7 for further discussion).

Langdon Elsbree classifies works in the style of Harrison's *Brown Dog* novellas by claiming that "these works are explicitly counter-myth by intent but . . . they may be read dialectically as a critique of the primary tradition of American myth and narrative paradigm."[68] Indeed, in Harrison's three *Brown Dog* texts, the original Myth is replaced by the anti-myth, a denial and finally an abrogation of the Myth that has come down to us; the disintegration of the American Dream is the substitution of the infinite potential of a relatively innocent "lighting out" with the finite, and most often aimless, kinetic impulse of the always-already. This critique of the American myth is repeated in all three of Harrison's narratives in an un-Twainian conflict between the protagonist and his society.

Brown Dog's and Huck Finn's initiation into the wilderness diverge in a moment of realization for Huck that he will not allow himself to be confined in a relationship with an abusive father who represents a society that increasingly allows such relationships. Brown Dog, on

the other hand, spends his life aimlessly wandering until he is presented with the one mission that brings his story full circle: a return to
the place where he feels comfortable in his aimlessness, a place that
evokes "a primitive religious feeling where the home ground is sacral,
so that when you're on a foreign shore you recall the hills, gullies,
creeks, even individual trees that have become the songlines of your
existence."[69] Even in his return, though, his predicament informs
another postmodern aspect of Harrison's text, that of uncertainty:
Brown Dog is never sure of anything, including his parentage or his
purpose in life, and his return engenders the sort of responsibility—
the care of Rose's two young children—that he has avoided all his life.
Paradoxically, his only identity is a profound lack of identity, a life of
one ephemeral event after the next defined by contradictions, limitations, and appetites.

Brown Dog's inability to define himself in terms of the society in
which he lives is symptomatic of the postmodern subject, one "suspicious of all identity. Its logic is one of disintegration: a disintegration
of the prepared and objectified form of the concepts which the cogni-
tive subject faces, primarily and directly. Their identity with the subject is untruth."[70] Because of Brown Dog's contentious relationship
with society, lies become central to his existence, and the absence of a
true ancestral heritage makes necessary his oblique relationship with
society. Still, through his return to the one place that Brown Dog calls
home, Harrison implies that the feelings of alienation and fragmentation that characterize the three narratives will be abated, if not
negated, when Brown Dog, outside the confines of civilization once
again, "half-stumbled down through a grove of poplar, cedar, and
birch to the lake where he knelt in the muddy reeds and rinsed his face
in the cold water. On the way back up the hill he took a longer route
through the woods, half-dancing through the trees like a circus bear
just learning his ungainly steps, slapping at the trees and yelling a few
nonsense syllables."[71]

In Harrison's *Brown Dog* series, that connection to home and the
contradictions that such a notion implies allow us to limn the disappearance of the Dream in terms of both the evolution of American literature and a constantly changing social context. The postmodern
stance—shifting narrative points of view in a self-referential text, the
essential "falseness" of the narrative, the inability of the protagonist
to establish any meaningful identity—announces that once and for all
the American Dream is untenable at the same time it suggests the

power of place and the strength of the individual who lives outside the constraints of society. It is important to realize that such a shift in the way that we view our myth-figures will always be unique to the time and place in which the myth is articulated, as Richard Slotkin points out, because "such changes in the myth's usage, appeal, and appreciation suggest that the operation of social and historical factors is at least as important as archetypal structure in shaping the special history of that myth."[72]

In delineating the myth-figure in his own time, Twain's escape fantasy for Huckleberry Finn involves his own symbiotic relationship with the society with which he is at odds. In keeping with the expression of an American ideal of individual freedom, the novel "narrates a confrontation of the American individual, the pure American self divorced from specific social circumstances, with the promise offered by the idea of America. This promise is the deeply romantic one that in this new land, untrammeled by history and social accident, a person will be able to achieve complete self-definition."[73] More than a century later, Harrison understands that the relationship between the individual and society has grown irreparably antagonistic, not entirely through the fault of the anti-mythic figure, but as a result of inexorable and inevitable changes in the structure of society. Brown Dog's escape from society entails a break from the confining rules and mores of a largely undefined, controlling, and paradoxically permissive culture, a culture that inevitably turns away from the "unchanged realities we must live amidst."[74] The initial inability of Harrison's protagonist to "connect all his disparities" is a symptom of society's disintegration, a bleak forecast for the idealists who believe that the American Dream is not dying as its messenger heads west. In the evocation of home in all its connotations, however, the Dream takes on meanings that create new and limitless possibilities for the individual.

·7·

Whose Myth Is It, Anyway?

The Evolution of the Myth-Figure in Jim Harrison's Novellas

When a writer approaches the 20,000-word mark, he knows he is edging out of the country of the short story. Likewise, when he passes the 40,000-word mark, he is edging into the country of the novel. The borders of the country between these two more orderly regions are ill-defined, but at some point the writer wakes up with alarm and realizes that he's come or is coming to a really terrible place, an anarchy-ridden literary banana republic called the "novella."
　　　　　　　　　　　　　　　—Stephen King, *Different Seasons*

The major issue here is the question of whether there is one narrative of progress or multiple stories, some of which contest mightily the whole notion of progress. It's a conflicted and contested battle over the meaning of being American.
　　　　　　　　　　　　　　　　　　　　　　—Barry Shank

History, if you're truly human, must reduce itself to the individual case.
　　　　　　　　　—Jim Harrison, *The Beast God Forgot to Invent*

Jim Harrison has written seven novels, though he is just as often recognized for a body of twelve novellas—three works from each of four collections that span more than two decades, from *Legends of the Fall* (1979) to *The Beast God Forgot to Invent* (2000)—that is rivaled in contemporary American literature only by neo-gothicist Steven Millhauser (*In the Penny Arcade, The Barnum Museum, Little Kingdoms*). Transcending the notions of gender that plague Harrison's critical reputation (about which Harrison seems not to care a great deal, though he has responded to those criticisms on more than one occasion), the novellas show how characters adapt: surprisingly, few of the characters, despite their many shortcomings, are abject failures at finding their way in society. As with Harrison's novels and poetry, the novellas range far-afield for their subject matter and their forms, from the *Brown Dog* series (discussed in chapter 6) to portrayals of women protagonists written in their own voices (also touched on in chapter 5 in an analysis of *Dalva* and *The Road Home*).[1] Those stories have garnered some of Harrison's strongest reviews, and the form is an apt bridge between the poetry that has been a lifelong passion and the novels that have sustained him as a writer since the early 1970s.

Though the novellas, are, by definition, more compact than Harrison's novels, he takes on many of the same themes that inform the longer works, including marital relationships, protagonists who find themselves at odds with society, the American Myth and the American Dream (in all their connotations from Campbell, Eliade, Frazer, Lévi-Strauss, and Cassirer to Slotkin, whose focus on the Myth and Dream and their relation to American history and literature is more appropriate for this study), and a profound loss of identity. Despite his disgust at society's venality, Harrison never fails to rely on the individual case for the meat of his narratives. Though he admires the socially oriented *Grapes of Wrath* and Steinbeck's work in general, the social commentary in Harrison is colored not always by the "facts" at hand, but by a razor-sharp wit that avoids the didacticism of the overarching statement and finds its targets with deadly accuracy. The highly personal, "real," and complex narrative that Harrison manages even in the limited space of the novellas is reminiscent of the elements of magical realism in Faulkner, particularly the ways in which "the mythical or legendary as well as the historic past becomes an actual presence in contemporary life," and a mixing of "mystical or magical elements with the everyday details of commonplace reality in an attempt to generate in the reader a firm belief in the validity and genuineness—the reality—of his fictions."[2] Attention to those elements in the novellas and Harrison's continued focus on the individual and his or her place in society results in the evolution of a new American myth that explodes the presuppositions of the Myth of the Frontier and finally creates a contemporary narrative that exalts the ordinary.[3]

The novellas in the four collections are held together by one of the many threads that run throughout Harrison's fiction, the characters linked by their essential inability to function within the constraints of a society that has become alien to them, either through their own machinations, or at the hands of someone who represents that society and who wishes to keep them in abeyance to society's mores. Harrison's characters are not unlike the author himself, "an expansive presence, full of chutzpah, with an amazing zest for life. He is a gregarious, shabbily dressed vicar, telling raucous jokes with irresistible brashness. He knows the difference between a fistful and a handful, seeing and looking, living and existing, riches and wealth, entertainment and art, books and literature."[4] The same qualities that inform Harrison's own life underpin his short masterworks. By immersing himself in his texts, and armed with an extensive knowledge of the Myth of the Frontier that has informed American literature for more than three centuries, Harrison has not only traced his own evolution as a writer, but has succeeded in the novellas in defining and redefining a new American Myth.[5] A study of one novella from each of the four collections (in this case, all four title stories: *Legends of the Fall, The Woman Lit by Fireflies* [1990], *Julip* [1994], and *The Beast God Forgot to Invent*), though hardly comprehensive, details the ways the traditional American Myth fails and begins to uncover the soul of a new myth-figure.[6]

Myths, Raphael Patai writes, "are the repositories of some of the finest attempts made by peoples throughout history to read a meaning into the problems of the human condition."[7] American myth-figures, of course, come in many shapes and sizes (though most of them are white and male), from the stories that have come down to us from the first days of European settlement in the New World—analyzed thoroughly and gracefully by Richard Slotkin in his trilogy of books dedicated to exposing the underlying structures of the Myth of the Frontier and our Gunfighter Nation—to the misinformation that is purposely spread on the internet, our newest and most insidious source for memetic transmission.[8] The definition of the word "myth" (because it is nebulous at best, the mention of the word itself is often enough to raise the hackles of any critic) creates some difficulties: if the term is used arbitrarily, given too much rein, it has no meaning; too closely defined, and it collapses under the weight of its own presuppositions and becomes equally meaningless. Given Harrison's own notions of the absurdity in our society and its power over the individual, I define myth and mythic characters in part, simply enough, as those who transgress the boundaries of society to fulfill their own visions and live their lives relatively free from societal constraints. The myth-characters are at once independent, yet dependent enough on society and its goals, against which they are defined, to initially rely on society to act as partner in a symbiotic dance that results in a character's expulsion (willingly or unwillingly) and leaves room for the possibility of future change, "self-realization, a keener self-understanding that resolves our lives in new directions."[9]

Since Harrison focuses his attention on the individual in the society/individual binary, if and when the myth-figures return, it is solely on their own terms; in Harrison's case, the mythic quest is not contingent upon the protagonist's return. Inherent in Harrison's dislike for the unsavory aspects of society is a disdain for images glorified by mass media that create a cultural shorthand—ultimately, a reductive form of communication that requires little real thinking, only acceptance—through which, if we are drawn in by those images and accept them, we view ourselves and the world around us not as we are, but rather as we see ourselves reflected in society's mirror. Harrison directs his scorn at, among others, academics, politicians, and celebrities. In order to avoid such facile types, the author grounds his fiction in an authentic contemporary context that celebrates the strength of the individual, gives their stories relevance in our own society, and precludes the "universal" aspects that we have come to expect from such myth-making (the way that the Custer myth, for instance, denotes the American frontier spirit of the late nineteenth century).

Also crucial in painting Harrison's vision of the new American myth-figure is the notion of escape and the ambivalence that breaking free engenders: escape can mean independence from a controlling society, on the one hand, but it can also include the alienation that such a break implies. As Bluefarb points out, "The element of escape thrusts back to early American beginnings and beyond to the European past and the flight from Europe itself."[10] Still, the characters in Harrison's novellas are trapped either geographically, psychologically, or both; very often, the more important question is not how to escape, but where to go. The impulse to escape, then, becomes not a celebration of freedom, but an act "born of desperation and hopelessness, so that escape finally [becomes] not so much an act of hope, optimism, and Emersonian self-reliance as of hopelessness and confusion."[11] Bluefarb makes a distinction between "escape" and "escapism," identifying the former as the more accepted route of departure and the latter as something much less savory and frowned upon by society. In Harrison's world, though, the distinction is blurred, the words merging to denote the same impulse: whether a character eludes society by escaping physically (escape) or going inward (escapism), the result is the same.

Also implicit in myth-making is a certain amount of physical and psychic violence, "the very pattern of American life: a content violently appropriated, a national life created in revolution and defined in the midst of Indian warfare, the degrading brutality of slavery and the conflict between competing national groups."[12] Violence is evident in Harrison, though not as we might expect to see it in narratives that presume to define a notion as broad and as sacred as the myth-figure: Tristan Ludlow suffers the loss of his brother in World War I and spends much of his life fighting to protect his place on the frontier or struggling against his own restlessness (which is often more violent than the physical battles); Clare spends a night in an Iowa cornfield sorting through the shards of her life with an inattentive husband and regretting the things she has missed; Julip's brother shoots her three lovers (though the intent to murder is not apparent, and they all survive); Joseph Lacort drowns himself after an accident has left him with no past and no future. The evolution of violence in the narratives is much like the narratives themselves, moving away from violence as a means to accomplishing the quest at the same time that the narratives become, not coincidentally, more introspective.

Indeed, Harrison's most violent and, because of the depth of its symbolism and its closeness thematically and chronologically to the traditional myth, least subtle novella is *Legends of the Fall,* a succinct portrayal of the immediate effect of several discrete myth-making events of the late nineteenth and early twentieth centuries—World War I, the Indian Wars, the Depression, Prohibition, and the advent of technology spawned by the automobile—on a wealthy Montana plains family. The result is a lean and taut expression of the life of a man who straddles two distinct epochs in our nation's consciousness: one that still condones, and perhaps admires, the actions of the myth-figure, and one that has thrown off the veil of innocence and Manifest Destiny that spawned the American Myth in favor of a more jaundiced view of a world too complex to allow such figures.

British anthropologist Mary Douglas, whose work Harrison particularly admires, delimits the function of myth, which is "to portray the contradictions in the basic premises of the culture," and also the relation of myth to society, in which the myth is "a contemplation of the unsatisfactory compromises which, after all, compose social life."[13] The end result of mythmaking is that, "In the devious statements of the myth, people can recognize indirectly what it would be difficult to admit openly and yet what is patently clear to all and sundry, that the ideal is not attainable."[14] With so much at stake in such a brief exposition, little wonder that most critical opinion that addresses the intricacies of the narrative points to the novella as either an abbreviated epic or saga. Keith Opdahl describes Harrison's novella as "honest and revealing," and the right style for the form, "mostly summary, as though we look from a distance, with a tone that catches the large perspective and mute struggle of the character himself."[15]

The cumulative effect of so rapidly layering events one on another can be dazzling or disappointing, and the critical reception of the novella reflects Harrison's ambitious attempt at demarcating the boundaries of an American myth in so short a narrative. William H. Roberson is alienated by the story's ambition and would have all characters in novellas drawn as subtly as those in Harrison's *The Woman Lit by Fireflies,* Jane Smiley's *Goodwill,* or Andre Dubus's *The Pretty Girl,* not with the rough brush that gives Tristan his mythic qualities and leaves the depths of his psyche and the motivations for his actions largely unstated, if not unsounded. Roberson writes that *Legends of the Fall* "is a dense and busy work, a novella of epic proportions . . . essentially composed of three parts, each comprised of adventure, violence, romantic obsession and death."[16] Critics have condemned the narrative as an exercise in "macho literature" (not a first for the detractors of Harrison's work, certainly), and Roberson's assertion that the narrative gives "no sense of fulfillment or strength at the conclusion," but "instead an emptiness and exhaustion, a sense of pity and loss" is a convenient evasion of the very point that Harrison makes in the narrative, where he circumscribes a culture that no longer exists. In fact, we are left increasingly to wonder if it ever existed, was perhaps a simulacrum of the American Myth.[17]

The opening scene anticipates the frenetic pace of its action, which is halted only by a brutally violent finale. Tristan Ludlow, the son of Col. William Ludlow, is an adventurer in the most capacious sense of the word—a man unable, like his brother Alfred, who becomes a popular politician with a disharmonious personal life, to satisfy himself within the conventions of society; unlike many American adventurers before him, however, Tristan's life is marked by random tragedies that pursue him around the world as he embarks on one extraordinarily dangerous adventure after another. Tristan is the quintessential myth-figure in a culture that, a generation later, will turn its back on such people. World War I provides the thematic underpinning that brings into focus the history Harrison creates and re-creates. From the time that his brother is killed in a German ambush, Tristan lives apart from that history and moves freely from World War I to involve himself in an increasingly violent and tightening circle of adventure that finally brings him back to his beloved Montana. Each successive striking out on Tristan's part is an attempt at redeeming his brother Samuel, and each adventure implicates Tristan further in the myth-making process and finally transforms the protagonist's story into a legendary tale of struggle against implacable and random events, the history that threatens to swallow him whole.

Tristan's freedom points up the conflict between the natural and the societal, and the violence that results informs nearly every action in his life to its conclusion many years after his fury at the death of his younger brother has become legendary in the Northwest: "Then Tristan went mad and there are still a very few old veterans up in Canada that remember his vengeance, because he was captured and restrained before it reached full flower."[18] His retribution on the murderers of his brother can never be complete, and he will spend the rest of his life trying to replace his brother, as in his marriage to Susannah, in which he attempts to create Samuel's replacement by being "a truly crazed lover though not for any biological reason, but the wound in his brain."[19] He also strikes back at society unceasingly, blindly, and often ineffectually in an attempt at erasing such a fundamental loss from his mind. The importance of place for Tristan as a repository for the family's history impels him to cut Samuel's heart from his badly mangled body and encase it in paraffin for burial in Montana. The obvious symbolism of Tristan's action reinforces his respect both for his brother and for his homeland, which contrasts to the lack of respect that both Tristan's brother Alfred and his mother command through their lack of spirituality and their unwillingness to live apart from "civilized" society. The land, according to One Stab, is imbued with and by history and, Harrison implies, is crucial for the articulation of myth. Shortly after Samuel's death, news of which had yet to reach Montana, One Stab contemplates the topography of the land around him, the heights of the mountains, which Tristan had taught him, and wonders, as if somehow cojoined to Tristan's own spirit, "What did the numbers mean if there were no sea near them? Some large mountains have no character while certain smaller ones are noble and holy places with good springs."[20]

After his brother's burial, Tristan is consumed by dreams of water, a foreshadowing of both his further connection to nature and a sym-

bol of his random journey through history. The water draws Tristan
to itself, and the land, the oceans, and history are intertwined in a battle for Tristan's soul: "A hundred years before he would have been content to travel the land, the mountains and rivers seemingly without
end, but now at twenty-one in 1915 there was little or none of that
left, and his compulsion was to see beyond the seven millionth wave
and further."[21] The transition period for the mythic figure has begun,
and Tristan takes to the water as the last bastion of unexplored wilderness, the ostensible hero, his "Acceptance of the call [to action amount-
ing] to acceptance of the possibility of so radical a personal alteration
as to constitute a death."[22] The necessity of Tristan's traveling forms
a counterpoint to his own obsession with the landscapes of home and
the history of his family. He travels with the will of an ascetic depriv-
ing himself of water, his own forced exile a punishment for being so
much a part of the land of his ancestors and, finally, so little a part of
the brother he could not protect or the new world that encroaches on
the old.

Tristan's attitude echoes Harrison's own complex mantra invoked
at the death of the individual, repeated again and again until the pattern enveloping and delineating the narrative's structure becomes
clear. That mantra is a sensual and rhetorically logical definition of the
myth-figure that allows (in fact, compels) Tristan to endure the
tragedy that provides a framework for the cycle of his life—especially
in his relationships with Susannah and Two—and for the larger history that pervades his consciousness and one that encompasses events
as broad as the "Indian Question" and the transgression of technology on pristine nature: "People finally don't have much affection for
questions, especially one so leprous as the apparent lack of a fair system of reward and punishments on earth. The question is not less
gnawing and unpleasant for being so otiose, so naïve." Harrison challenges the old rules of the frontier and recognizes in the new that
"Some of our strangest actions are also our most deeply characteristic: secret desires remain weak fantasies unless they pervade a will
strong enough to carry them out." That force of will not in the name
of Manifest Destiny but rather toward a much more personal end—
revenge—paints Tristan as a mythic figure whose actions transcend
history and implicate him alone within the history of his family as he
attempts to "ingest sixty years of his grandfather's experience." By
assimilating his grandfather's knowledge, he subsumes an ephemeral
accretion of events, like those that form his own brother Samuel's life;

still, those events only feed Tristan's compulsion, as "Oddly, and like many men compelled to adventure with no interest in the notion of adventure but only a restlessness of the body and spirit, Tristan did not see anything particularly extraordinary about his past seven years."[23] The implication, one that is repeated throughout the narrative, is that Tristan has made little conscious decision to leave, but will leave nonetheless.

Of the events that compel him to continue his rather aimless quest, Tristan's dissolution of his relationship with Susannah recalls the death of Two, whom he had married in perhaps the most uneventful and undoubtedly the happiest time in his life. More than any other event, his wife's death pushes him "well past simple notions of vengeance and perhaps grief had coarsened and poisoned him to the point that he knew there was no evening the score with the world."[24] In the subsequent downward spiral of vengeance, Tristan rages against his brother Alfred, a politician and businessman, a convenient symbol of society's degeneration. Alfred's discovery that Tristan and Susannah are continuing their affair despite Susannah's relationship with Tristan's brother points up the inherent conflict between the two cultures that Harrison describes and the inherent weakness, in terms of the mythic figure, of "civilized" society: "Alfred said only to Tristan, 'I want to kill you,' and Tristan released himself from Susannah and handed Alfred the pistol. Alfred stared at the pistol then pressed the muzzle to Tristan's temple. . . . Alfred turned the pistol to his own head and Tristan knocked it from his hand. Alfred slumped to the floor weeping."[25] The confrontation is a metaphor for the myth-figure: strong, but with no overweening desire to control; firm in his demand for independence, but willing to allow society to slouch its way toward Bethlehem.

The final assessment of Tristan's status as myth-figure is summarized in the legend that grows out of Tristan's grief after the death of his wife Two: "It is still argued by old men in the area whether it was alcohol, jail or grief, or simply greed that made Tristan an outlaw: but this is only gossip to nurse the drinks of pensioners and interesting in that forty years later Tristan was still an object of fascination, somehow the last of the outlaws, rather than a gangster."[26] By defining Tristan as an outlaw, society recognizes his privileged position on the outside. Were society to suggest otherwise, it would be implicit in numbering him as one of their own. Tristan's constantly shifting position relative to society is one that casts him as a visionary whose spir-

ituality confounds those around them. Both the protagonist's continued interaction with society and society's interest in his actions point
up the changing definition of the myth-figure: neither Tristan nor society, it seems, is ready to wholly embrace the myth-figure nor to boldly
renounce him.

In part because of his closeness to One Stab, Tristan's profound
understanding of the ways that history manifests itself most closely
mirrors Dalva, and the similarities are worth noting. Tristan's dream-
state on his grandfather's schooner is similar to Dalva's own visions of
the landscapes, scarred and burned, as she observes them from 30,000
feet in the air: "Tristan had in his fever achieved that state which mys-
tics crave but he was ill-prepared for: all things on earth both living
and dead were with him and owned the same proportion." And in
much the same way that Dalva and her family must piece together
their own histories from Northridge's journals, Harrison leaves many
of the events of Tristan's own life unspoken: "No one but his far-flung
crew knows much of Tristan's next six years except for a few details,
all the more teasing because of their incompleteness."[27] Regardless of
the absence of knowledge, then, it is possible to construct as viable a
history for these six years as for any period of time, despite the dearth
of "facts" at hand. Such is the nature of history, the culling of a finite
number of noteworthy events that stand out in a universe of detail; as
with Dalva's notion that some people choose to "step into and then
out of" history, Harrison presents one side of the story at the expense
of the other. He also assumes the cynical notion that tales of contentment are not worth telling: "What doomed [Tristan] again (for there
is little to tell of happiness—happiness is only itself, placid, emotionally dormant, a state adopted with a light heart but nagging brain) was
a trip to Great Falls with Two and the ranch hands to drive a group
of fall steers to the railhead."[28]

The form of the novella precludes the full development of the characters while it allows Harrison the opportunity to focus on the chaos
and fragmentation—with seven years of peerless bliss between—of
Tristan's life. The desire to detail and convey the depth of Tristan's solitude is indicative, Leslie Fiedler writes, of literature that tries to find
"techniques for representing a universe in which we share chiefly a
sense of loneliness: our alienation from whatever things finally are, as
well as from other men's awareness of those things and of us."[29] The
idea of discovering and delineating such spiritual seclusion shares an
important element with Harrison's notion of the myth-figure that has

finally made his break from the "cluster of images and values that grew out of the confrontation between the uncivilized and the civilized world" that had, for so long, defined the American Myth. In *Legends of the Fall,* the hollowness of existence for a character who feels so deeply the weight of his own past and those of others allows him to transcend, for a time at least, the even more disjointed present.

The nostalgia for sanguine days on the Great Plains or America's love affair with the "Noble Savage" does not cloud Harrison's pragmatism. He is well aware that writing that glosses over the less savory aspects of our society will fail, and in the process distort the events that still influence us. Harrison's own narrative intrusions, written as clear manifestations of the author's vision, provide clues to the paradoxical conclusion of this myth: "The best words are ambiguous, and the more richly ambiguous the more suitable for the poet's or the myth-maker's job. Hence there is no end to the number of meanings which can be read into a good myth."[30] Myth, then, because it relies on the myth-teller as much as it does the hero's deeds, very often ends in an indeterminate or unsatisfying fashion. Any attempt to construct myth, given the double context of the writer and his characters, will invariably result "in frustration and futility, underscoring the Keatsian outlook that only in appreciation for the creative act or work of art itself can there be any real feeling of lasting satisfaction."[31] In this case, the end of the story is apparent long before its conclusion, a statement of the very definition of an ambiguous, but nonetheless definable, collective unconscious that underscores the nature of myth: "There's little more to tell. Susannah was buried next to Samuel and Two and the reader, if he or she were a naïve believer, might threaten God saying leave him alone or some such frivolity. No one has figured out how accidental is the marriage of blasphemy and fate."[32]

The Woman Lit by Fireflies, chronologically the next in Harrison's novella collections, is different enough from *Legends of the Fall* in content and form to signal a distinct evolution in Harrison's articulation of the myth-figure. Written in a female voice, the story eschews the Frontier Myth, whose relevance has been called into question by its very underpinnings as a unifying narrative for the oppression of America's native peoples and the capitalist impulse. The story centers on the refashioning of the protagonist's own psyche in her imaginary conversations with her daughter, Laurel, her dead friend Zilpha Underwood, and her therapist, Dr. Roth. When the protagonist, Clare, decides to leave her husband, who has grown increasingly distant as a result of his focus on career and financial success, a "specific giddiness began to overtake her when she thought of the goodbye. This is the way, after all, I've spent my life, she thought."[33] The abuse that Clare suffers is psychological rather than physical; the result of Donald's control over her for three decades is subtle and insidious. Clare's predicament, then, is not in relation to the frontier as we have come to know it—vast geographical spaces peopled by enemies of our own making—but rather one of the individual will rising above an extremely personal circumstance. Clare's essential struggle with herself "allows us to understand our human transcendence less as a war with nature and more as a purification or harmonizing of our natural inclinations. . . . Human nature becomes something which needs to be explored."[34]

Nearly all of that struggle takes place in Clare's memory: she recalls a tour of the museums of Moscow and Leningrad that she had planned with her friend Zilpha but which had never transpired because "Donald had jinxed the visa with a phone call to a friend in the State Department, the sort of favor that is due a major Republican fund raiser like Donald."[35] Later, she remembers giving birth to her daughter, Laurel, and thinks that "there was a tinge of déjà vu in the present rain. I had two children and lived with a man nearly thirty years. *I don't seem to have a real idea what occurred to me. Maybe nobody does, or just a few.*"[36] Donald's attitude toward Clare—her absence, it seems, affects him much more profoundly than her presence—internalizes her struggle and forces her to come to terms with her own wants and needs. As the society that Harrison portrays implies, Donald lives his life as he cares to, though Harrison makes no attempt at hiding his disdain for anyone who lives a life utterly devoid of introspection.

Clare's struggle for independence is typical of Harrison's characters, who comprehend both the big picture and the minute details that make a life unique. Clare's love for animals, which she has imparted to Laurel, who is a veterinarian, is juxtaposed to history's larger events, in this case Cortez's conquering of Mexico, in which, Clare thinks sardonically, "Cortez had destroyed the city and murdered hundreds of thousands of citizens—that was to be expected—but the burning of Montezuma's aviaries seemed to stand for something far more grotesque and the image of the conflagration passed through her mind daily."[37] When she finds herself alone at night in an Iowa cornfield, after she has escaped Donald at a rest stop, she experiences a brief taste of the sort of introspective life about which she has only dreamed.

Clare's mythic quest begins simply enough when she dons a beret that she had bought thirty years before in Paris but never had the courage to wear. The indecision that causes Clare to lend such importance to the beret comes from never being asked to make her own decisions. In addition to her simple act of rebellion against her husband, Clare's transformation is expedited by migraine headaches—again, it is worth noting that every stimulus that prompts Clare to action comes from within—which make her feel as though she "was moving within the heart of time. Normally she stood aside and lived on her comments to herself on what was happening to her, but when the pain moved to the left she moved inside herself, and this had the virtue of being novel within the framework of suffering." Here, Clare's own psychic escape is combined with a physical component and a dream—her first in months—of her own death, "which simply didn't hold her interest."[38] Harrison's overt symbolism at the outset of Clare's journey prepares us for the inevitable: after Clare questions her own motives, she reconciles her old life with the new one that she has chosen free of her husband and, implicitly, a society that has controlled her since her carefree days in college.[39]

Without leaving her hideout, Clare's transition is completed in a series of events during the night: she slips into a stream-of-consciousness reverie remembering the death of her dog Sammy and "wonders if she deserved it" when she is surrounded by fireflies. After another light dream during which she recalls an event from her distant past, she "felt herself floating in memory from her beginning, as if on a river but more quickly along the surface than what had happened to her. Now she saw when it was she had slept on the ground without covers up at the cottage when she was seven. . . . When Clare woke again the fireflies were gone."[40] The water imagery that Harrison uses to affect the change is significant: water for Harrison is neither linear nor predictable, and very much part of the same continuum along which history itself moves; by imagining herself on the water, Clare is at the whim of her unconscious and her own history. That she dreams of an event from her childhood is also important in connecting her with the past, another simple act which finally propels her into the future. In addition, Clare attributing importance to the fireflies that float around her in the darkness and the dreams that figuratively carry her through memory and into the uncharted territory of her own independence is reminiscent of Stephen Dedalus's epiphany in Joyce's *Ulysses,* a

> *problem-solving* act . . . not only revealing a moment profoundly lived in, but resolving the terms of thought itself in the persistent search for under-

standing. It reaches no conclusions and does not symbolize anything at all
. . . for the thrust of its presence is to create a potential space to move in.
It contains the tensions in the moment of knowing itself, so that we learn
more about thinking, perception, and the limits of consciousness than we
do about a specific conclusion to be reached.[41]

Clare's escape is an end unto itself, and she has little idea of what the
future holds except that she wants to return to Paris. Her night in the
cornfield, though, allows her a "space" within which to move as she
considers her options.

With the psychic space that Clare creates, the reconciliation process—
a piecing back together of what she has dismantled by leaving her husband—can continue. She reconstructs her relationship with her ana-
lyst, Dr. Roth, who "liked to think that, all efforts of the glitz media
to the contrary, life is Dickensian, and that pathos is invariably the
morning's leading news item. Clare with dusty knees and a verbless
prayer would, no doubt, amuse him."[42] Though there has been no
physical relationship between the two, Clare realizes that she had, for
a time, loved him. She recalls a lull in one of their conversations when
Dr. Roth asked her to pull a quotation from a ledger of literary bits
and pieces that Clare had begun during her college days, "from
Aeschylus down to E. M. Cioran, with a preponderance coming from
the early modernist period in world literature from 1880 to 1920. Her
intended but never finished honors thesis was to be on Apollinaire and
there were many translated quotes, but her temperament seemed to
have been most captured by Rilke. Dr. Roth's own sense of balance
had been disturbed when he came across Yeats's notion to the effect
that life was a long preparation for something that never occurred."
The ledger is prescient of Clare's own current predicament, a connection to her past that hints at her expansive spirit and suggests that any
relationship whose context is a controlling society will be untenable
for her. She realizes that "the highest hopes of her twenties had dis-
sembled to the degree that she was relegated to writing checks to distant organizations and trying to save the occasional pond, creek or
sorry woodlot in Michigan."[43] Harrison's own fascination with the
symbolist and modern poets informs his view of myth by stressing the
fragmentation of experience and its bittersweet and contradictory
reality, the necessary end to our quests.[44] That notion is reinforced by
Dr. Roth's declaration to Clare that "'The only reality you are ever
going to get is the ordinary one you make for yourself. In other words,
there's no big breakthrough." Again, the importance of Clare's simple

act of defiance when she puts on the beret is made clear. The one book that Clare carries with her on her escape is the *Tao Te Ching*, which a counselor at her pain clinic told her could cure her of her migraines. Even so, the reason for carrying the book with her is as banal as the notion that it could cure her: "the translator was the same as that of her favorite volume of Rilke, *The Sonnets to Orpheus*."[45]

Clare's relationship with Dr. Roth validates her own evolving notions of life: she sees herself as the foundation of society, imposed upon by that society, the uncomplaining wife who supports her husband and allows him to achieve the success that he so richly deserves. Dr. Roth alerts her for the first time to the fact that "the overexamined life was not worth living, and that the quasi-upper-class life had become the shabbiest of self-improvement videos. Goddamn but her mind was so exhausted with trying to hold the world together, tired of being the living glue for herself, as if she let go, great pieces of her life would shatter and fall off in mockery of the apocalypse." Later, she muses that "The sheer taffy in self-awareness exhausted her. Saying that you were no more inflexible than your husband was small-minded dogshit, and she laughed out loud. She wanted more life, not Robert's Rules of Order." Once again, the contrast is between society and the individual, and Dr. Roth makes clear to Clare that "All of this mythological freedom we grow up on which we usually get to express standing around in a field wearing a baseball mitt" or "sailing a quarter-million-dollar sailboat down the Detroit River hoping the water won't corrode a hole in the bottom" is what holds us in abeyance to society.[46] Clare understands that her predicament is hardly important to anyone but herself, though she is unable to disappoint society's expectations; it is a role she has come to know too well in her adult life. In fact, she realizes the lengths to which society will go in order to maintain its control over her when she relates that "One of the favorite local psychiatrists was an ardent pill pusher in his efforts to remove any socially embarrassing symptoms. The probable cause in her case would be obvious to all—the deaths of Zilpha and [her dog] Sammy—but her marriage, which was considered to be improbably solid, would not be questioned."[47]

Although she has made her break from Donald, Laurel, who would normally support such an endeavor, finds Clare's dream of revisiting Paris with her newfound freedom "silly," claiming that "Paris isn't the same as it was thirty years ago. You'll be disappointed."[48] Because of her practicality and her own stable home life Laurel, with whom Clare has had several imaginary conversations during her night in the corn-field, cannot understand the motivation behind Clare's dream, seeing only the necessity of escaping Donald. Clare's quest does not result in the myopic admiration with which we often view our myth-figures, and the omniscient narrator who observes Clare's departure from the rest stop and records her thoughts reads her mind one last time, as if to confirm what seems odd coming from the mind of someone who has just accomplished a significant goal: "The beauty and dread of time was that nothing was forgiven. Not a single minute. The years she had spent in consideration of this act were not only lost, irretriev-able, but the recognition of the loss was so naïve as to leave her breath-less. . . . *If she had the whole thing to do over she would have done it differently, but then no one has anything to do over.*" When Clare makes her way back home and decides that she would like to relive the days when she first bought the beret, her attitude is both ambiva-lent and accepting of whatever life offers her: "Clare felt a little lost but then she always had, and supposed easily that it was the condition of life. Lying back on the bed, under the whir of the fan on the night-stand, she decided that she felt less lost than before her night in the thicket, she would write letters to Dr. Roth and Laurel. If it rained, she would wear her beret to dinner."[49]

Harrison's accomplishment in questioning the traditional myth and creating something much more contemporary, in this instance describ-ing Clare's self-imposed exile to freedom, is akin to Camus's notion of "'terrible freedom,' that once you decided not to commit suicide, whether physically or figuratively, you assumed the responsibility of freedom"—nothing short of a delineation of the current state of Amer-ican society in relation to its past. The myth, in this case, remains a story based on the history of our culture that has "acquired through usage . . . a symbolizing function that is central to the cultural func-tioning of the society that produces" it. [50] Although the myth-figure in *The Woman Lit by Fireflies,* in the traditional sense of the Frontier Myth, is hardly heroic enough to warrant a narrative, Clare's story has become part of the mythic tradition as Harrison defines it.

Julip is similar to *The Woman Lit by Fireflies* only in that it is writ-ten from a woman's point of view, and its importance to the evolution of the myth-figure in Harrison's novellas lies not in its rigorous phi-losophy of life—the story is, perhaps, apart from the novellas *Revenge* or *Sunset Limited,* the most linear of Harrison's works—but rather in its analysis of imminent mortality and its celebration of youth. Julip, a young dog trainer who has had affairs with three older men, undertakes a quest more immediate than Clare's: to free her brother from jail for shooting her three lovers. Julip's youth and her connection with nature—Harrison tells Joseph Bednarik that "Julip survives these men and survives everything because she has this very specific skill in relationship with animals. It's a tremendous focus for her life, like in our darkest times we always have our poetry"—are her strengths.[51] Though young, she is wary and observant (as she must be to train her dogs) and Harrison contrasts her toughness to the more refined tastes of her lovers.

Julip's childhood, only a few years in the past, is profoundly influenced by her memories of being summoned to a hall in the plantation where her mother works. There she saw

> two Edward Curtis prints that had troubled, mystified, attracted her: Two Whistles, his face powdered and a crow perched on his head, and Bear's Belly, the Arikara medicine man cloaked in the skin of a bear. After being chided or spanked she wanted to hide within the bearskin robe of Bear's Belly, having been drawn to the eyes of the man who promised an earth without the small-time bullshit of punishment. It was strange, she thought, that in Wisconsin Indians were subjected to abuse that far exceeded that of blacks in the South. Somehow, though, the message inherent in the memory of these two men was that it was important not to approach life with the attitude of a hurt child. It got you nowhere in life, she had decided, and it certainly was the way to ruin a potentially good bird dog during training. Life and bird dogs required a firm hand.[52]

Julip's "felt sense" of the power of art—informed by her own romantic vision and a sense of the beauty inherent even in photographs that, in the context of Harrison's fiction, recall the extirpation of Native American lives and the appropriation of their culture—are enough to begin her on her quest: "Naïve as it was, there is no response to art so genuine as the desire, the often heart-rending pull, to be within the work."[53] Julip's desire is much more intuitive than Clare's, much less visceral than Tristan's; in that sense, Harrison's notion of where the novella will take him has evolved from the physical violence that characterizes the American Myth of the nineteenth century to a quest that extols the individual virtues of innocence and discovery.[54]

In order to transcend into the mythic, though, Julip must confront her lovers one by one and ask them to support her brother Bobby's move from prison to a psychiatric ward. Her quest is not one away from society, as the other two have been, but rather back into it, where she must act in harmony, at least for a time, with the elements that have alienated her. For Julip, even though the society that she encounters, embodied by her lovers, is familiar to her, the ground rules that she must follow are difficult for her to define. The reconciliation will test her "capacity to encounter the foreign and to inhabit one's own culture as a provisional and shifting horizon whose form is, in many respects, quite arbitrary yet which hangs together by its own internal coherence."[55]

One roadblock for Julip in her attempt at freeing Bobby from prison is the story of her own life. Julip has been told by her mother, from whom she is estranged, that her father committed suicide, and the circumstances surrounding his death have always bothered her. When she discovers that he was, in fact, killed in a hit-and-run accident, she suffers through "a strange, wakeful night, her imagination seemingly electrified by the details of her life, and a fresh anger emerging from the fact that her father had simply been killed rather than committing suicide."[56] Perhaps we could surmise that Julip has spent the intervening years searching for a father figure, though the importance of her father's death is in her own act of identity-making, which is simultaneous to her quest: without the "truth" of her father's death (and only when she realizes that she had not known the truth does the fact become significant for her, of course), Julip is destined to be lied to by society, and society will once again have succeeded in co-opting the myth-narrative from the individual for its own broad uses as a controlling narrative. Rather, by actively searching out the truth of her own past, Julip re-creates the events of her past—much as she does in subsequent meetings with her lovers, the "Boys"—and gains control of her own identity.

Identity-making in Julip's life is not as difficult a process as that loaded phrase implies. Rather, it requires only a knowledge of the self in relation to society—the impulse might be to deem it "cynical" or to refer to the "lack of maturity" that characterizes such a person for society—and a desire to escape from society's strictures. Her lovers' attraction to Julip, then, is based in part not on her worldliness or her beauty, but on her simple philosophy of life informed by the pictures from her childhood and her closeness to nature, characterized by her vocation. Her value as a myth-figure to her jaded lovers is her youth and her relative innocence, and she "didn't know how much they had come to depend on her, more in spirit than in presence. The fact was that more than her supposed attractiveness, her vividness, she was so ordinary that she reminded them of the value of life aside or beyond work and exhaustion. She was totally without their distortions and had grown tired of drawing them out of the hundreds of funks that success is heir to."[57] The three—an artist, a writer, and a photographer, all successful—act as anti-mythic characters, victims of a profound ennui that forces them to relive the dreams of their youth on Key West to experience the shortening of time, when "one feels less reason to keep the deepest passions quiet to please others or to gain protection."[58] For them the structure of society has become abundantly clear, and the "horizon was as invisible as it was when they were nineteen, but now its nature was deeply sensed. An actual surprise would have astounded them now that their time was sliced so precise and thin."[59]

The intimation of death, or at least the winding-down of lives that are too deeply inculcated in the machinations of society to be redeemed, is a concept with which Julip is unfamiliar. She knows little of the world that the Boys inhabit (although, in her relationships with them, she appropriates the wants of society for her own benefit) or the literature that is so often important to Harrison's characters. She recalls that "The only class she cared for at junior college had been an introduction to anthropology where a very old English feminist taught them that in nearly all cultures in the history of humankind men had worked to deprive women of their free will," and Julip considers that if she had not become a dog trainer, she would have "emulated this woman." After a staid meeting with Charles, the photographer, Julip recalls another event from her childhood and compares it to her emotion: "There was the pathetic, anguished feeling of living within a pop tune sung by any of a hundred singers she loathed. She still had genuine emotion and it was difficult to endure the fake." When Julip succeeds in getting the Boys to acquiesce to her demand to free Bobby from prison, she has succeeded in transcending the limitations of her education, her class, and her gender. When she last leaves the Boys, "she glanced at each of them and for the briefest chilling moment they looked like petrified babies suspended in dreamless sleep."[60] Harrison again points up the differences between Julip and her older lovers; with that last look, she is satisfied to return to a life not as part of society, but to a life more suited to the training of dogs.

The latest of Harrison's novellas, *The Beast God Forgot to Invent*, serves as a fitting conclusion to his construction of a peculiarly post-heroic myth. Having moved from the visceral (*Legends of the Fall*) on a rough continuum to the story at hand, which deals with the purely cerebral predicament of his protagonist, Harrison details the late life and death of Joseph Lacort, whose brain has been irrevocably damaged in a motorcycle accident. Lacort has become what Harrison has implied all along in his notion of what our relationship with nature should be: because he has no memory of the past, he can hardly imagine a future; because he lives only in the immediate present, he is the perfect tabula rasa upon which nature can leave its mark and through which his interaction is unmediated by any preconceived notions of what that relationship *should* be.

Despite Lacort's inability to offer his own narrative, Harrison neatly provides contextual grounding from outside the protagonist's frame of reference through his narrator, Norman Arnz, who, in the course of writing the story, is completing a coroner's inquest of Lacort's death by drowning in Lake Superior. The novella's opening recalls the poignant first line of *The Road Home,* a combination of folk wisdom, world-weariness, and a profound understanding of the human condition: "The danger of civilization, of course, is that you will piss away your life on nonsense."[61] From there, Arnz weaves his narrative in a roundabout manner, providing context for the story that will follow and describing the myth of Joseph Lacort. In doing so, he invokes the "discounted sociologist Jared Schmitz, who was packed off from Harvard to a minor religious college in Missouri before earning tenure when a portion of his doctoral dissertation was proven fraudulent." What Arnz knows of Schmitz's work is a bit of ersatz philosophizing that allows him to make sense of Lacort's accident. Schmitz's single contribution to the canon, it seems, is the notion that "in a culture in the seventh state of rabid consumerism the peripheral always subsumes the core, and the core disappears to the point that very few of the citizenry can recall its precise nature."[62] What that notion implies is nothing less than the privileging of the marginal characters in Harrison's fiction over the "core" element of society. The fact that Arnz is taking the time to record Lacort's life and his spectacularly banal death suggests that the myth permeates the society through which Arnz writes.

Arnz is another of Harrison's bibliophiles who attempts to make sense of his own world through literature. His response to news of Lacort's condition is to describe the scene as "wretchedly Dickensian, or from our own Steinbeck," and he is "full of ire despite that fact that I could scarcely swallow from melancholy." Arnz's friend Roberto sends him books such as Slobodkin's *Simplicity and Complexity in the Games of the Intellect* and *Neural Darwinism* that "shoved me over the edge into a prolonged anxiety attack that my poor soul had been spoiling for," and caused him to reassess his own position in a society that little appreciates the fragility of consciousness. Despite his vast knowledge of E. O. Wilson's *Biophilia*, Freud, Jung, Dostoevsky, Yeats, and García Márquez, he decides that he will never float free of the societal gravity imposed upon him when he realizes that "the banality in my thinking was the old time trap. My invented genius had to go to meetings, seduce women, raise unruly children, drink wine and perhaps martinis, make a living." Lacort has to deal with no such constraints, though Arnz questions his halting admiration for Lacort, for whom "All human activity would be distracting. Or maybe ultimately supporting."[63]

The two worlds that Arnz straddles in the narrative—the landscape of Lacort's own invention and the much more familiar society through which Arnz has moved in his six decades—are an interesting deconstruction of Harrison's own life: Arnz's attitudes on academia are transparent and too closely aligned with Harrison's to be coincidental, and he concludes that "I'm quite tired of being a querulous old fuck and I am beginning to wonder if this persona isn't simply another cultural imposition." The result of the narrator's close association with the author is a complex narrative that presumes to bring to a close the more or less indeterminate narratives that have marked Harrison's novellas to this point. Arnz's statement that "I am scarcely interesting even to myself. I am the personification of Modern Man, the toy buyer who tries to thrive at the crossroads of his boredom"[64] implicates Harrison, his narrator, and the protagonist in a struggle to locate themselves relative to society's imposed boundaries.

The result of Lacort's accident and the necessity of Arnz relating his predicament to the coroner is clear: the mythic beasts that Lacort claims to see (both the "beast" of the title and Harrison's play on words with Lacort's character) and the powers over nature that he appears to possess inculcate him in a world that is distinctly "Other." Lacort "announced that he had seen something quite extraordinary, a brandnew mammalian species, a beast that he didn't know existed," and his newfound communion with nature is quite different from his personality before the accident. Arnz suggests that Lacort "might need his tripartite beast or monster for the same reason that Claude Lévi-Strauss pointed out, to the effect that the creation of such mythological beasts was as necessary as nest building. . . . Maybe Joe's beasts were similar to our own impulse in the creation of our early religions, a map of gods."[65] By allowing Lacort to create, in essence, his own identity, Harrison reinforces Lacort's own status as myth-figure and places him even further outside society. That Arnz invokes Lévi-Strauss in relation to Lacort also suggests that Lacort has already attained myth status.[66]

When Arnz mentions that "Frankly I didn't care for him before his injury. Despite his financial success downstate he would become immediately loutish up here, aping his local friends,"[67] he suggests that Lacort, unlike any of the three earlier protagonists, had previously been part of the society that he now dismisses, not a character in any way subjugated to the whims of that society; rather than having the protagonist progress through a series of life-altering events, Harrison slams him irrevocably into myth by eliminating any possibility of his return. By doing just that, however, Harrison illustrates the extent to which society has co-opted the individual: if Lacort is able to gain release from society only by eliminating his past and his future (in fact, Arnz describes Lacort's individual universe as "totally holographic, so that he moves dimensionally within time's enclosure but quite unrelated to it"), the implication is that society controls time (and history) itself.[68]

Still, even as a nominal member of that society, Arnz is unwittingly drawn into Lacort's predicament through his close association with him after the accident. Always the thinker, Arnz is bothered by the fact that the research that Lacort's girlfriend Ann sends him on closed-head injuries disturbs him to his core:

> But why would I be so overwhelmed by these stories, a sophisticated student of language, of the best of world literature not to speak of legal documents, histories, the best newspapers and magazines? The answer I suppose lay in the charm of folkloric stories, primitive or "naïve" art, the origins of third-world music, the recorded oral tales of our own Natives. A trucker swerves to miss a school bus (of course!). There are massive head injuries and his head becomes a partially cooked rutabaga. . . . Jesus Christ, this tale floored me.
>
> Reading these stories by the dozens reminded me how nearly all of our printed discourse is faux Socratic and contentious, a discourse without nouns of color and taste, a worldwide septic tank of verbiage that is not causally related to the lives we hope to lead. It is the language of the enemy and politicians lead the pack, with this verbal shit spewing out of their

mouths on every possible occasion. Analogic, ironic, what we call common usage leaking its viruses from between book covers.[69]

Arnz's questioning of the efficacy of language and its potential for oppression, here represented by maudlin tales of people even worse off than Lacort, offers fitting closure to the four collections of novellas. All the analysis of the situation that Arnz (I.Q. 157, we find out) can muster cannot define Lacort's dilemma any better than Lacort himself is able. The literature that Arnz has read, finally, pertains to him and to him alone, and any searching after a coherent narrative around which we can wrap our minds to explain the life and untimely death of Lacort is as useless as "the language of the enemy" is insidious. The only option remaining to Arnz—and by extension, to any reader of the narrative—is to accept the story on its own merit, devoid of the context of history. Harrison, finally, has constructed a myth-figure whose identity is irreducible from the individual. Even then, the narrative is negotiable.

The historical innocence with which Lacort views the world manifests itself most profoundly in his sense of place: without being bound by history—as Harrison repeatedly points out, such a context can be stifling—he is free to "re-map the world, or the only world his senses could tolerate," though finally, "there was not enough of this world to make his life tolerable." Lacort's death is equally important as his life. Arnz points out that "the word 'suicide' is a banality that doesn't fit this extraordinary situation. Perhaps he felt summoned by the mystical creatures he thought he had seen." The importance of Lacort's life takes on new meaning when his body is found by fishermen thirty miles from shore. "One of the fishermen claimed Joe was 'nearly alive' when they pulled him aboard but the two others weren't sure." The fact that Arnz feels compelled to mention to the coroner that Lacort was seemingly alive when he was pulled from the water implies that the myth of Joseph Lacort will survive: the mysterious circumstances surrounding his death recall other myth characters from Christ to the pop figures Elvis Presley and Jim Morrison. Lacort has transcended the life that Arnz and others like him have lived, and Arnz finds himself trying to come to grips with both Lacort's death and his own situation, "trying, moment by moment, to think of what I should do next. Joe had left us to ourselves."[70]

The construction of a new myth-figure in Harrison's novellas is both subtle and profound. If, as Slotkin writes, "Myth is history successfully disguised as archetype," then what Harrison articulates in his novellas is all the more remarkable for the way in which he gives extraordinary meaning to the lives of ordinary characters and situations. [71] Slotkin draws on the myth of Custer and Whitman's articulation of that myth for the title of his seminal treatise on the Frontier Myth, *The Fatal Environment,* and claims that "it is myth, as much as any other aspect of reality, that creates the 'fatal environment' of expectations and imperatives in which a Custer, or a war correspondent, or a whole political culture, can be entrapped. One of the ways of escaping the fatality of that environment is through the demystifying of specific myths and of the mythmaking process itself."[72] Harrison manages in the course of these four novellas to both demystify the Frontier Myth and its analogues and, through the construction of individual lives whose meaning is most profound to the individual, not to society, demystify the myth-making process itself. By focusing on the individual rather than the society at large, these narratives personalize and humanize the mythic quest and unravel the overarching Myths to the point of their negation.

Epilogue

It is the act of communication that distinguishes the work of art from an incoherent cry of pain or joy, and it is the presence of pain or joy in the act of communication that separates literature from other forms of writing, such as journalism, or the preparation of technical reports. Whether what is communicated is evaluated as "great" or as a work of genius is in some measure culturally and historically determined. . . . The primary task of literary criticism involves more than making value judgments about what is great art and what is second class. The challenge is to understand the experiential core of art, and how private fantasy derived from this base is made over into something public that has the power to move audiences and to capture their imagination.

—Leo Schneiderman, *The Literary Mind: Portraits in Pain and Creativity*

It is possible to tread water until you are unable to do anything else.
—Jim Harrison, "A Natural History of Some Poems"

Putting the finishing touches on this collection of essays is a task that I have scrupulously avoided until now. To be satisfied with such a thing—the notion of truly completing any work, be it a novel, a novella, an essay, a poem—is a sure sign of the complacency that reduces literature to a cultural shorthand whose relevance has evaporated fifteen minutes after the ink has dried. With these essays, I hope only to have scratched the surface of the critical possibilities that await future scholars when they examine Harrison's work. In truth, I have given no attention to a handful of Harrison's novellas and many of the essays that were outside the scope and the critical avenues that I travel here. Also, the poetry that is such an integral part of his life as a writer remains essentially untouched—both by itself, and in relation to the fiction (combined with the essays, the poetry might be seen without difficulty to form an overarching narrative in the body of Harrison's work, though that's a matter for much future debate and analysis).

I have been careful to keep Harrison's work in its original context, the canvas covered in something that perhaps resembles a pointillist painting. Such close readings limn the boundaries of a body of work that struggles against classification, though the vagaries of literary criticism required me to, on occasion, "cut off the horse's legs to fit him into the box" (another of Harrison's favorite aphorisms in any discussion of the academy, the joke being, I suppose, that once you cut off his legs, you're beating a dead horse). The structure of these essays is meant to mirror Harrison's own style with an eclectic mix of philosophy, popular reception, literature, history, and research. Because of the dearth of critical study on Harrison to this point, the threads I have traced in these essays are diverse and any of those avenues contains enough rich material for a host of scholarly essays and a book-length treatment of the most viable issues. Still, several of those themes have found their way to the top, in one form or another, in all seven chapters: history, both its making and its profound and sometimes seemingly random influence on the events that follow; the inevitable relationship of man to nature; the Frontier Myth and the American Dream in all their connotations (scholars, as they are wont to do, have come up with as many definitions for the Myth and Dream as there are essays written about those concepts); a critique of contemporary society; the complexity of interpersonal relationships; the influence of place on our perception; the powerful role of wants and needs in our lives; our continuing struggle with and against technology in an attempt to come to terms with our own aspirations; the way we view time; the ways we view ourselves. These themes are all part of the rich tradition of American literature. None is original to Harrison.

The true value of Harrison's work to scholars, rather, is that rarely in our literature, and arguably at no time in the last three decades of the twentieth century—notwithstanding a host of beautiful writers too numerous to begin mentioning here, for fear of the conspicuous omission—did an author succeed in synergizing these familiar themes into works of such varying length, scope, and form into literature that holds up to the rigors of close multiple readings. Perhaps most important, Harrison's work evokes emotions in its readers that define a purely American sensibility. At the same time, through a passion and a capacious memory both of which must be witnessed to be believed, the author invokes the best literature in the world and an obsession with *art* that should inspire anyone even the least bit interested in the life of the mind.

One of the most perplexing problems in placing the disparate themes in Harrison's works into a viable critical paradigm is the author's own outspoken distaste for critical theory and a paradoxical stance—for instance his waffling on the issue of irony in his narratives—that makes reaching any absolute conclusion about the work a virtual impossibility: the harder the work is squeezed, the more difficult it becomes to reach "logical" conclusions about Harrison's intentions. Such is the nature of Harrison's mind and his ability to reconcile the seemingly irreconcilable elements in his fiction.

Are such contradictions antithetical to the creation of important literature? No! in thunder.

In fact, Harrison's unwillingness to make grand statements for his characters outside the defined boundaries of their own narratives, each a discrete whole written in a particular time and place, is the one aspect of his fiction among many that, if given sufficient critical exposure, might lead to an acceptance by both literaty scholars and the reading public of the loose ends that give our best literature the texture and life that it so richly deserves and needs to thrive. Of course, I hope these essays will be of some value to Harrison scholarship in the future. To be sure, Harrison is not done writing: he is producing fiction, poetry, essays, including *The Raw and the Cooked,* a collection of food pieces published in November 2001, and a memoir at an astounding pace, considering that he has published consistently and prolifically for more than thirty-five years.

I would be remiss if I didn't end with a poem, in this case, "Looking Forward to Age," from *The Theory and Practice of Rivers,* which seems to me to summarize Harrison's artistic vision and his life in a few scant lines that might take a future biographer several hundred pages to articulate:

> I will walk down to a marina
> on a hot day and not go out to sea.
> I will go to bed and get up early,
> and carry too much cash in my wallet.
> On Memorial Day I will visit the graves
> of all those who died in my novels.
> If I have become famous I'll wear a green
> janitor's suit and row a wooden boat. (35)

Harrison, who accepts the passing of time as he works to understand the impulses that drive him to continue, is prescient of his own mellowing. The images that surround and envelop death, the most human of all events, are stated as a simple and staid continuation of the spirit. The literature that comes out of the author's own experiences is invariably autobiographical, as he readily admits, although the effect is that of a magician who gives away the secrets of his craft beforehand and still manages to captivate his audience.

The search for "truth" in an author's work is at the foundation of any project like this. I have annotated many passages in this study with the author's own words, the surest source of truth I could hope to find. The essays, the bibliography, and the notes in this study are a means for future researchers to begin excavating below the surface—where they will discover, on their own terms and in ways much different from those that I use to examine the dominant tropes, the rich complexity of the life in Jim Harrison's work, and the work that is Jim Harrison's life.

Notes

Introduction

1. Jim Harrison, "Fording and Dread," in *Just before Dark* (Livingston, Mont.: Clark City Press, 1991), 259.

2. Harrison writes instead that his "interest is in the 'art novel,' which has never been a market-driven genre" (interview, *American Literary History* 11.2 [summer 1999]: 276).

3. Harrison admits that the lure of a life in the university, at least in the early days, was strong: "The hardest thing was during our poorest years when I got offers to be the poet in residence at some place. . . . I remember about five years ago this university had offered me $80,000. . . . I thought, 'My God, that's quite a draw!' but I wrote back and said, 'Thank you, but someone has to stand on the outside'" (interview by Robert J. DeMott and Patrick A. Smith, tape recording, Leelanau, Mich., 28–30 August 1997).

4. Mike Norton, "A Peek at Jim Harrison's World: Flamboyant, Controversial Novelist Mellows—Just a Little," *Record-Eagle (Traverse City, Mich.),* date unknown, 2(D).

5. Ruth Pollack Coughlin, "The Man Who Likes Empty Spaces," *Detroit News,* 14 August 1990, C1+.

6. Ibid.

7. Jim Harrison, review of *All My Friends Are Going to Be Strangers,* by Larry McMurtry, *New York Times Book Review,* 19 March 1972, 5+.

8. Jim Harrison, interview by DeMott and Smith.

9. Harrison's lifelong passion for literature is illustrated by his founding in 1968, along with friend and fellow Michigan State alumnus Dan Gerber, the literary journal *Sumac,* which featured work from some of America's finest writers, including Galway Kinnell, Charles Simic, Louis Simpson, Gary Snyder, Hayden Carruth, Denise Levertov, Ezra Pound, James Tate, and William Kittredge. In 1997, the journal received renewed critical attention when a collection of work originally featured in the nine-issue run was edited by Joseph Bednarik and published by Michigan State University Press.

10. Jim Harrison, interview by DeMott and Smith. Harrison echoes that notion in the preface to *"What thou lovest well remains": 100 Years of Ezra*

Pound when he writes, "Pound was the medicine man who opened our language in the manner of Moses and the Red Sea. At least he did for many of us down through Olson, Duncan, Ginsberg, Levertov, Snyder, Dorn, Eshelman, Frank O'Hara, and on a more conservative note, Wright, Kinnell, Simpson, etc. Those who don't think so should return to the texts. The only place you don't see the indomitable mark is in the whining psychologies produced in net tonage out of writer's schools" ("History as Torment" [Boise, Idaho: Limberlost Press, 1986], x).

In *The Road Home,* Dalva's son, Nelse, reiterates the notion: "The rich and the upper middle class were now seething with resentment over protecting their position and were demanding an enforceable mono-ethic which was gradually turning the country into a fascist Disneyland" ([New York: Atlantic Monthly Press, 1998], 224).

Harrison also discusses the value of literary criticism and offers a further indictment of writing schools:

> Certain distortions come to mind because scholars, like the rest of us, are often creatures of fashion. For instance, there is a truly vast array of work done on the poets Robert Lowell and Sylvia Plath for reasons having nothing to do with the quality of their work while more difficult poets like Robert Duncan and Gary Snyder are largely ignored. Alfred Kazin, Harold Bloom, and Helen Vendler are all relatively large-minded but suffer from the barrier of Eastern xenophobia. Of course the front lines of battle are quite different from the milieu of Pentagon tacticians or historians of war. I have grave doubts if so-called 'creative writing' has a place in the university where peer pressure has tended to construe a uniform product and the MFA has become a somewhat suspect license. Of course the university is ultimately the place a writer might turn to for fair judgment given the utter venality of the marketplace and many of the reviewing mediums. It is also pleasant to see the immodest silliness of deconstruction disappear (interview, *American Literary History,* 276).

11. Review of *Farmer,* by Jim Harrison, *New Yorker,* 30 August 1976, 90.

12. Peter S. Prescott, review of *Legends of the Fall,* by Jim Harrison *Newsweek* 94 (9 July 1979): 72.

13. Jim Harrison, "The Art of Fiction CIV: Jim Harrison," interview by Jim Fergus, *Paris Review* 30 (1988): 71.

14. Jim Harrison, "First Person Female," *New York Times Magazine,* 16 May 1999, 100.

15. William H. Roberson, "'Macho Mistake': The Misrepresentation of Jim Harrison's Fiction," *Critique* 29.4 (1988): 242.

16. Julia Reed, "After Seven Acclaimed Novels, Jim Harrison Is Finding It Harder to Elude Fame," *Vogue,* September 1989, 502, 506, 510.

17. John Keats, *Complete Poems and Selected Letters,* ed. Clarence DeWitt

Thorpe (New York: The Odyssey, Inc., 1935); Harrison, "First Person Female," 100.

18. Harrison, interview by DeMott and Smith.

19. Jim Harrison, *Julip* (New York: Houghton Mifflin/Seymour Lawrence, 1994), 199.

20. Harrison, *Outlyer and Ghazals* (New York: Simon and Schuster, 1971), 26.

21. Harrison, "The Art of Fiction CIV," 64.

22. Jim Harrison, "PW Interviews Jim Harrison," *Publisher's Weekly* 237.3 (3 August 1990): 60.

23. Jim Harrison, "From the *Dalva* Notebooks, 1985–87," in *Just before Dark,* 287.

24. Ihab Hassan, *The Dismemberment of Orpheus: Toward a Postmodern Literature* (Madison, Wis.: University of Wisconsin Press, 1982), 267–68.

25. Jim Harrison, "Fording and Dread," in *Just before Dark,* 260.

26. Harrison's view on the American Dream is cynical in the extreme: "The whole purpose of America [now] is for its inhabitants to behave well so the less than one percent who have the dough can continue accumulating it freely. It's completely batty" (interview by DeMott and Smith).

Chapter 1

1. In *The Selected Poetry of Rainer Maria Rilke,* Stephen Mitchell translates these lines from Rilke's "Portrait of My Father as a Young Man": "Oh quickly disappearing photograph / in my more slowly disappearing hand."

2. Harrison, interview by DeMott and Smith.

3. Quentin Anderson, *Making Americans: An Essay on Individualism and Money* (New York: Harcourt, 1992), 29.

4. Harrison often describes his fiction in poetic terms and, as I repeat throughout these essays, his fiction is a synthesis of poetic imagery, a poet's eye for detail, and a storyteller's voice. In writing both poetry and fiction, Harrison attempts to "bear down on the singularity of images. Movement. Those suites were good training for moving from image to mood. It's like Mailer says, 'Boy, if you're worried about getting people in and out of rooms, you've already blown it'" (Kay Bonetti, "An Interview with Jim Harrison," *Missouri Review* 8.3 [1985]: 74).

5. Kathy Stocking, "Writer Jim Harrison: Work, Booze, and the Outdoor Life—and an Absolute Rage for Order," *Detroit Free Press,* 5 June 1977, 26.

6. Jim Harrison, *Wolf: A False Memoir* (New York: Simon and Schuster, 1971), 11–12. Harrison himself would have been only twenty-three at the end of the four-year period that the narrative spans (1956–60). He was thirty-three when the book was published. The references to Christ in the narrative are frequent and often obvious, although I comment on several of them in the essay.

Other references, such as an offhand remark about a beautiful girl who shuns him at the Longwood Cricket Club in Boston ("She turned again with a cool stare, not thirty-three feet away" [87]), seem less relevant to the overarching themes of the narrative, as does a particular night in the Huron Mountains on which Swanson counted "one hundred thirty-three scabs, large and small, both actively suppurating and lightly irritating" (82) on his body. Later, he remarks that he had spent $333 for "an incredibly unsuccessful hatchet job" (152) on an eye operation. The reference is to Harrison's own damaged left eye, the result of an accident when the author was eight years old.

7. Harrison, *Wolf,* 215.

8. Randall Roorda, "Sites and Senses of Writing in Nature," *College English* 59.4 (April 1997): 395.

9. Robert E. Burkholder, *Dictionary of Literary Biography Yearbook 1982,* ed. Richard Ziegfield (Detroit: Gale Research/Bruccoli Clark, 1983), 268.

10. M. L. Rosenthal, "Outlyers and Ghazals," review of *Outlyer and Ghazals,* by Jim Harrison, *New York Times Book Review,* 18 July 1971, 7+.

In fact, Harrison won an NEA grant and a Guggenheim in the 1960s, long before he penned his first novel.

11. Janis P. Stout, *The Journey Narrative in American Literature* (Westport, Conn.: Greenwood Press, 1983), 14.

12. Joyce Carol Oates, "Going Places," review of *Wolf,* by Jim Harrison, *Partisan Review* 37.3 (summer 1972): 463. Edward Reilly implicitly takes issue with critical responses such as that by Oates by explaining that the impetus for the novel was perhaps not primarily artistic, as "Harrison was so broke, he mailed the only copy of the manuscript to his brother John to photocopy, but it was lost in the mail for about a month because of a postal strike. John finally went to the New Haven post office and dug the package out of a mail bin" (*Jim Harrison* [New York: Twayne Publishers, 1996], 25). This could in part explain the lack of organization that Oates finds in the narrative, although we must remember that the novel is Harrison's first attempt at writing long fiction.

In his analysis of Barry Hannah's first novel *Geronimo Rex* in the *New York Times Book Review,* Harrison, fresh off having his own first novel published, details the vagaries of breaking into fiction writing:

> You might look at the world of the first novel as a gunny-sack race in the gathering twilight at a county fair, a festival that is on the verge of obsolescence anyhow. It is very hot and dusty even in the lengthening shadows of the grandstand (capacity 300). One can smell the lime in the toilets underneath and hear the bawling of the cattle in the stock barns. A mixed group of 50 have entered the race this year. The prize is a warm watermelon that someone has deftly entered with a razor blade and filled with a coral snake wrapped around an eyeball and a tumor. This is all plainly not as healthy as summer camp or the 4-H (14 May 1972, 4).

13. Jonathan Yardley, "Also Extravagantly Free-Male," review of *Wolf: A False Memoir,* by Jim Harrison, *New York Times Book Review,* 12 December 1971, 4.

14. Christopher Lehmann-Haupt, "The Woods Are Ugly, Cold, Wet," review of *Wolf: A False Memoir,* by Jim Harrison, *New York Times,* 24 November 1971, 33.

15. Reilly, *Jim Harrison,* 26.

16. Harrison, *Wolf,* 137–38.

17. Edward Reilly relates the tragedy of the death of Harrison's father and sister in his book *Jim Harrison:* "In 1962, tragedy invaded the Harrison house when their father and younger sister Judith were killed in a head-on car crash with a drunk driver" (8). Harrison writes about the two in "David," a poem about his father's death, and "A Sequence of Women," a poem about his sister's death and its lasting effects on his life (from *The Shape of the Journey*).

18. Roorda, "Sites and Senses of Writing in Nature," 385.

19. Although *Wolf* deftly handles some difficult philosophical questions, it had an unspectacular genesis that belies its complexity. Harrison wrote the novel at the suggestion of Thomas McGuane, after a hunting accident had left him in traction in a hospital in Traverse City, Michigan (Reilly, *Jim Harrison,* 25). Edward Reilly, to whom I defer many times in this study, especially for Harrison's biographical information, relates that McGuane surmised that "since Harrison had a Guggenheim grant, he should write a 'sort of autobiographical novel.' 'What had happened,' says Harrison, 'was I had a terrible hunting accident. I'd fallen down a cliff and it really screwed up my back and I had to be in traction at Munson [Medical Center in Traverse City]. I just sat there and said, gee why don't I write a novel'" (25).

Jonathan Yardley is the first critic to draw the inevitable comparison between the fiction of Harrison and his friend Thomas McGuane:

> These two Michigan writers possess extraordinary talent, but they are also extravagantly free-male, male-animal. That may be a refreshing alternative to a plastic society, but by the same token it manufactures a fraternity of he-men who use women in the fashion of town pumps and romanticize about an ecologically balanced utopia where, fishing pole in hand and Rover by his side, a man can be a man—while the rest of the world staggers on in its admittedly lamentable, but inescapably real, way. Such husky romanticism is hardly unique to the Upper Peninsula—some of the best young Southern writers are currently making a fetish of portraying themselves as good ole boys—but it seems to thrive in the Michigan woods ("Free Male," 38).

Yardley's assertion that the "macho" image surrounding these two, and later the group that would include Dan Gerber, Guy de la Valdéne, Jimmy Buffett,

Jack Nicholson, Peter Fonda, Hunter Thompson, and others associated with the freewheeling Key West lifestyle of the 1970s, undoubtedly is the germ for much later Harrison-bashing on the point of Harrison's perceived antifeminism.

20. Geoffrey Galt Harpham, *The Ascetic Imperative in Culture and Criticism* (Chicago: University of Chicago Press, 1987), xii.

21. Reilly, *Jim Harrison,* 37.

22. Harrison, *Wolf,* 109.

23. Ibid., 173.

24. Ibid., 11, 89.

25. Winifred Gallagher, *The Power of Place: How Our Surroundings Shape Our Thoughts, Emotions, and Actions* (New York: Poseidon Press, 1993), 146–47.

26. Harrison's play with Christ imagery is apparent when Swanson writes that he would make love to a woman and "Then I would sleep for three days and three nights and roll the stone back up the hill again until she arrived" (133). Here, the author combines the story of Christ's resurrection with the myth of Sysiphus.

27. Harrison, *Wolf,* 105.

28. Ibid., 83. In *Of Wolves and Men* (1978), Barry Lopez writes convincingly of the wolf's rightful place in our environment and its importance as a symbol in literature:

> The possibility has yet to be realized of a synthesis between the benevolent wolf of many native American stories and the malcontented wolf of most European fairy tales. At present we seem incapable of such a creation, unable to write about a whole wolf because, for most of us, animals are still either two-dimensional symbols or simply inconsequential, suitable only for children's stories where good and evil are clearly separated.
>
> Were we to perceive such a synthesis, it would signal a radical change in man. For it would mean that he had finally quit his preoccupation with himself and begun to contemplate a universe in which he was not central. The terror inherent in such a prospect is, of course, greater than that in any wolf he has ever written about. But equally vast is the possibility for heroism, humility, tragedy, and the other virtues of literature ([New York: Scribner's], 270).

Lopez's chapter "*Canis Lupus Linnaeus*" ends on a somber note concerning the survival of the wolf in northern Michigan when he claims that "an experiment to establish transplanted wolves into old range where there was sufficient wild food for them came to an inconclusive end when all four animals, each wearing a plainly visible radio collar, were killed" (72). Five years after *Of Wolves and Men* was published, James Hammill, a Michigan wolf biologist, claims that Dick Thiel and Larry Prenn, two biologists from the Wis-

consin Department of Natural Resources, sighted a wolf in the Upper Peninsula of Michigan in January 1983. Hammill considered the sighting significant, given "the pattern of wolf persecution, habitat destruction and extirpation by humans" (1) that characterizes man's treatment of the wolf population
in the area. Hammill writes that wolves had already been nearly eliminated
from the Lower Peninsula by the middle of the nineteenth century, and only
the unrestricted hunting of the wolves in the 1950s can explain their decline:

> Intensive logging of virgin forests occurred throughout the Upper Penin-
> sula during the early 20th century. The subsequent regrowth set the stage
> for an unprecedented increase in prey and relatively low human pressure.
> However, wolf numbers continued to decline until remnant animals were
> thought to be single individuals, immigrants from more stable populations
> in Ontario, Canada, or in Minnesota. The decline in this remnant popula-
> tion can be tracked by the bounty records from the Upper Peninsula dur-
> ing the 1950's. The number of wolves bountied in 1956 was 30; 1957,
> unknown; 1958, seven; 1959, one. In 1960 Michigan repealed the bounty,
> and in 1965 granted the wolf full protection by law (1).

The wolf has made something of a comeback. Twenty years after Harrison gives
little hope for the restoration of the wolf to its habitat in the Upper Peninsula,

> at the close of 1992, we could verify the existence of at least 20 wolves. . . .
> The Upper Peninsula includes more than 16,000 square miles of rugged
> forest with abundant prey and enough wild places to afford the wolf a
> chance to survive. The recovery plan that eventually will come of this effort
> will take into account people's desires and concerns and the potential of
> the land to produce wolves (Hammill, 1).

29. Roorda, "Sites and Senses of Writing in Nature," 405.
30. Harrison, *Wolf,* 102.
31. Ibid., 127.
32. Ibid., 155–56.
33. Ibid., 70.
34. Gallagher, *The Power of Place,* 149.
35. Roderick Nash, *Wilderness and the American Mind* (New Haven,
Conn.: Yale University Press, 1973), 9.
36. Harrison, *Wolf,* 70–71. This aspect of Harrison's work is particularly
important in terms of his analysis of technology and its effect on the environment in *Sundog* and *A Good Day to Die* (see chapter 2). Swanson writes,
"My pitifully radical sensibilities run to dynamite or plastic explosives. But
I've got no urge to hurt people, the idea repels me. And there's more implicit
drama here than I deserve: I mean if I could blow up Dow or Wyandotte
Chemical I might if no one were to be hurt or go jobless" (114).

37. Harrison, *Wolf,* 115.

38. Roorda, "Sites and Senses of Writing in Nature," 394.

39. Harrison, *Wolf,* 132.

40. Leslie Fiedler, *Love and Death in the American Novel* (New York: Stein and Day, 1966), 186.

41. The paraphrase is from Samuel Taylor Coleridge's *The Rime of the Ancient Mariner* (1798): "Forthwith this frame of mine was wrench'd / With a woeful agony / Which forc'd me to begin my tale / And then it left me free."

42. Louise H. Westling, *The Green Breast of the New World: Landscape, Gender, and American Fiction* (Athens: University of Georgia Press, 1996), 38.

43. Certainly an ironic setting for Swanson's quest. The Huron tribe was driven from the area during settlement.

44. Frederick Turner, *Beyond Geography: The Western Spirit against the Wilderness* (New York: Viking Press, 1980), 9.

45. Ibid.

46. Harrison, *Wolf,* 18.

47. Ibid., 141.

48. Swanson thinks,

All of them were the same. Convinced of this, they revolved their particularities around a single head, the body's parts too were interchangeable. When young there was the breathlessness of looking up the word "sin" in the dictionary after a morning spent in Bible school. . . . The dead woman who played the piano for Wednesday night prayer meeting is in heaven now and can see what you do to yourself at night and what you do to others at home or work or play. Nothing can be hidden from the dead and they can't help us though they must weep for us. . . . A friend of mine had given their Negro maid five dollars of Christmas money to raise her dress way up. What did she look like I don't know her underpants were on underneath the dress. Five dollars. . . . But when I came up through the waters in my white flannel pants everything was new and the Holy Ghost was in the baptismal font felt in my chest, which was at bursting. Maybe held the breath too long. It lasted, the ghost, for a week or so even if my father said you won't have to take a bath joking. Or am I a heathen? Billy Sunday saved my father for two days but he got drunk on the third. Backsliding they call it (34–36).

49. Harrison, *Wolf,* 38.

50. Ibid., 40.

51. Harrison, interview by DeMott and Smith.

52. Harrison, *Wolf,* 41.

53. Ibid., 70.

54. Ibid., 48.

55. Swanson recalls,

Off Newbury Street again and up the stairs where she waited. All faint and pink as a quartz mine. No aquacities here. Corn shucks. Tamales.

Really too hot for fuckery. Room livid and airless. We lay there sweating as animals apparently don't. I hear only through their mouths: running dog pink tongue. I ached as metal might. . . .

Waitresses smelling of lamb stew. I dressed quickly and went down the stairs and into the street. I went into the first bar and drank two glasses of beer then a shot of bourbon dropped into the third glass as they do in Detroit. A time bomb. For hygiene. In the toilet I aimed at the shrinking deodorant puck then a cigarette butt. In youth they were Jap airplanes to be shot at. A witticism at eye level on the wall: "Boston College eats shit." No doubt about that, Jesuits with platesful. The cook ladled seconds. Lurid goo us, they say, gimme all the luv ya got.

And more: she raises herself on an elbow. Her eyes narrow and focus in the dim light of the room" (51–52).

56. John Rohrkemper, "'Natty Bummpo Wants Tobacco': Jim Harrison's *Wilderness, Great Lakes Review* (fall 1982-spring 1983): 24.
57. Harrison, *Wolf,* 93. In *Dalva,* the protagonist also considers the geography of the country from above (in this case from an airplane) and, like Swanson, sees a deeper symbolism in our misunderstanding and misuse of the land:

The upshot was that from an airliner the entirety of the United States, except for a few spotty wilderness areas, looks raked over, tracked up, skinned, scalped—in short, abused. . . . What I mean, she said, is that in out-of-the-way places there's still a certain spirit, I mean in gullies, off-the-road ditches, neglected creek banks and bottoms, places that have only been tilled once, then neglected, or not at all, like the Sand Hills, parts of northern Wisconsin, the Upper Peninsula of Michigan, or the untellable but grazed plains of Wyoming, Montana, Nevada, the desert, even the ocean in the middle of the night. (123).

Dalva's disdain for the abusers of the land recalls Swanson's own derision for the "malling of America" that he sees in the Midwest on his way to the West Coast.

58. Harrison, *Wolf,* 121.
59. Ibid., 101.
60. Rachel Carson, *Silent Spring* (Boston: Houghton Mifflin, 1962), 85.
61. Harrison, *Wolf,* 96.
62. Ibid.
63. Harrison often mentions that his reading of Loren Eiseley has influenced

his own writing, and there is an interesting parallel to Swanson's waiting for the osprey to return in Eiseley's essay collection *The Immense Journey.* In his essay "The Bird and the Machine," Eiseley reads that man will be capable of replicating animals in their minutest detail, and he recalls his experiences as a naturalist, in particular his short-lived task of collecting birds for a zoo. He muses that "Sometimes of late I find myself thinking the most beautiful sight in the world might be the birds taking over New York after the last man has run away to the hills" (187), and, importantly, he also draws a valuable distinction concerning animals and machines which Harrison implies in his own fiction. After Eiseley has succeeded in capturing a female hawk's mate, and finally releases the bird because he cannot bear to keep it caged, he decides that the crucial difference between animals and machines is that "The machine does not bleed, ache, hang for hours in the sky in a torment of hope to learn the fate of another machine, nor does it cry out with joy nor dance in the air with the fierce passion of a bird" ([New York: Random House, 1957], 193). That Swanson cannot get the upper hand on the bird is not surprising, given his admitted lack of understanding of the wilderness; that he nonetheless attempts to commune with nature and appreciates the majesty of the bird is one of Swanson's redeeming characteristics.

64. Harrison, *Wolf,* 103–4, 125.

65. Robert Packard, *Refractions: Writers and Places* (New York: Carroll & Graf, 1990), 5.

66. In much the same way that Warlock, the title character of Harrison's 1981 novel, is unable to describe places without food imagery, Swanson's inability to recall events without remembering in intimate detail the places in which they occurred is another form of obsession in Harrison's characters.

67. Ronald Primeau, *Romance of the Road: The Literature of the American Highway* (Bowling Green, Ohio: Bowling Green State University Popular Press, 1996), 69.

68. Ibid.

69. Harrison, *Wolf,* 109.

70. Ibid., 113.

71. Ibid., 163.

72. Ibid., 122. In *The Road Home,* Harrison, through Dalva's son, Nelse, articulates the nature of language: "People are limited by their central obsession, from which the nature of their language emerges, whether it is sports, raising cattle, the stock market, anthropology, art history or whatever. I added location, thinking of the xenophobia notes from the four hundred or so locales in my journals" (222).

73. Leigh Gilmore, "Policing Truth: Confession, Gender, and Autobiographical Authority," in *Autobiography and Postmodernism,* ed. Kathleen Ashley, Leigh Gilmore, and Gerald Peters (Amherst: University of Massachusetts Press, 1994), 55.

74. Harrison, *Wolf,* 173.

75. Ibid., 181.

76. Ibid., 192, 190.

77. Randall Roorda, *Dramas of Solitude: Narratives of Retreat in American Nature Writing* (Albany: State University of New York Press, 1998), 11.

78. Harrison, *Wolf,* 200–1.

79. Frederick Turner, *Spirit of Place: The Making of an American Literary Landscape* (San Francisco: Sierra Club Books, 1989), 7.

80. Harrison, *Wolf,* 216.

81. Ibid., 225.

82. Ibid.

83. Christopher L. Salter and William J. Lloyd, *Landscape in Literature* (Washington, D.C.: Association of American Geographers, 1977), 5.

84. Gallagher, *The Power of Place,* 12.

Chapter 2

1. The title of the novel is derived from the war cry of the Nez Percé Indians. That Harrison's narrative predates Abbey's by two years is a fact that, as far as I can ascertain, has never been published before. Abbey probably knew little, if anything, about Harrison's second novel before he published *The Monkey Wrench Gang,* although in his *Confessions of a Barbarian* he does bemoan the fact that Harrison, who gave the novel a favorable review in the *New York Times* (see Jim Harrison, review of *The Monkey Wrench Gang,* by Edward Abbey, *New York Times Book Review,* 14 November 1976, 59), "misrepresents the book as a 'revolutionary' tract for the old 'New Left.' Jeez! No mention of the comedy, the wordplay, the wit, humor, and *brilliance!*" ([New York: Little, Brown, 1994], 245). The journal entries in *Confessions,* which date from 1951–89, explain in part the similar thematic concerns of the two novels through a sort of Jungian "collective unconsciousness," an "eco-type" that becomes prevalent in intellectual thought and eco-literature in the middle of the century, when technology finally catches up with (and in many ways surpasses) our notions of the necessity of stewardship in nature. As early as 1959 (the Glen Canyon Dam, which is a prime target of Abbey's outlaws, was completed in 1966), Abbey is prescient of the deleterious effects of technology on nature. He writes,

It seemed to us that Glen Canyon became more beautiful and wonderful with every mile. We cursed the engineers and politicians who had condemned these marvels and the wildlife sheltered by them to death by drowning.

How much dynamite, we wondered aloud to each other, would be needed to destroy the dam? How delightful and just, we imagined, to have

our dynamite so integrated into the dam's wiring system, that when the
president or the secretary of the interior and the Four Corners' governors,
together with their swarms of underlings, the press and hordes of tourists
had all assembled for the Grand Opening, it would be the white pudgy fin-
ger of the biggest big-shot, pressing the little black button on the beflagged
switchboard, that would blow to hell and smithereens the official himself,
his guests, the tourists, the bridge, and Glen Canyon Dam. A sad and hopeless fantasy. . . . (*Confessions of a Barbarian,* 152).

In *Seeking Awareness in American Nature Writing,* Scott Slovic writes a
similar argument for *The Monkey Wrench Gang* that I write for *A Good Day
to Die:* the essence of both books lies not on the surface, at the plot level, but
rather in the psyches of the characters themselves. Slovic contends that Abbey
"is trying to prompt a more basic kind of consciousness among his readers,
to provoke not a singleminded political movement but rather an awareness
on the individual level of the need to question moral and aesthetic assumptions. *The Monkey Wrench Gang* is less a clear-cut call to action than a call
to feeling" ([Salt Lake City: University of Utah Press, 1992], 103–4).
    In his own review of Abbey's book, Harrison echoes the disaffirmation of
the three protagonists. The time had come and gone, it seems, for the sort of
"call to action" that could change our nation's view of ecology in one wide
stroke of the brush:

> Edward Abbey wrote the book in an atmosphere of political vacuum as a
> sort of soldier of the void when the only possible audience the book could
> truly resonate against, the New Left, had largely turned to more refined
> dope, natural foods, weird exercises, mail order consciousness programs,
> boutiques and Indians (jewelry). Surely a base of warhorses is left, a core
> of politically astute veterans who have changed their pace but not their
> intentions, but the sense of mass movement is deader than Janis Joplin (59).

    2. I mention several times in these essays the importance that Harrison
places on avoiding didacticism, to deal with the contradictions of his subjects
in the way that Keats calls for in his notion of "negative capability." That
Harrison wrote *Sundog* more than a decade after *A Good Day to Die* is
important to our understanding of Harrison's evolving philosophical views,
which are initially more closely related to Abbey's own advocacy of subversive action and later move toward an understanding and acceptance of the
role that the Strangs of the world play in bringing about positive change by
respecting the power of nature at the same time that they harness it for the
benefit of mankind.
    3. Jim Harrison, *Sundog* (New York: E. P. Dutton/Seymour Lawrence,
1984), 45–46.
    4. Jim Harrison, review of *The Monkey Wrench Gang,* by Edward Abbey,

New York Times; Slovic, *Seeking Awareness in American Nature Writing,* 108.

5. Edward C. Reilly, "The Tragedy and the Folly: Harrison's *A Good Day to Die*—An Earlier Version," *Publications of the Mississippi Philological Association* (1986): 23; Joseph Meeker, *The Comedy of Survival: Studies in Literary Ecology* (New York: Scribner's, 1972), 9–10.

6. Meeker, *The Comedy of Survival,* 9–10.

7. Wendy Smith, "*PW* Interviews Jim Harrison," *Publisher's Weekly* 237.3 (3 August 1990): 60.

8. Sara Blackburn, *New York Times Book Review,* 9 September 1973, 4–5.

9. William H. Roberson, "'A Good Day to Live': The Prose Works of Jim Harrison," *Great Lakes Review* 8.2–9.1 (1982–83): 30.

10. William Crawford Woods, "What a Strange Accomplishment," review of *A Good Day to Die,* by Jim Harrison, *Washington Post,* 9 September 1973, 4.

11. Jim Harrison, *A Good Day to Die* (New York: Simon and Schuster, 1973), 14.

12. Harrison, "The Art of Fiction CIV: Jim Harrison," 63.

13. In *The Sporting Club,* McGuane's protagonist Vernor Stanton, an enigmatic member of the exclusive Centennial Club, also destroys a dam and drains the lake at the club, precipitating its downfall and uncovering some of its more unsavory traditions—including an orgy which was photographed for posterity, thereby undermining the club's raison d'être and exposing the folly of class politics.

14. Harrison, *A Good Day to Die,* 121.

15. Ibid., 37.

16. Ibid., 149.

17. Ibid., 23.

18. Ibid., 152.

19. Ibid., 22.

20. Ibid., 27. The narrator responds to Tim's saying "I've never seen the Grand Canyon" (26), a thought that prefigures the opening of the *Monkey Wrench Gang,* in which the four protagonists demolish the bridge over Glen Canyon: "Like a solitary smoke signal, like the silent symbol of calamity, like one huge inaudible and astonishing exclamation point signifying *surprise!* the dust plume hangs above the fruitless plain, pointing upward to heaven and downward to the scene of the primal split" (Abbey, 7).

21. Reilly, "The Tragedy and the Folly," 23.

22. Reilly, *Jim Harrison,* 49.

23. Harrison, *A Good Day to Die,* 34.

24. Ibid., 34–35.

25. Ibid., 35.

26. Ibid., 45.

27. Ibid., 55.

28. Ibid., 69.

29. Reilly, *Jim Harrison*, 43.

30. Harrison, *A Good Day to Die*, 56.

31. Ibid., 59.

32. Ibid., 77.

33. Ibid., 81. Ironically, the *Blaster's Handbook* goes into great detail on the methods that were used to clear the way for some of the world's great structures, including the Grand Coulee Dam. Naturally, the DuPont Company, which published the book, espouses the progressive uses of its explosives: "Now there are explosives specially designed and carefully made to serve some phase of all modern industry and enterprise, and these can be safely and skillfully applied to achieve that end" (1). The preface to the text seems to apply to Tim: "The distinction between good practice and bad is not always obvious, and all but experienced blasters should avoid unproved innovations." Tim could have benefited from a closer reading of Appendix II of the text, titled "Dont's."

34. Harrison, *A Good Day to Die*, 109.

35. Ibid., 114.

36. Ibid., 115.

37. Westling, *The Green Breast of the New World*, 91.

38. Harrison, *A Good Day to Die*, 119.

39. Ibid., 125.

40. Ibid., 128.

41. Reilly, *Jim Harrison*, 48.

42. Harrison, *A Good Day to Die*, 139.

43. Ibid., 149, 141. In his article "Twisted Footnote to Wounded Knee," Robert Venables writes, "on December 29, 1890, in a ravine near Wounded Knee Creek, South Dakota, the U.S. Army, supported by American Indian mercenaries, slaughtered approximately 300 Lakota men, women and children—75 percent of Big Foot's Lakota community. Two-thirds of the massacred Lakotas were women and children. Only 31 of the 470 soldiers were killed, many by 'friendly fire' of fellow soldiers" (1). He points out that the Lakota had already surrendered when they were brought to Wounded Knee and exterminated. The Army used rapid-fire Hotchkiss guns to expedite the killing. The "twisted footnote" to which Venables refers is an editorial by L. Frank Baum, the author of the children's story *The Wizard of Oz* (1900), in the *Aberdeen Saturday Pioneer* immediately after Sitting Bull's assassination on 15 December 1890, in which Baum writes, "We cannot honestly regret [the Indians'] extermination, but we at least do justice to the manly characteristics possessed, according to their rights and education, by the Redskins of America."

More ironic, perhaps, is the American Indian Movement's occupation of Wounded Knee in March and April 1973, the same year in which Harrison published *A Good Day to Die*. A group led by Leonard Peltier and Leonard Crow Dog (whose wife Mary Crow Dog details the occupation in her first book *Lakota Woman*), the man who revived the Ghost Dance (for a related discussion, see chapter 5 of this study), "brought the issue of conditions on the reservations to the attention of all America. They won the respect and support of many Native Americans nationwide and earned the hatred of the Federal Bureau of Investigation as well as President Richard Nixon" (Jeremy Schneider, "From Wounded Knee to Capitol Hill: The History, Achievements, and Legacy of the American Indian Movement," <http:\\icarus.uic.edu/~jschne1/wounded_knee.html>, 16 November 1997, 2). During the seventy-one-day siege one Oglala Sioux, Buddy Lamont, was killed, "shot through the heart and died instantly during a heavy firefight. . . . He is buried on the hill by the ditch, joining the ghosts of all the other Sioux killed at Wounded Knee. His headstone says: 'Two thousand came to Wounded Knee in 1973. *One Stayed*'" (Mary Crow Dog, *Lakota Woman* [New York: HarperPerennial, 1990], 143).

44. Reilly, *Jim Harrison*, 47.

45. Fiedler, *Love and Death in the American Novel*, 359.

46. Ibid.

47. Harrison, *A Good Day to Die*, 175.

48. Ibid., 172.

49. Ibid., 173, 175, 176.

50. Mark Busby, "The Significance of the Frontier," in *The Frontier Experience and the American Dream: Essays on American Literature*, ed. David Mogen, Mark Busby, and Paul Bryant (College Station: Texas A & M University Press, 1989), 95.

51. Richard Slotkin, *Gunfighter Nation: The Myth of the Frontier in Twentieth-Century America* (New York: Atheneum, 1992), 317–18.

52. Reilly, *Jim Harrison*, 45.

53. Harrison, *A Good Day to Die*, 175.

54. See Harrison's poetry collection *Letters to Yesenin* (1973) for a similar rendering of alternating thoughts on suicide and survival, and the author's own mortality. Sergei Esenin, a Russian poet, hanged himself on 28 December 1925. He was thirty years old; Harrison was thirty-five at the time he published the collection. In his biography of Yesenin, Gordon McVay quotes Georgy Ustinov, who writes, "'Esenin died in Ryazin fashion, as the yellow-haired youth I had known . . . Sergei Esenin wrapped twice around his neck the rope from a suitcase imported from Europe, kicked the night table from under his feet, and hung facing the blue night, looking out onto St. Isaac's Square'" (*Esenin: A Life* [Ann Arbor, Mich.: Ardis, 1976], 292).

55. A. C. Greene, "The Man-God of the Michigan Jungles," review of *Sundog*, by Jim Harrison, *New York Times Book Review*, 15 July 1984, 14.

56. Michiko Kakutani, "Books of the Times," review of *Sundog,* by Jim Harrison, *New York Times,* 21 May 1984, 17.

57. Richard Deveson, "Call of the Wild," review of *Sundog,* by Jim Harrison, *NS,* 23 August 1985, 28.

58. *Publisher's Weekly,* review of *Sundog,* by Jim Harrison, 13 April 1984, 52.

59. Ibid.

60. Bonetti, "An Interview with Jim Harrison," 76.

61. Pico Iyer, "Romancing the Home," *The Nation,* 23 June 1984, 767.

62. Ibid., 770.

63. Harrison told Kay Bonetti that he added the subtitle for the narrative— *The Story of an American Foreman . . . as told to Jim Harrison*—"just to have fun. Like Nabokov. I did that to throw people off the track. It is a little bit myself, but I had to have a contrast to Strang. I had to have somebody coming from way outside, coming into that world. You could say they're almost extremities of the right and left lobes of the same brain" (70).

64. Harrison, *Sundog,* x.

65. Ibid., 2.

66. Meeker, *The Comedy of Survival,* 9.

67. Harrison, *Sundog,* xi.

68. Ibid., 3.

69. Ibid., 19.

70. Ronald Weber, *The Literature of Fact: Literary Nonfiction in American Writing* (Athens: Ohio University Press, 1980), 27.

71. The narrator enumerates the accomplishments and quirks of Strang's life:

Education limited to kindergarten and first grade by seizures caused by accident. Petit mal epilepsy now totally controlled by Tagonet and other drugs. . . . Started working for his older brother, a subcontractor, on the Mackinac Bridge. By age twenty he is helping building schools and missions in Kenya for the United Nazarene Mission . . . then on to the Sudan on an irrigation project off the White Nile. Then to Amritar for another irrigation project for a Swiss company, down to Hyderabad for a flood control project. Hospitalized for amoebic dysentery, returned to Miami for treatment. Then on to Baja California for work on La Paz Reservoir, a dam in Costa Rica, more dams in Peru, Venezuela, Brazil, becoming in his thirties somewhat a trouble shooter. . . . Two years in Uganda working on a dam project for the French, left when Amin came in. Back in Venezuela with a year's stop in Holland on their immense storm surge barrier called the Delta Project. Back to Brazil on the Tucurui Dam on the Tocantius River. Last two years ending with disaster in Venezuelan highlands. Whew. Old Pasternak said it takes a lot of volume to fill a life (11).

72. Harrison, *Sundog,* 45.
73. Ibid., 14.
74. Bonetti, "An Interview with Jim Harrison," 69.
75. Harrison, *Sundog,* 35.
76. Ibid., 24–25.
77. Ibid., 25. Although Strang claims not to know politics, the narrator describes a conversation during which Strang

> quipped one day he had never spotted one of our congressmen in either South or Central America and had seen no evidence to the contrary that they were simply a bilious clot of lawyers. . . . I imagined both Congress and the Soviet Presidium being packed off to a boatless Elba. I saw Reagan and Andropov mooning each other across the Atlantic, asses up like huge, pink, metallic scorpions, while the other continents waited in terror for the results (142–43).

Later, Strang takes aim at the problem of hunger in the United States, a partial defense of his own position as a builder of dams:

> You could easily feed the hungry people in this country on the extra dough the defense contractors swindle out of the Pentagon. . . . None of these fat fuckers in Washington or Lansing will ever have to serve his kid a cup of bouillon for dinner a week hard-running. That's for sure, because they're all lawyers, and lawyers think everything is a matter of the right language. . . . In our own Republican and Democratic demographics, the few million hungry can't swing an appreciable vote. The smart political money is after the ladies and homosexuals. I hope these groups are ready for the mudbath (192).

78. Harrison, *Sundog,* 30–31. Strang's use of Thompson's text illustrates his ability to imagine holistically how dam structures might affect their surroundings. *On Growth and Form* deals in large part with the adaptive nature of physical structures in plants and animals and, at first glance, seems only tangentially related to the design and building of dams. Perhaps most relevant to any discussion of dams are the chapters "The Spiral Shells of the Foraminifera," "On Form and Mechanical Efficiency," and "On the Shapes of Eggs, and of Certain Other Hollow Structures," as Strang points out that dams, contrary to popular belief, are essentially hollow structures that must support the great weight of their own frames as well as the water behind them. That Strang has educated himself well is, as the narrator observes, beyond question.

Later, the narrator writes that "The textbook on dam engineering is the best tonic for insomnia I've ever possessed" (73).

79. Harrison, *Sundog,* 31.

80. Ibid., 168.

81. Ibid., 35.

82. Karl, Strang's older brother, is not unlike Tim in *A Good Day to Die*. Although Karl has taught Strang to live life to the fullest despite his epilepsy, "Karl, as noble as he seemed to me as a boy, always ran so stridently counter to all authority, to the way we structure society, that he was doomed from the beginning. I don't just mean the cliché of the Midwest preacher's son sowing wild oats; I mean a hard-core, violent man, at odds with the world" (82). Both Karl and Tim have seen military action (Karl "had a long and wonderful war which [he] joined at fourteen, and stayed in until 1948" [204]), and Karl's presence in the text cannot be overstated in terms of his providing a contrast to Strang's character. Karl is in prison for assaulting four undercover policemen and exacting revenge on his niece's rapists by manually emasculating them. When Strang expresses his distaste for the subject, Karl replies, "Of course you're ashamed. You're a fine Christian person. I'm not" (205).

83. Harrison, *Sundog*, 39.

84. Ibid., 132–33, 135, 167.

85. Ibid., 51.

86. Ibid., 83, 71.

87. Ibid., 56. Perhaps Strang's father is justified in railing "against the gods of Mammon and Moloch" in his diatribe against the dam. Even though Strang's motives as a dam-builder are clearly altruistic (along with some of Halliburton's own obsession with wringing every last bit out of a too-short life—Halliburton himself died at thirty-nine in a shipwreck), as both the narrator's own tapes and Strang's actions confirm, criticisms of the Hoover Dam project and others like it are not uncommon. Donald C. Jackson writes that

> Donald Worster portrays twentieth-century water development in the West as being subject to the control of a centralized bureaucracy (termed an "elite of water bearers") oriented toward serving the economic interests of a select group of landowners and powerful businessmen. Working through the politically attuned (and largely subservient) Bureau of Reclamation, the West's authoritarian "hydraulic society" has, in Worster's view, guided water development from a singular, self-serving perspective. In so doing, it has established "a coercive, monolithic and hierarchical system, ruled by a power elite based on the ownership of capital and expertise" (*Building the Ultimate Dam: John S. Eastwood and the Control of Water in the West* [Lawrence, Kan., University Press of Kansas, 1995], 251).

Additionally, in recapitulating the dam-building theories of John S. Eastwood, who espoused the "multiple-arch" dam and decried the popularization of the "earthfill" dam, Jackson writes, "More problematic [than the dam's structure] would be his reaction to a society in which the values of unrestrained economic and technological growth have begun to be questioned by a significant portion of the citizenry" (253).

In his history of the Hoover Dam, Joseph E. Stevens writes of the workers who were involved in the creation of the monolith,

> Bravado aside, every injury, every death, served to resurrect the nagging doubts about job safety, the disquieting questions about the trade-off between accidents and speed that had surrounded the Hoover Dam project from the beginning. Billboards with the bold black message 'Death is so Permanent' were displayed prominently around the site as part of the well-publicized safety program Six Companies started in 1932 (*Hoover Dam: An American Adventure* [Norman: University of Oklahoma Press, 1988], 202).

88. Joseph W. Meeker, *The Comedy of Survival: Literary Ecology and a Play Ethic*, 3d ed. (Tucson: The University of Arizona Press, 1997).

89. Harrison, *Sundog*, 58–59, 107, 63. Strang recalls with particular delight the Delta Project,

> the only unique engineering marvel I've ever been privileged to work on. The idea was simple enough: dam the estuaries of the Eastern Scheldt south of Rotterdam and prevent a repeat of the 1953 storm that killed eighteen hundred people. Halfway through the project, the Dutch, unlike we ever do, changed their minds when they discovered the first two dams destroyed the rich marine life of the estuary, the mussel, cockles, and oysters. They spent nearly a billion more dollars to protect the eleven million dollar annual gross of the Scheldt seafood industry. This sounds a bit insane if you have the soul of the accountant. The engineers erected about sixty 25,000-ton piers with gates that slide up and down as a storm surge barrier. This was a visionary act, so much so that all the major equipment had to be invented (222).

90. Harrison, *Sundog*, 72.
91. Ibid., 73.
92. Ibid., 87, 89.
93. Ibid., 91.
94. Ibid., 151.
95. Ibid., 127, 142, 145.
96. Ibid., 154.
97. Ibid., 160, 191.
98. Ibid., 224, 225.
99. Ibid., 239, 240–41.
100. Meeker, *The Comedy of Survival*, 41.
101. Reilly, *Jim Harrison*, 18.
102. Stories, both in the sense that they carry the plot of the narrative and

that they are composed of "facts" that can neither be confirmed as "truth" nor decried as "false." One cannot help but draw a connection here to Swanson's story in *Wolf.*

Chapter 3

1. Jim Harrison, *Farmer* (New York: Viking Press, 1976), 1.
2. In his essay "Bird Hunting," Harrison defends his native Michigan:

Tom McGuane, the novelist, said to me about the Midwest, "Mortimer Snerd must have bred five thousand time a day to build that heartland race." True, but the land as I find it, and daily walk it, is virtually peopleless, with vast undifferentiated swamps, ridges, old circular logging roads; a region of cold fogs, monstrous weather changes, third-growth forests devoid of charm, models, and actresses, or ballerinas, but somehow superbly likable (*Just before Dark,* 167).

3. Wallace Stegner, "The Writer's Sense of Place," in *Regionalism Reconsidered: New Approaches to the Field,* ed. David Jordan (New York: Garland Publishing, Inc., 1994), 93.
4. Francesco Loriggio, "Regionalism and Theory," in *Regionalism Reconsidered,* 3.
5. Judy Gerstel, "A Vulnerable Predator: Jim Harrison Writes with a Keen, Compassionate Eye," *Detroit Free Press,* 15 August 1990, 1D; David Jordan, ed., *Regionalism Reconsidered,* xv.
6. Gilbert Fite, "Panel: The Realities of Regionalism," *South Dakota Review* 26.4 (1988): 83–84.
7. William Stafford, "Panel: The Realities of Regionalism," 89.
8. Christopher Lehmann-Haupt, "Celebrations of the Natural," review of *Farmer,* by Jim Harrison, *New York Times,* 26 July 1976, 21.
9. Webster Schott, "Farmer," review of *Farmer,* by Jim Harrison, *New York Times Book Review,* 10 October 1976, 32.
10. Harrison, *Farmer,* 3–4.
11. Ibid., 151.
12. David Marion Holman, *A Certain Slant of Light: Regionalism and the Form of Southern and Midwestern Fiction* (Baton Rouge: Louisiana State University Press, 1995), 51.
13. Harrison, *Farmer,* 153.
14. Barry Lopez, "The American Geographies," in *Finding Home: Writing on Nature and Culture from Orion Magazine,* ed. Peter Sauer (Boston: Beacon Press, 1992), 116.
15. Ibid., 123.
16. Harrison, *Farmer,* 26.

17. Ibid., 147.

18. Ibid., 124–25.

19. Roberson, "Macho Mistake," 237.

20. Harrison, *Farmer,* 125.

21. Schott, "Farmer," 32.

22. Harrison, *Farmer,* 15.

23. Ibid., 99.

24. Ibid., 57.

25. Ibid.

26. Ibid., 83.

27. Ibid., 46.

28. Gary Snyder, *The Practice of the Wild: Essays* (San Francisco: North Point, 1990), 60.

29. Harrison, *Farmer,* 14.

30. Joseph is haunted throughout his life by an accident that has left him with a permanent limp. During a particularly bad fever, Joseph recalls the event and reaches

for his leg to see if it was covered with bandages as it had been thirty-five years ago. He heard his mother scream *I can't stop the bleeding it won't stop bleeding. His father running from the field with him held in his arms. He was dazed and his pants were torn and his leg was hot and twisted. They were buzzing wood with a belt off the neighbor's tractor attached to the big saw and they gunned the tractor to cut a big log. He backed into the belt when he threw his dog a stick and before anyone could move the belt had gripped his pants toward the roller which mangled his leg, even ripped the skin from his crotch* (70).

Later, "Joseph looked at the scar running down the inside of his leg from thigh to ankle. In places it zigzagged like lightning and at the knee the scar formed a knot, then continued rather thinly on down to his ankle where it made a left turn across the bridge of his foot. What a mess, he thought, but a mess appeared to be the rule of late" (130). When Joseph's mother dies, the doctor recounts Joseph's father's reaction to the accident: "So when the accident happened to you he blamed himself and became softer then. It was always heartbreaking to us all when he would carry you into the tavern on Saturday and you would be happy and he'd just sit there watching you drag your cast around the room talking to everyone like nothing had happened" (97). Physical disability is not an uncommon theme in Harrison's fiction, as I have documented throughout these essays. The theme certainly deserves greater critical attention in the future.

31. Harrison, *Farmer,* 5.

32. Ibid., 60, 6.

33. Diane Dufva Quantic, *The Nature of the Place: A Study of Great Plains Fiction* (Lincoln: University of Nebraska Press, 1995), 138.

34. Harrison, *Farmer,* 8.

35. Leo Marx, *The Machine in the Garden: Technology and the Pastoral Ideal* (New York: Oxford University Press, 1964), 23.

36. Harrison, *Farmer,* 78.

37. Jill Franks, "The Regionalist Community," in *Regionalism Reconsidered,* 87.

38. Harrison, *Farmer,* 11.

39. Loriggio, "Regionalism and Theory," in *Regionalism Reconsidered,* 19.

40. Harrison, *Farmer,* 13, 41.

41. Ibid., 41, 134.

42. Ibid., 47.

43. Ibid., 20. Joseph's attempts to see a coyote are not unlike Swanson's in *Wolf,* or Strang's mention of the wolf in *Sundog.*

44. Harrison, *Farmer,* 136.

45. Ibid., 29.

46. Ibid., 136.

47. Ibid., 32, 74, 49.

48. Ibid., 36, 61.

49. A notion not dissimilar to Harrison's "soul history," although Joseph and his family do not struggle against that history to the extent that Dalva does (see chapter 5).

50. Harrison, *Farmer,* 77, 71, 75.

51. Ibid., 144, 137, 154, 157.

52. Ibid., 158.

53. Ibid., 160. Bruno Barreta's film adaptation of *Farmer,* starring Dennis Hopper, is titled *Carried Away.*

54. Harrison, *Farmer,* 160.

55. Ibid., 2.

Chapter 4

1. Harrison, *Just before Dark,* 23. Jo Brans eloquently sums up the American love of food and eating in her *Feast Here Awhile: Adventures in American Eating:* "I have a passion for food. In this book, I have tried to represent the America of our time through the passionate cooks and eaters of our time, both the professionals and those numerous others who, like me, are enthusiastic amateurs in the sense of *amo, amas, amat*—people who just love food, love to eat it, love to prepare it, love to talk about it, and love to read about it. And we are legion" (New York: Ticknor and Fields, 1993, 6). Harrison himself, in an interview with Marc J. Sheehan, brings the act down to the low-

est common denominator when he comments that "I think anything you do two or three times a day should require your absolute attention. It's always amused me that the second position to the *Roshi,* or master, in a big Zen monastery is always the *Tenzo,* or cook" ("The Writer as Naturalist: Michigan Poet/Novelist Jim Harrison Talks about Food, Buddhism, Politics, and the Art of Writing," *Lansing Capital Times,* September 1990, 19).

2. Harrison drew the title for his column from Claude Lévi-Strauss's book of the same name. In the "Overture" to his *The Raw and the Cooked,* the author writes that "The aim of this book is to show how empirical categories—such as the categories of the raw and the cooked, the fresh and the decayed, the moistened and the burned, etc., which can only be accurately defined by ethnographic observation and, in each instance, by adopting the standpoint of a particular culture—can nonetheless be used as conceptual tools with which to elaborate abstract ideas and combine them in the form of propositions" ([Chicago: Chicago University Press, 1983], 1). The author claims as one of his theses that some cultures "view culinary operations as mediatory activities between heaven and earth, life and death, nature and society" (64–65). And in his essay "The Opossum's Cantata," Lévi-Strauss makes a bold claim for the importance of food preparation in the perpetuation of our cultures and myths: "Not only does cooking mark the transition from nature to culture," he writes, "but through it and by means of it, the human state can be defined with all its attributes, even those that, like mortality, might seem to be the most unquestionably natural" (164).

Harrison's column makes good use of a catchy title (it is, after all, in *Esquire*), and his essays follow a train of thought that is similar to that of Lévi-Strauss. For both writers, food—the raw and the cooked—is essential not only in maintaining our bodies and our spirits (the "eat or die" mentality), but also as a way of defining our culture through the culinary choices we make every day.

The penchant for Harrison and his friends to seek out and devour the finest in food and drink is legendary. In a feature titled "The Sporting Club" (*Outside,* March 1989), a reference to the title of Thomas McGuane's first novel, Jim Fergus details the exploits of Harrison, McGuane, de la Valdéne, and Chatham. The article ends with a description of an extravagant feast, followed by a quotation from Harrison's essay "A Sporting Life": "It is finally a mystery what keeps you so profoundly interested over so many years. The sum is far more than simply adding those separate parts. In the restorative quality there is the idea that as humans we get our power from the beauty we love most" (117).

Undoubtedly, one of the beauties to which Harrison repeatedly refers is that of preparation and consumption. He also revels in writing descriptions that evoke memories of the endless possibilities for an imaginative gourmand: "It's interesting to see," Harrison writes, "in the manner of a pharmacist, how particularized the food nostrum can be: for clinical depression you must go to Rio to a *churrascaria* and eat a roast sliced from the hump of a zebu bull; also try the *feijoada*—a stew of black beans with a dozen different smoked meats, including the ears, tails, and snouts. For late-night misty boredom, go to an Italian restaurant and demand the violent pasta dish known as *puttanesca,* favored by the whores of Rome. After voting, eat collard greens to purge yourself of free-floating disgust. And when trapped by a March blizzard make venison *carbonnade,* using a stock of shin bones and the last of the doves. If it is May and I wish to feel light and spiritual, I make a simple sauté of nuggets of sweetbreads, fresh morels, and wild leeks, the only dish, so far as I know, that I have created." ("Meals of Peace and Restoration," in *Just before Dark,* 10)

3. David Bevan, ed., *Literary Gastronomy* (Amsterdam: Rodopi, 1988), 4.

4. J. D. Reed, "Hick Gumshoe," review of *Warlock,* by Jim Harrison, *Time,* 9 November 1981, K12.

5. Jim Harrison, *Warlock* (New York: Delta/Seymour Lawrence, 1981), 6.

6. T. O. Treadwell, "Fantasist in the Shopping Mall," review of *Warlock,* by Jim Harrison, *Times Literary Supplement,* 15 January 1982, 48. Treadwell also astutely remarks that "Harrison is a self-conscious writer and knows that 'warlock' derives from the Old English *wárloga* which means, literally, 'liar against the truth,' and thus gets at Lundgren's refusal (like Bottom's and Quixote's) to see his relationship with the rest of the world in an objective light. Out of this refusal comes comedy, but something deeper too" (48). That "something deeper" is Harrison's understanding that viable literature, in this instance, is created with one eye on the truth and tongue planted firmly in cheek.

7. Thomas Maher Gilligan, "Myth and Reality in Jim Harrison's *Warlock,*" *Critique: Studies in Contemporary Fiction* 25.3 (1984): 148.

8. Paul Stuewe, "Sex in Venice: Essays from Bloomsbury and Uris's Jerusalem," *Quill and Quire,* January 1982, 39; William H. Roberson, "'A Good Day to Live': The Prose Works of Jim Harrison," *Great Lakes Review* 8.2–9.1 (1982–83): 36.

9. Curiously, the novel's first edition does not contain this disclaimer or any other attempt by Harrison to discuss the context of the narrative. In the frontispiece, he draws a tongue-in-cheek connection between food imagery and the body of the narrative when he writes, "The meat and potatoes of the story of Johnny Lundgren, a.k.a. Warlock, not to speak of the gravy, is a grim tale of crime and vengeance set in a framework of mythic simplicity. . . . In a way, he does battle with Earth herself, whose vast, globy body has never been known to smile."

10. Harrison, *Warlock,* preface.

11. Mark Twain, *Adventures of Huckleberry Finn* (Berkeley: University of California Press, 1985), xxv.

12. Mikhail Bakhtin, *Problems of Dostoevsky's Poetics,* ed. and trans. Caryl Emerson (Minneapolis: University of Minnesota Press, 1984), 123.

13. Jean-Anthelme Brillat-Savarin, *The Philosopher in the Kitchen* (1826; New York: Penguin Books, 1981), 117. Brillat-Savarin's treatise on the intricacies of eating contains a curious allusion to Napoleon who, according to the author, wished (like Warlock) to be a gourmand but was not: "The moment he felt hungry, it was necessary that he should be fed" (119). Brillat-Savarin also contends that gourmands are predestined, an interesting notion in light of Warlock's own Calvinist upbringing.

14. Roberson, "Macho Mistake," 236.

15. Harrison's notion of "reality" for his characters is closely related to his own "reality" as a writer who is often in the spotlight. When asked whether the reconstitution of reality is a major theme in his fiction, Harrison replied: "Your only alternative as an artist is to survive, and I think that's basically why I feel like an alien in New York, because you have to survive in this time—and I think Faulkner did that to a certain extent too—you really have to create a habitat for your soul. I have to create my own environment, or I can't endure. At all. I wrote that last essay, "Dream as a Metaphor for Survival," for the *Psychoanalytic Review,* on dislocation. If you don't create your own habitat, that dislocation is permanent" (DeMott and Smith interview, 28–30 August 1997).

16. Harrison, *Warlock,* 8. Harrison relates the importance of dreams in his own life in "Dream as a Metaphor for Survival": "[Dreams] seem curiously simpleminded, like surreal children's stories. But within a socio-historical framework it is the primitive aspects of psychoanalysis that appeal to me. There never was a culture in fifty thousand years that ignored dreams (except our own) or wherein, as Foucault puts it, a healthy mind did not offer wisdom and succor to a weak and sick one" (*Just before Dark,* 317). The importance of dreams in *Warlock,* then, cannot be overstated, particularly in terms of the recurring interconnection of the protagonist's dreams with the sensory impulses associated with his appetites.

17. Harrison, *Warlock,* 121.

18. Harrison, *Just before Dark,* 36.

19. Harrison, *Warlock,* 9.

20. Ibid., 4.

21. Bevan, *Literary Gastronomy,* 19.

22. Harrison, *Warlock,* 10.

23. Ibid., 11.

24. Ibid., 14, 169.

25. Harrison, *Just before Dark,* 33.

26. Harrison, *Warlock,* 26.

27. Eira Patnaik, "The Succulent Gender: Eat Her Softly," in *Literary Gastronomy,* 61.

28. Paul Fieldhouse, *Food and Nutrition: Customs and Culture* (London: Croom Helm, 1986), 200.

29. Sanford Ames, "Fast Food/Quick Lunch: Crews, Burroughs and Pynchon," in *Literary Gastronomy,* 21.

30. Harrison, *Warlock,* 47.

31. Reilly, *Jim Harrison,* 89–90.

32. Harrison, *Warlock,* 50.

33. Ibid., 52–54. Warlock's directives parallel the "Names of Virtues with their Precepts" that Benjamin Franklin outlines in his *Autobiography.* Franklin lists thirteen precepts, the first of which is particularly relevant to Warlock's own quest: "I. TEMPERANCE. Eat not to Dulness. Drink not to elevation" ([New Haven: Yale University Press, 1964], 149). The irony here, despite Harrison's suggestion to the contrary in the preface to the novel, is obvious.

34. Fieldhouse, *Food and Nutrition,* 210–11.

35. In his essay "Midrange Road Kill," Harrison details his own bouts with depression and describes the disease in terms of the loss of individuality with which the sufferer contends as he attempts to break free of the cycle of banality: "When entering a depression, you become a consensus human, a herd creature going through the motions that the wolves, the interior predators, can spot a mile away. You go through the motions of consensus: eating food from consensus cookbooks and restaurants; imbibing consensus perceptions, beliefs, and knowledge from consensus newspapers and magazines, feeling consensus feelings offered by consensus television, music, and drama, and reading poetry, fiction, and nonfiction from consensus publishers. You have become the perfect midrange road kill" (*Just before Dark,* 30). Harrison's description closely mirrors Warlock's own situation, particularly as pertains to food and his ineffectual renderings of recipes from "consensus cookbooks." The plight of Warlock in this narrative is not dissimilar to that of many of Harrison's other protagonists.

36. Harrison, *Warlock,* 56–57.

37. Ibid., 57, 59, 65, 66.

38. Ibid., 72. Warlock's meeting with Clete and the simplicity of Clete's life recalls Harrison's statement in "Then and Now" on the efficacy of a life simply lived: "Luckily, we eat in the present tense, else we might travel further into madness. That goes for fishing, too. When you combine fishing, eating, and a little drinking, you are riding the cusp of sanity as you did, quite happily, the schoolyard swing or that rope at the swimming hole that arced you out out over a deep hole of cold, clear water" (*Just before Dark,* 15). Earlier, the narrative mentions Clete's own rather unsportsmanlike method of fishing: "[Warlock] found Clete standing with a bow and arrow beside his crystalline spring fed trout pond. The trout were fed on pellets and couldn't be caught on flies and worms because flies and worms didn't smell or look like pellets.

Clete would throw pellets to bunch up the trout, then shoot an arrow attached to a string in their midst" (71). The passage points up the close connection between the trout and their usefulness as food.

39. Harrison, *Warlock,* 106, 72, 99.

40. Richard White, "Are You an Environmentalist or Do You Work for a Living?: Work and Nature," in *Uncommon Ground: Toward Reinventing Nature,* ed. William Cronon (New York: W. W. Norton and Company, 1995), 185.

41. Leon R. Kass, *The Hungry Soul: Eating and the Perfecting of Our Nature* (New York: The Free Press, 1994), 84.

42. Harrison, *Warlock,* 86. To wit: "Lunch was one of the most splendid of his life, Warlock felt, a little dreamily. An entire bottle of a Bordeaux, a Beychevelle '67, had soothed his frayed synapses. . . . There was an array of English dishes including a steak and oyster pie, a mixed grill including a broiled kidney, a pork cutlet, lamb chop, bacon, a woodcock of all things, a broiled stuffed tomato and a side of fresh spinach. Warlock's heart went out to the doctor who ate a bowl of stewed millet and ice water.

"The boobs at the Mayo Clinic tell me I have the worst gout they've ever seen. It's been controlled by allopurinol but I'm only able to dine twice a week at most. . . .

"Ten years ago I weighed nearly three hundred pounds and now I weigh one fifty. I'm in my sixties but I fully recaptured my sex life" (108).

43. David A. Booth, "Learned Ingestive Motivation and the Pleasures of the Palate," in *The Hedonics of Taste,* ed. Robert C. Bolles (Hillsdale, N.J.: Lawrence Erlbaum Associates, Publishers, 1991), 29.

44. Bolles, ed., *The Hedonics of Taste,* 3.

45. Gout is an ailment of the extremities that results from overindulgence in rich foods, red meat, and alcohol. Harrison himself has suffered from gout, and describes the ailment as excruciating not only for the physical pain that it causes the sufferer, but for the ruthless limitations that it necessarily puts on one's table habits.

46. Harrison, *Warlock,* 109.

47. Ibid., 120.

48. Ibid., 121.

49. Ibid., 121, 129.

50. Ibid., 136, 137.

51. Kass, *The Hungry Soul,* 126.

52. Harrison, *Warlock,* 139–40.

53. Ibid., 142.

54. Ibid., 144, 146. Warlock's ingenuous acceptance of the vagaries of "reality," and the dream that prompts Warlock's epiphany, calls into question the validity of his visions—most of which are accompanied by detailed descriptions of meals. Carl Sagan, for one, describes research that explains

the suggestibility of the subjects: "The greater the lag time between viewing the film and being given the false information, the more people allow their memories to be tampered with. Loftus argues that 'memories of an event more closely resemble a story undergoing constant revision than a packet of pristine information'" (*Science as a Candle in the Dark: The Demon-Haunted World* [New York: Random House, 1996],139). Perhaps the meals provide a context for Warlock's memories; perhaps the meals themselves are, in a sense, more memorable than the events that accompany them, a notion that is corroborated by a number of writers, including Paul Auster, Mark Winegardner, Janet Burroway, and Harrison himself.

55. Harrison, *Warlock,* 260, 255.

56. Ibid., 154.

57. Pierre Bourdieu, *Distinction* (Cambridge, Mass.: Harvard University Press, 1984), 196.

58. Harrison, *Warlock,* 159–160.

59. Kass, *The Hungry Soul,* 183.

60. Harrison, *Warlock,* 186.

61. Ibid., 207.

62. Ibid., 215–16.

63. Ibid., 221, 224.

64. Ibid., 256–57, 262.

65. Food and drink and its preparation have taken on more importance in the lives of Americans in the last four decades than at any other time in our history, as evidenced by our obsession with weight-loss programs, fad diets, and pills that very well may not allow us to live long enough to enjoy our new-found fitness. According to the Department of Agriculture, the average American ate 49 more pounds of food in 1983 than in 1963, and consumed 270 more calories a day. "As a nation," writes Jo Brans, "we are eating more, and, if the proliferation of gourmet cookbooks is an indication, though we may not be cooking more, we are cooking more ambitiously" (*Feast Here Awhile,* 3).

66. Harrison, *Warlock,* preface.

67. Harrison, *Just before Dark,* 4.

Chapter 5

1. Henry Claridge, "Writing on the Margin: E. L. Doctorow and American History," in *Essays on American Literature since 1970,* ed. Graham Clarke (London: Vision Press, 1990), 9.

2. Philip Roth, *Reading Myself and Others* (Hammondsworth: Penguin Books, 1985), 176.

3. Kathleen Stocking, "Hard Cases: Conversations with Jim Harrison and Tom McGuane, Riders of the Purple Rage," *Detroit News Magazine,* 12 August 1980, 19.

4. Harrison, *Just before Dark,* 300.

5. Lois Tyson, *Psychological Politics of the American Dream: The Commodification of Subjectivity in Twentieth-Century American Literature* (Columbus: Ohio State University Press, 1994), 1.

6. Marc Chenetier, "History in Contemporary American Fiction, or 'The Constrained Nightmare,'" in *History and Post-War Writing,* ed. Theo D'haen and Hans Bertens (Amsterdam: Rodopi, 1990), 147.

7. That we as a nation are obsessed with specific details of history and base much of our national mythology on those tenuous "facts" is a paradox that requires more fleshing out than I can give here (see chapters 6 and 7 for further discussion on the Frontier Myth and Harrison's response to it). That we remember what we want to remember and conveniently disregard the rest is a notion toward which Harrison takes umbrage.

8. The name of Dalva's great-grandfather provides a nice historical irony. John Wesley Powell was the first director of the Bureau of American Ethnology, established in 1879. The function of the bureau, according to Helen Carr, was to "gain the kind of understanding of tribal life that would enable officials best to persuade the Indians to accept the American way of life" (*Inventing the American Primitive: Politics, Gender and the Representation of Native American Literary Traditions, 1789–1936* [Cork, Ireland: Cork University Press, 1986], 155). Harrison's use of "John Wesley" as one of the three voices in the narrative juxtaposes the altruistic intentions of Dalva's great-grandfather with those of the bureau, which attempted to assimilate "the Indians" into an "American" way of life to gain control of Native American land. The allusion to Powell hints at the complexity and attention to historical detail that Harrison brings to his work.

9. Harrison, *The Road Home,* 48.

10. Jim Harrison, *Dalva* (New York: E. P. Dutton/Seymour Lawrence, 1984), 306. Dalva reiterates the notion shortly before her death: "I clumsily explained my own modest theory that we can only go so far without thinking, and then our minds must be refilled by the 'thinginess' of life—landscape, creatures, any sort of travel, people we could not imagine not having existed" (*The Road Home,* 390–91).

11. Harrison, *Dalva,* 175.

12. Ibid., 247.

13. Harrison, interview by DeMott and Smith. Harrison continues: "But I'd been going to the sandhills of Nebraska repeatedly because there's something hauntingly beautiful in the landscape, such a lush improbable area with the Niobrara River valley and the big cattle swaggering in pit-high grass, the water and the lushness of the landscape and the people are indeed pleasant because they're five hours away from a real airport. And so I had gone out there and I was thinking about that whole thing, what happened in America from 1865 on, and then I caught her great-grandfather's voice and then I actually did dream her

sitting on a balcony in Santa Monica looking at the Pacific Ocean and remembering Nebraska, although I think that in times of that kind of emotional pressure, then the dreams become so utterly vivid, so there she appeared an attractive vision indeed" (interview by DeMott and Smith).

14. Harrison, interview by DeMott and Smith.

15. Harrison, "First Person Female," 99. He continues: "I tend to think of art as essentially androgynous and that gender is a biological rather than a philosophical system. . . . On an almost absurd level I thought once that since I'm blind in my left eye, I'm missing half of life—and if I'm writing only as a man, I'm cut in half again. Being down to a scant quarter isn't enough to sustain my life" (101).

16. James I. McClintock, "Dalva: Jim Harrison's 'Twin Sister,'" *Journal of Men's Studies* 6.3 (spring 1998): 320.

17. Ibid., 322. In the essay "Religious and Social Dimensions of Jung's Concept of the Archetype: A Feminist Perspective," Demaris S. Wehr provides a useful definition of the two terms: "The anima and the animus are two especially powerful archetypes. Both Emma and Carl Jung used the terms anima and animus to indicate the unconscious contra-sexual element (the anima being the feminine component of the male psyche and the animus the masculine component of the female psyche) in the male and female personalities. These are lopsided concepts given that the cultural positions of men and women differ, with men generally having and women generally lacking, power and respect" (*Feminist Archetypal Theory: Interdisciplinary Re-Visons of Jungian Thought* [Knoxville: University of Tennessee Press, 1985], 34).

18. Michiko Kakutani, *New York Times,* 8 March 1988, p. C25: John Clute, "Elegiac Heirs," review of *Dalva,* by Jim Harrison, *Times Literary Supplement,* 24 March 1989, 299.

19. Harrison, *Dalva,* 4.

20. Ibid., 57. The same idea informs much of Harrison's own writing. In relating a story to Kay Bonetti of watching a man commit suicide from the Golden Gate Bridge, Harrison constructs a history, much as Dalva does, from his own experiences: "We [Harrison and his wife] looked back and a man had just jumped off the bridge, missed the water by twelve feet and his head was even gone. You know the impact of three hundred feet onto cement, your head vaporizes. My wife and the driver were contorted with horror, and trembling, and I immediately started making sentences. That's my only defense against this world: to build a sentence out of it" (86).

21. Harrison, *Dalva,* 109.

22. Northridge's viability as a character in the novel despite his physical absence in the narrative bears out Dalva's earlier assertion that her family has always relied on journals as a way to validate themselves. By affirming the truth of that statement, Harrison implies the inherent difficulty (often the *impossibility*) of reconstructing history. Rather, we must filter history through

our own perceptions (history becomes more of a recreation than a reconstruction, perhaps), because once we are removed from the event itself, objectivity is lost.

23. Harrison, *Dalva,* 150–51.

24. Ibid., 114.

25. Ibid., 37. Dalva's insistence that we must hold ourselves accountable for the sins of the past is the same notion that Harrison presents as a symptom of society in the Brown Dog Series. Without quite understanding why or how, Brown Dog lives outside history and in a continuous present.

26. Harrison, *Dalva,* 147–48.

27. Ibid., 112.

28. Reilly, *Jim Harrison,* 129.

29. Carr, *Inventing the American Primitive,* 67. Northridge II echoes this notion in *The Road Home* in a passage that he has transcribed from Kipling: "I never got over the wonder of a people who, having extirpated the aboriginals of their continent more completely than any modern race has ever done, honestly believed that they were a godly little New England community, setting examples to brutal mankind. This wonder I used to explain to Theodore Roosevelt, who made the glass cases of Indian relics shake with his rebuttals" (128). He continues: "One need not read very deeply in history, despite the otiose trappings of patriotism, to see how irrationally vicious we were with our Natives. We have rebuilt Germany in a scant dozen years and have utterly ignored our first citizens, and are confident in this sodden theocracy that the God of Moses and Jesus has been quite enthused over our every move" (143).

30. Harrison, *The Road Home,* 375.

31. Harrison, *Dalva,* 135.

32. Ibid., 176.

33. Ibid., 196.

34. Ibid., 140, 141.

35. Reilly, *Jim Harrison,* 130.

36. Harrison, *Dalva,* 4.

37. Ibid., 5.

38. Ibid., 7.

39. Reilly, *Jim Harrison,* 131.

40. Harrison, *Dalva,* 13.

41. Ibid., 12. Dalva echoes the general tone of *The Road Home,* a railing against the venality and greed of society, when she writes that in her work with the children, "Oddly, it wasn't the poverty that ground against the sensibilities so hard that depressed me the most but the attitude of many of the more fortunate who weren't satisfied with having money unless there were many who didn't have it. This was particularly true in Santa Monica during the Reagan years when my occupation was largely seen as laughable, if not

contemptible. Even quasi-religious people like to quote Jesus as saying, 'The poor you have with you always,' neglecting to add that he didn't say to sit on your ass and don't do anything about it" (*The Road Home,* 372).

42. Harrison, *Dalva,* 15.

43. Ibid., 19, 14.

44. Ibid., 56.

45. McClintock, "Dalva: Jim Harrison's 'Twin Sister,'" 327.

46. Thomas McNamee, "O Pioneers!," review of *The Road Home,* by Jim Harrison, *New York Times Book Review,* 8 November 1998, 11.

47. Wendy Smith, "Returning to the Earth," review of *The Road Home,* by Jim Harrison, *Washington Post Book World,* 15 November 1998, 4.

48. Ibid.

49. Harrison, *The Road Home,* 3, 24.

50. Ibid., 21, 45, 46. Those simulacra are defined by Paul later when he tells Northridge II that "there was a word in Portuguese called *saudade* that appeared to represent our farm and lives, a homesickness or longing for something vital that had been irretrievably lost and only the dream of it could be recovered" (*The Road Home,* 64).

51. Harrison, *The Road Home,* 43, 112, 149, 42.

52. Ibid., 56, 35.

53. Brian Edwards, *Theories of Play and Postmodern Fiction* (New York: Garland, 1998), 25.

54. Harrison, *The Road Home,* 154.

55. James Hillman, *The Dream and the Underworld* (New York: Harper & Row, 1979), 64. A *nekyia* is an archetypal descent.

56. Hillman, *The Dream and the Underworld,* 106–7.

57. Ibid., 133.

58. Harrison, *The Road Home,* 35.

59. Nelse, especially, is indignant over what he sees: "It struck me for the thousandth time that when you were on the move you noted the bottom third. . . . Those in Washington who could help simply had never noticed these people, that there was something about the xenophobic power trance in politics that made them unable to extrapolate any other reality than the effort toward reelection. They were making a mighty effort to rigidify the society to protect the top, and the bottom third were being openly sacrificed" (*The Road Home,* 194). Later, he takes on academics, one of Harrison's favorite targets of derision: "After quite a bit of exposure to Natives, though, the scholarly texts I had read as a student and the quasi-serious books I had read afterward didn't seem to jibe with my experiences. I clumsily accounted for this by thinking that though the books may have represented a lot of field work they were written elsewhere, say in a college town or in Washington, D.C., where people, no matter how fresh to the job, are only in touch with themselves" (204).

Dalva, too, is angered by the way that her society chooses to remedy its problems: "I avoided a contingent of thoroughly white bliss-ninnies nearby, who are the source of much humor among Native Americans, along with the representations of them on television and in the movies. There is a false identification and wan hope of brushing against those who are falsely considered to have an almost genetic virtue, which in itself creates the additional difficulty of distance from the true problems" (*The Road Home,* 383).

Naomi understands the continuing implications of the history of the area when she writes, "My own family place was over southeast of Gordon, not all that far in Nebraska terms from where Mari Sandoz of Old Jules fame was raised. No white person ever looked more clearly at our extirpation of the Natives. . . . Perhaps my heart is weaker now because I no longer can bear to look at some of her books, especially *Crazy Horse* and *Cheyenne Autumn.* The cruelty of what happened to our first citizens is too great in dimension. But it's not just the books, it's because I was born and raised with stories of Native tribulations that had become the darkest part of our own family history" (*The Road Home,* 306).

The notions of the three characters are deeply embedded in Harrison himself, who tells Joseph Bednarik that "What's out of bounds for me is somebody else's religious rituals. The most disgusting appropriation of what's Native American. That just terrifies me. How could they do that? Just like that old Chippewa shaman seeing his first picture of a white man who shot a deer with his foot on the deer—Oh, God—you don't fool with that. Oddly enough, that's just like if a Catholic went into a teepee and saw all these priest vestments hanging there as wall decoration. I mean there's something tremendously inappropriate about one writer fooling with another person's secret religion or public religion or using it for his own purposes" ("A Conversation with Jim Harrison," 110).

The connection here between what Nelse, Dalva, and Naomi observe and what Northridge watched with horror a century before is clear.

60. Jim Harrison, "The *Salon* Interview: Jim Harrison," interview by Jonathan Miles, *Salon,* December 1998. The difficulty for Harrison of writing Nelse's character also manifests itself in Nelse's narrative: Nelse muses that "One thing I've noted over and over about men my age in my lost journals was the sense of their free-floating pissed offness which was still of indeterminate source to me" (*The Road Home,* 198).

61. Nelse recalls that "My adviser, a melancholy young assistant professor who soon thereafter went back to his own father's auto dealership in Texas, had told me that I'd get in trouble for doing something so unscientific as talking to actual Natives when there was ample research material available written by qualified people. . . . He actually sneeringly called me a *romantic humanist*" (*The Road Home,* 170).

62. Harrison, *The Road Home,* 180.

63. McNamee, "O Pioneers!," 11.

64. Harrison, *The Road Home*, 230, 279.

65. Ibid., 186, 190. Dalva comments about Nelse that "It is hard to imagine a young man who knows more about wild areas and less about what the civilized world has to offer" (*The Road Home*, 419).

66. Harrison, *The Road Home*, 194–95. He strains to recall "what a young English professor had said about Foucault, a Frenchman, and levels of discourse but I couldn't remember the main points other than power controls discourse. At the time it only meant to me that the environmental movement was screwed because they were forced to do their dealings in the language of the enemy camp, the government and developers" (*The Road Home*, 210).

67. Harrison, *The Road Home*, 191. In defining Nelse's "mating urge," Harrison plays on the moral code that he finds so offensive in the reception of Northridge II's relationship with Willow when Nelse falls madly in love with a married stripper.

68. Harrison, *The Road Home*, 190.

69. Michael Roemer, *Telling Stories: Postmodernism and the Invalidation of Traditional Narrative* (Lanham, Md.: Rowman & Littlefield, 1995), 8.

70. Harrison, *The Road Home*, 302, 321.

71. Roemer, *Telling Stories*, 131.

72. Harrison, *The Road Home*, 201, 301, 332.

73. Ibid., 288, 337, 355.

74. Ibid., 397.

75. Ibid., 409.

76. Ibid., 437, 383, 391, 394.

77. McClintock, "Dalva: Jim Harrison's 'Twin Sister,'" 326.

78. Harrison, *The Road Home*, 364–65, 445.

Chapter 6

1. "It would be difficult to persuade me that the story of the Prodigal Son is not the legend of a man who didn't want to be loved. . . . The secret of that life of his which had never yet come into being, spread out before him. Involuntarily he left the footpath and went running across the fields, with outstretched arms, as if in this wide reach he would be able to master several directions at once. And then he flung himself down behind some bush and didn't matter to anyone."

Several times in this collection I allude to the fact that Rilke has influenced Harrison's work; Harrison's constant attention, both in his poetry and fiction, to Rilke's work is especially relevant in the context of Robert Hass's discovery of Rilke in Paris. Hass writes that "A friend promised to take me to a cafe, not far from Rue Monsieur-le-Prince, where Rilke was said to have breakfasted in the early years of the century when he was working as Rodin's secretary. I was glad for the pilgrimage because, of all poets, Rilke is the hardest to locate in a place. He was born a year after Robert Frost, in 1875, a little too soon to be a young modernist, and the dissimilarity between his work and Frost's is so great that the fact does not help to anchor for me a sense of his life" (xi). Perhaps what has impelled me to view Harrison's work from so many different angles is its essential "dissimilarity" from the work of Harrison's contemporaries.

Hass's exuberant affirmation of Rilke's work also seems fitting in a discussion of Harrison: "It is wonderful just to be able to watch the world come flooding in on this poet, who had held it off for so long. Human feeling is not so problematical here. It does not just evaporate; it flows through things and constitutes them. And, in the deepest sense, it is not even to the point" (xli).

2. Thomas Docherty, ed., *Postmodernism* (New York: Columbia University Press, 1993), 11.

3. I resist calling this group of three related novellas the *"Brown Dog* trilogy," as Harrison has entertained the notion of turning the series as it exists now into a tetralogy.

Harrison's Phillip Caulkins explains the meaning of the title *The Seven-Ounce Man* in the novella *The Beige Dolorosa,* from *Julip:* "My difficulties with the law, were, as Ballard called them, 'ounces,' but ounces eventually added up to pounds" (207).

4. Langdon Elsbree, "Our Pursuit of Loneliness: An Alternative to This Paradigm," in *The Frontier Experience and the American Dream,* ed. David Mogen et al. (College Station: Texas A & M University Press, 1989), 159.

5. Patrick A. Smith, "A Man's Man's World," review of *The Beast God Forgot to Invent,* by Jim Harrison, *January Magazine,* 26 November 2000, <www.januarymagazine.com/fiction/beastharrison.html>.

6. Jerry Leath Mills, "Three Novellas, Three Lessons in Life," review of *Julip,* by Jim Harrison, *Atlanta Journal-Constitution,* 22 May 1994, N12.

7. Jonis Agee, "The Macho Chronicles," review of *Julip,* by Jim Harrison, *New York Times Book Review,* 22 May 1994, 41.

8. Alexander Harrison, "Seeking New Frontiers," review of *Julip,* by Jim Harrison, *Times Literary Supplement,* 25 November 1994, 20.

9. Judith Freeman, "Woman's Intimations," review of *The Woman Lit by Fireflies,* by Jim Harrison, *Los Angeles Times Book Review,* 19 August 1990, 5.

10. Docherty, *Postmodernism,* 3.

11. John Barth, "The Literature of Exhaustion," *Atlantic Monthly* 220.2 (August 1967): 34.

12. John Barth, *The Floating Opera* (Garden City, N.J.: Doubleday, 1967), 191.

13. David Mogen, *The Frontier Experience and the American Dream,* 17.

14. In Richard Slotkin's *The Fatal Environment,* one of three epic criticisms of the American Frontier and its lasting influence on our society, the author poses the question "Whose Myth Is It?" and writes, "It is essential to

my approach to myth to insist that the substance of mythic materials and genres is provided by human 'authors': men and women who fabricate or compose
the stories, and promulgate them; who bring to the work their needs, intentions,
and concerns. However, this premise of human authorship is the very thing that
myth is organized to deny" ([New York: Atheneum, 1985], 26). By exposing
the archetype as a construction that is inherently flawed by its human author—
the idealization of the mythic hero transcends literature and becomes a simulacrum of the legends that we have created and perpetuated—Slotkin has hit
upon the very thing that allows Harrison to so ably articulate our conception
of the "anti-mythic" character (and later, as I write in chapter 7, an evolving
myth-figure who grows out of the ashes of the Frontier Myth). Slotkin goes on
to explain that "Archetypes do not exist 'in nature.' They are abstractions of
mythic structures, derived from the study of comparative mythologies by pro-
cedures of scholarly analysis. Our current catalogue of archetypes is the end
product of a century of scholarship ranging over every extant culture, and many
others now known only through archaeology. . . . The weakness of the archetypal approach is that it must scant the historical particular in the search for
the universal structure" (27–28). The implication of Slotkin's analysis is that
Brown Dog is an anti-mythic figure because he does not readily fit any of our
mainstream archetypes that constitute the creation of the mythic figure.

15. Mogen, *The Frontier Experience and the American Dream,* 22.

16. Charles Newman, *The Post-Modern Aura: The Act of Fiction in an
Age of Inflation* (Evanston, Ill.: Northwestern University Press, 1985), 9.

17. Smith, "A Man's Man's World."

18. Reilly, *Jim Harrison,* 135.

19. Frederic Jameson, *Postmodernism,* or The Cultural Logic of Late Capitalism (Durham, N.C.: Duke University Press, 1991), 17.

20. In the introduction to *Postmodernism,* editor Thomas Docherty asserts
that the term "postmodern" "was probably first used by Arnold Toynbee in
1939, and prefigured by him in 1934." In Volume V of his epic *A Study of
History,* Toynbee "suggested that the modern now comes to an end during
the First World War, 1914–18, and that the postmodern begins to articulate
and shape itself in the years between the two wars, between 1918 and 1939,"
Arnold J. Toynbee, *A Study of History* (London: Oxford University Press,
1976), 1–2.

21. Gerald Vizenor, *Narrative Chance: Postmodern Discourse on Native
American Indian Literatures* (Albuquerque: University of New Mexico Press),
1989.

22. Wylie Sypher, *Comedy* (Baltimore: Johns Hopkins University Press,
1956), 252–53.

23. Twain, *Adventures of Huckleberry Finn,* 362.

24. Jim Harrison, "The Art of Fiction CIV," 55.

25. Jim Harrison, "An Interview with Jim Harrison," interview by Kay
Bonetti, audiocassette, American Audio Prose Library, 1985.

26. Jim Harrison, *The Woman Lit by Fireflies* (New York: Houghton Mifflin, 1990), 3. Harrison first details the preserving effects of the cold water on bodies in *Sundog,* when he shares with Strang "the unspoken lore of Lake Superior, where the bodies of drowned sailors never float to the surface; the water near the bottom is always too cold for the bodies to deliquesce and gain buoyancy. For some reason, sailors want to be buried on land, say back near the Indiana farm where they started" (111).

27. Harrison, *Julip,* 85.

28. Joan Penzenstadler, "La frontera, Aztlan, el barrio: Frontiers in Chicano Literature," in *The Frontier Experience and the American Dream,* 162.

29. Twain, *Adventures of Huckleberry Finn,* 18.

30. Ibid., 1.

31. George C. Carrington Jr., *The Dramatic Unity of Huckleberry Finn* (Columbus: Ohio State University Press, 1976), 3.

32. Joseph Carroll, *Evolution and Literary Theory* (Columbia: University of Missouri Press, 1995).

33. In his text *The Society of the Spectacle,* Guy Debord takes a cynical approach to a construction of history based solely in the present. And although I tend to reject such overarching claims as Debord makes for the essential falseness of such a construction, his statement neatly defines Brown Dog's own inability to connect with his past:

> The claim that a brief freeze in historical time is in fact a definitive stability—such is, both consciously and unconsciously expressed, the undoubted basis of the current tendency toward 'structuralist' system building. The perspective adopted by the anti-historical thought of structuralism is that of the eternal presence of a system that was never created and that will never disappear. This fantasy of a preexisting unconscious structure's hegemony over all social practice is illegitimately derived from linguistic and anthropological structural models—even from models of the functioning of capitalism—that are misapplied even in their original contexts; and the only reason why this has occurred is that an academic approach fit for complacent middle-range managers, a mode of thought completely anchored in an awestruck celebration of the existing system, crudely reduces all reality to the existence of that system. ([New York: Zone Books, 1994], 141–42)

Debord implicitly calls for a transcendent view of history rather than the structuralist view that Brown Dog is subject to and that the historian Michael in *Dalva* perpetuates for his own gain; Harrison, aware of the danger of "anti-historical" thought, describes Brown Dog's place in the "system" at the same time that he gives credence to a more liberating view of history. In Harrison's novellas, it is easy to dismiss the implications of Brown Dog being trapped always-already in the present.

Writer Janet Burroway states the problem more succinctly: Because we no longer pay heed to history, "spectacle becomes reality, and it no longer makes sense to talk about our confusing reality and spectacle, because they're the same thing. These changes that we so readily accept profoundly affect our reality, because it becomes artificial to live by the natural" (personal interview).

34. Harrison, *Julip,* 93.

35. Ibid., 94, 95.

36. The quasi-tragic fact of Brown Dog's future is that, at best, he can live as he has been living—only in the present, with very little of his past on which he may buttress his future. Brown Dog's inability to make good use of the totems that come his way (both the chief in the beginning and the bearskin that Delbert gives to Brown Dog as a symbol of strength) is indicative of his ultimate inability to create an identity for himself. Both objects, if he were, in fact, to "connect" to the Native American history that is such an important theme in the narratives, could draw him into the "social groups" defined by the objects. Indeed, as Lévi-Strauss posits, "wherever social groups were defined by unilineal descent and where genealogical links were vague or fictitious, the only way to guarantee the identity and continuity of these groups was to make use of differential terms transmitted by heredity and which were often drawn from the animal and vegetable kingdoms" (*Anthropology and Myth* [London: Basil Blackwell, 1987], 26).

37. Walter Blair writes that "beginning in the sixteenth century, in hundreds of picaresque novels and their offspring, rascals, servants, social parasites, shady ladies and teen-age dropouts, many as illiterate and as busy with adventures as Huck, somehow got prose autobiographies assembled and published" (in *The Critical Response to Mark Twain's Huckleberry Finn* ([New York: Greenwood Press, 1991], 110).

38. Harrison, *The Woman Lit by Fireflies,* 3–4.

39. Jim Harrison, *The Beast God Forgot to Invent* (New York: Atlantic Monthly Press, 2000), 116. In *Westward Ho,* Brown Dog discovers with bemusement that society knows much more about him than he assumes. Bob Duluth, for whom Brown Dog has become a chauffeur, "had all of this information [about Brown Dog] at his fingertips. Up until two years ago when he had met Shelley he had led a totally private life, mostly because, he now supposed, nobody was interested" (134).

40. Elizabeth Deeds Ermarth, *Sequel to History: Postmodernism and the Crisis of Representational Time* (Princeton, N.J.: Princeton University Press, 1992), 88.

41. Ibid.

42. Harrison, *The Beast God Forgot to Invent,* 128.

43. Ibid., 104, 139. Brown Dog's realization that the only familiar aspect of his world was his own body recalls Wittgenstein's notion of language and the creation of reality in *Philosophical Investigations.* It also echoes Nelse Carlson's contention in *The Road Home* that "I have no control of the world beyond my own skin" (230).

44. Ernst Behler, *Irony and the Discourse of Modernity* (Seattle: University of Washington Press, 1990), 111.

45. Twain, *Adventures of Huckleberry Finn*, xxv.

46. The shifting perception of Brown Dog's character is defined in his travels to Los Angeles, where he feels out of place, and he is "Quite unmindful in his ordinariness that his straits were dire indeed, or that some in his immediate area of a great university, not to speak of the film business, would mistake this ordinariness as extraordinary" (*The Beast God Forgot to Invent*, 112).

47. Harrison, *Julip*, 114.

48. Harrison, *The Beast God Forgot to Invent*, 124.

49. Harrison, *The Seven-Ounce Man*, 147.

50. Harrison, *Brown Dog*, 59.

51. Harrison, "The Art of Fiction CIV," 58.

52. Bennett Kravitz, *Dreaming Mark Twain* (Lanham, Md.: University Press of America, 1996), 83. To be sure, the story of Huck is not one of unadulterated freedom, but rather of an "American Dream" that has not yet been defiled to the point of its negation. In his astute essay "*Huckleberry Finn:* 'Self' Construction and the Pursuit of the Virgin Land," Bennett Kravitz posits that "Huck has latched on to one of the most prominent of 'American Dreams,' one that appears—in Pierre Macherey's terms—in the margins or the 'non-dit' of the text: the dream of domination in the guise of creating a new world, or settling a 'virgin' land. By setting out to construct a new world—one in which he will become an active self-fashioner rather than the passive participant he had been in the widow's 'sivilized' world—Huck imagines he will be able to avoid the very conflicts Twain has assembled for him throughout the novel" (81). Additionally, "Whenever Huck succumbs to his own ambition, and actually believes he is his own creator, Mark Twain reminds him that civilization is always ready to encroach on his 'virgin' territory" (83). The important point here, and the irony of Twain's narrative, is that Huck ostensibly escapes, but that escape is contingent upon society's implicit cooperation in facilitating that "lighting out." Brown Dog has no such recourse. Without question, Huck actively seeks his own freedom (albeit, I argue, with the permission of the society that has until his escape kept his ambitions at bay); Brown Dog, on the other hand, incessantly *reacts* to society and is not, like Huck, in unspoken concert with society. While much of Huck's own adventure is, arguably, a reaction to the stimuli with which he is presented, his final escape is an individual act of will, not a stipulation placed on him by society. That society does, in fact, facilitate his escape speaks to the nature of the mythic hero in a time when society still allowed such heroes to exist.

53. Harrison, *Julip*, 168.

54. Susan Derwin, "Impossible Commands: Reading *Adventures of Huckleberry Finn*," *Nineteenth-Century Literature* 47.4 (1993): 442.

55. Twain, *Adventures of Huckleberry Finn*, 66.

56. Harrison, *The Beast God Forgot to Invent,* 145. That sense is reiterated in Brown Dog's "darkest hour" in Los Angeles: "Traffic was tied up on Sunset due to an accident and B. D. felt poignantly the utter crush of civilization. . . . B. D. wanted to turn turtle like he did when he and Lone Marten had driven through the profound ugliness of Las Vegas, and where he simply raised his shirt collar and sank into its dark confines, preferring his own rank air" (*Westward Ho,* 168–69).

57. Reilly, *Jim Harrison,* 147.

58. Frederic Jameson, *Postmodernism: or, the Cultural Logic of Late Capitalism* (Durham, N.C.: Duke University Press, 1991), 361.

59. Jean-François Lyotard, "Answering the Question: What is Postmodernism?" in *Postmodernism,* ed. Thomas Docherty, 42.

60. An editing oversight on Harrison's part adds a particularly ironic twist to a discussion of identity in the three Brown Dog novellas. In *Brown Dog,* Shelley's surname is "Newkirk."

61. Harrison, *The Seven-Ounce Man,* 174.

62. D. H. Lawrence, *Studies in Classic American Literature* (Garden City, N.Y.: Doubleday, 1953), 68–69.

63. Harrison, *Julip,* 86.

64. Twain, *Adventures of Huckleberry Finn,* 270–71.

65. Steven Connor, *Postmodern Culture: An Introduction to Theories of the Contemporary* (London: Basil Blackwell, 1989), 125.

66. Harrison, "The Art of Fiction CIV," 57.

67. Mogen, *The Frontier Experience and the American Dream,* 21.

68. Elsbree, "Our Pursuit of Loneliness," 33.

69. Harrison, *The Beast God Forgot to Invent,* 128.

70. Thedor Adorno, *Negative Dialectics* (New York: Seabury Press, 1973), 145.

71. Harrison, *The Beast God Forgot to Invent,* 186.

72. Slotkin, *The Fatal Environment,* 28.

73. Nina Baym, *Feminism and American Literary History: Essays* (New Brunswick, N.J.: Rutgers University Press, 1992), 11.

74. Turner, *Beyond Geography,* 19.

Chapter 7

1. In chapter 6, an analysis of the Brown Dog series, I define the American Dream and the American Myth in terms of the postmodern. The similarities between the Brown Dog series and the four novellas under consideration are too numerous to mention. To study them all in the same context, however, would have been unwieldy and, perhaps, a bit contrived. I also see a genuine connection between Brown Dog and Huckleberry Finn, one that does not exist to as great an extent in Harrison's other nine novellas.

The line between defining and not-defining, as Harrison himself knows well, is a fine one indeed. That any such analyses come dangerously close to tautology is an aspect of literary criticism about which every writer is aware. The dilemma is summed up nicely by Harrison when he tires of discussing his own work: "It is what it is . . . ."

2. Wayne Ude, "Forging an American Style," in *The Frontier Experience and the American Dream,* ed. David Mogen, Mark Busby, and Paul Bryant (College Station: Texas A & M University Press, 1989), 50–64.

3. Slotkin's definition of the Myth of the Frontier: "The Myth of the Frontier is arguably the longest-lived of American myths, with origins in the colonial period and a powerful continuing presence in contemporary culture. Although the Myth of the Frontier is only one of the operative myth/ideological systems that form American culture, it is an extremely important and persistent one. Its ideological underpinnings are those same 'laws' of capitalist competition, of supply and demand, of Social Darwinian 'survival of the fittest' as a rationale for social order, and of 'Manifest Destiny' that have been the building blocks of our dominant historiographical tradition and political ideology" (*The Fatal Environment,* 15).

4. Beef Torrey, "Collecting Jim Harrison: Untrammeled Renegade Genius," *Firsts: The Book Collector's Magazine,* May 1999, 47.

5. In his essay "The Significance of the Frontier in Contemporary American Literature," Mark Busby defines the sensibility that Harrison uses to create his new myth-figure: "Most . . . writers express a deep ambivalence toward the frontier. On one hand, they nod longingly toward some frontier American values and recognize positive traits associated with the pastoral frontier. On the other hand, they acknowledge the limitations that a nostalgic, rearward-looking frontier emphasis produces, and they recognize the problems spawned by playing what McMurtry calls 'symbolic frontiersman'" (*The Frontier Experience and the American Dream,* 95).

6. Undoubtedly, the novellas that fall outside the scope of this study will be dealt with on their own merits and in a collection devoted solely to their contents. Certainly, each of the twelve novellas deserves more than mere plot summary.

7. Raphael Patai, *Myth and Modern Man* (Englewood Cliffs, N.J.: Prentice-Hall, 1972), 30.

8. Witness recent attempts at canonizing grunge rocker Kurt Cobain by claiming that he was murdered or a rumor that falsely announced the untimely death of rock icon and pop culture hero Lou Reed. Leslie Fiedler, anticipating nearly forty years ago what Harrison would articulate in his novellas, writes that "The study of popular culture threatens itself to become a branch of Popular Culture" (*No! in Thunder: Essays on Myth and Literature* [London: Lowe & Brydone, 1963], 184). In essence, a culture begs the question of its own existence and its intellectuals are effete and live their lives

largely by proxy—a simulacrum of the Beat lifestyle that Harrison so vehemently questions in *A Good Day to Die* and *Wolf,* and also in the novellas at hand.

9. My own notion of the mythic quest and the initial willingness or unwillingness of the protagonist to undertake that quest is a departure from the traditional belief articulated by Leo Marx, who sees the mythic quest as "a separation from the world, a penetration to some source of power, and a life-enhancing return" (*The Machine in the Garden,* 3–4). Leonard Biallas echoes Marx when he writes, "there has to be a willingness to give of the self before a person can grow, before arriving at a 'oneness' or reunion with all creation, with the spiralling self, and with the numinous forces active in each life. It is the giving of the self to the quest, the consent to the struggle, that opens up possibilities for a fuller life and a new relationship with the world" (*Myths: Gods, Heroes, and Saviors,* 169).

In the case of Joseph Lacort in *The Beast God Forgot to Invent,* the point is moot, since Lacort, because of his closed-head injury, does not consciously undergo any progression toward a goal. The quest is simply in his living, the single tool at his disposal his wide-eyed innocence for a world that is new enough to him to be harmless. In addition, even though the notion of the "spiralling self" is a good one, Biallas does not allow for that self to exist outside the societal constraints that all four of the protagonists at hand seek to escape. To view myth-making as a process that always aggrandizes the communal disregards the individual's struggle for "self-realization." The point is a minor one, perhaps, but one worth making.

10. Sam Bluefarb, *The Escape Motif in the American Novel: Mark Twain to Richard Wright* (Columbus, Ohio: Ohio State University Press, 1972), 3.

11. Ibid.

12. Fiedler, *No! in Thunder,* 175.

13. Mary Douglas, *Implicit Meanings: Essays in Anthropology* (London: Routledge & Kegan Paul, 1975), 156.

14. Ibid.

15. Keith Opdahl, "Junk Food," review of *Legends of the Fall,* by Jim Harrison, *Nation,* 7 July 1979, 24.

16. Roberson, "A Good Day to Live," 33.

17. Ibid., 35.

18. Jim Harrison, *Legends of the Fall* (New York: Delta/Seymour Lawrence, 1979), 217.

19. Ibid., 226.

20. Ibid., 219.

21. Ibid., 226.

22. Turner, *Beyond Geography,* 115.

23. Harrison, *Legends of the Fall,* 231, 236, 234, 248.

24. Ibid., 262–63.

25. Ibid., 271.

26. Ibid., 255.

27. Ibid., 243, 245.

28. Ibid., 253.

29. Fiedler, *No! in Thunder,* 17.

30. Douglas, *Implicit Meanings,* 167.

31. Wiley Lee Umphlett, *Mythmakers of the American Dream: The Nostalgic Vision in Popular Culture* (Lewisburg, Pa.: Bucknell University Press, 1983), 35.

32. Harrison, *Legends of the Fall,* 272–73.

33. Harrison, *The Woman Lit by Fireflies,* 178.

34. Colin Falck, *Myth, Truth, and Literature: Towards a True Post-Modernism* (Cambridge, England: Cambridge University Press, 1989), 145–46.

35. Harrison, *The Woman Lit by Fireflies,* 199.

36. Ibid., 196–97.

37. Ibid., 180.

38. Ibid., 188, 187.

39. Harrison's sense of irony here is sharp: Donald, who prides himself on his financial savvy, thought "Clare's taste in wine . . . a wasteful vice she had inherited from her mother. Frequently, he noted, the wine on a dinner bill equaled the price of the food, and when he picked up a case of Mersault or Chambertin at the wine store he liked to joke out loud: 'Here goes another three shares of General Motors.' The old clerk at the wine store invariably smiled his mask of a smile knowing it was Clare's money in the first place, a point which would appall Clare herself in that she was so fair-minded as to be frequently rendered immobile" (181–82).

40. Harrison, *The Woman Lit by Fireflies,* 239, 240–41.

41. Eric Gould, *Mythical Intentions in Modern Literature* (Princeton, N.J.: Princeton University Press, 1981), 145.

42. Harrison, *The Woman Lit by Fireflies,* 189.

43. Ibid., 192, 222–23. Predictably, Donald's attitude toward charity is much different from Clare's: "Donald didn't mind when she asked him to write a large check for the American Indian College Fund or the NAACP, two of her favorite charities, saying something to the effect that 'those folks got the wrong end of the stick,' as if all American history had been a business deal. Maybe it was. Donald tried to hedge at her support of the Nature Conservancy and Greenpeace because he felt the bird watchers and 'little old ladies in tennis shoes' were cramping certain resort complexes in northern Michigan that were otherwise good investment potentials" (215).

44. The point is corroborated by Colin Falck, who writes, "The technical innovations of modernism—its renderings of the stream of consciousness, its systematic derangements of the senses, its narratorial shifts of time and of viewpoint, its frequent aggressions against its own medium—are all ways of

breaking with the world's appearances and of finding deeper meanings behind the 'common sense' spatio-temporal framework of superficial representation" (*Myth, Truth, and Literature,* 150).

That Harrison moves easily between the romantic, modern, realist, and postmodern modes of literature suggests the difficulty of pinning down his literary sensibility.

45. Harrison, *The Woman Lit by Fireflies,* 193, 200.

46. Ibid., 225, 207, 230.

47. Ibid., 217.

48. Ibid., 195.

49. Ibid., 230, 244, 247.

50. Ibid., 235; Slotkin, *The Fatal Environment,* 16.

51. Joseph Bednarik, "A Conversation with Jim Harrison," *Northwest Review* 33.2 (1995): 107.

52. Harrison, *Julip,* 19.

53. Ibid.

54. In *The Violence Mythos,* Barbara Whitmer draws a conclusion that gives an interesting context to the novella's evolution in Harrison's work:

> Authority depends upon the social participant's consent to belief in the authority's legitimacy. This assumes a consent to the legitimacy of power underlying authority. These relationships differ from strength, force, and violence. Power refers to an ability to act in concert. It belongs to the domain of the group, not to the individual. When someone is said to be 'in power,' what is meant is that he/she is empowered, or given permission, to act in the name of the group. If the group disappears, so does the power of the person 'in power.' Thus power rests upon acceptance and support in the group context.
>
> Strength, in contrast, refers to the singular, the individual. Strength is the property inherent in a person or object and belongs to its character. It may prove itself in relation to other things, but it is independent of them. ([Albany, N.Y.: State University of New York Press, 1997], 67)

Whitmer's implication, in the context of Harrison's novellas, is that the protagonists have evolved from characters whose violence is implicitly part of their culture (Tristan) and implicates them in that culture (the Myth of the Frontier) to those who remain outside the group—thus appropriating their own "strength" and asserting their independence from the group.

55. Michael Bell, *Literature, Modernism, and Myth: Belief and Responsibility in the Twentieth Century* (Cambridge, England: Cambridge University Press, 1997), 37–38.

Bell posits that, as the century progressed, there was "a gradual shift of emphasis from the metaphysical to the political aspect of myth, since myth is not just a subjective projection, or an 'internal coherence theory,' it is a way of getting truly to see the world" (38).

56. Harrison, *Julip*, 34.

57. Ibid., 53.

58. Linda A. Westervelt, *Beyond Innocence, or the Altersroman in Modern Fiction* (Columbia, Mo.: University of Missouri Press, 1997), 2.

59. Harrison, *Julip*, 59–60.

60. Ibid., 61, 63–64, 80.

61. Ibid., 3. Harrison's opening line of *The Road Home*, written by John Wesley Northridge II in the middle of the century: "It is easy to forget that in the main we die only seven times more slowly than our dogs" (3).

62. Harrison, *Julip*, 3.

63. Ibid., 62, 69, 64.

64. Ibid., 12, 13.

65. Ibid., 10, 75.

66. The notion of a "meta-myth" created by Lacort in his sighting is intriguing but well outside the scope of this essay.

67. Harrison, *Julip*, 7.

68. Harrison, *The Beast God Forgot to Invent*, 57.

69. Harrison, *Julip*, 17–18.

70. Ibid., 96, 4, 97.

71. Slotkin, *The Fatal Environment*, 20.

72. Ibid.

Bibliography

Primary Sources (chronological)

Fiction

Wolf: A False Memoir. New York: Simon and Schuster, 1971; New York: Strode, 1971; New York: Dell, 1981; New York: Delta/Seymour Lawrence, 1989.

A Good Day to Die. New York: Simon and Schuster, 1973; New York: Delta/Seymour Lawrence, 1981, 1989.

Farmer. New York: Viking Press, 1976; New York: Delta/Seymour Lawrence, 1980, 1989.

Legends of the Fall. New York: Delta/Seymour Lawrence, 1979 (limited signed edition); New York: Delta/Seymour Lawrence, 1979 (regular first edition); New York: Delta/Seymour Lawrence, 1979 (three-volume boxed set); New York: Delta/Seymour Lawrence, 1980, 1982, 1989.

Warlock. New York: Delta/Seymour Lawrence, 1981 (limited signed edition and regular first edition); New York: Delta/Seymour Lawrence, 1982.

Sundog. New York: E.P. Dutton/Seymour Lawrence, 1984; New York: Washington Square Press, 1991.

Dalva. New York: E.P. Dutton/Seymour Lawrence, 1988; New York: Washington Square Press, 1989.

The Woman Lit by Fireflies. New York: Houghton Mifflin, 1990; New York: Washington Square Press, 1990, 1991.

Julip. New York: Houghton Mifflin/Seymour Lawrence, 1994; New York: Washington Square Press, 1995.

The Road Home. New York: Atlantic Monthly Press, 1998.

The Beast God Forgot to Invent. New York: Atlantic Monthly Press, 2000.

Collected Nonfiction

Just before Dark: Collected Nonfiction. Livingston, Mont.: Clark City Press, 1991; New York: Houghton Mifflin, 1992.

Poetry

Plain Song. New York: W.W. Norton, 1965.

Walking. Cambridge, Mass.: Pym Randall Press, 1967 (100 numbered plus 20 signed and lettered copies).

Locations. New York: W.W. Norton, 1968.

Stony Brook Holographs. Stony Brook, N.Y.: Stony Brook Poets Foundation, 1968.

Outlyer and Ghazals. New York: Simon & Schuster, 1971.

Letters to Yesenin. Fremont, Mich.: Sumac Press, 1973 (1,000 softcover, 100 numbered, and 26 lettered hardbound copies).

Returning to Earth. Berkeley, Calif.: Ithaca House, 1977.

Letters to Yesenin and Returning to Earth. Los Angeles: Sumac Poetry Series Center Publications, 1979.

Selected and New Poems, 1961–1981. New York: Delacorte/Seymour Lawrence, 1981; New York: Delta/Seymour Lawrence, 1982.

The Theory and Practice of Rivers and Other Poems. Seattle: Winn Books, 1986 (signed limited edition).

The Theory and Practice of Rivers and New Poems. Livingston, Mont.: Clark City Press, 1989, 1990.

The Shape of the Journey: New and Collected Poems. Port Townsend, Wash: Copper Canyon Press, 1998.

Selected Articles and Essays

"Grim Reapers of the Land's Bounty." *Sports Illustrated* 35 (11 October 1971): 38–40ff.

"To Each His Own Chills and Thrills." *Sports Illustrated* 36 (7 February 1972): 30–34.

"Old Faithful and Mysterious." *Sports Illustrated* 36 (14 February 1972): 68–72ff.

"Where the Chase Is the Song of Hound and Horn." *Sports Illustrated* 36 (20 March 1972): 64–69ff.

"Plaster Trout in Worm Heaven." *Sports Illustrated* 36 (10 May 1972): 70–72ff. Reprinted in *Just before Dark*, 55–62.

"Machine with Two Pistons." *Sports Illustrated* 39 (27 August 1973): 36–38ff.

"Guiding Light in the Keys." *Sports Illustrated* 39 (3 December 1973): 78–81ff. Reprinted in *Just before Dark*, 109–19.

"Fishing." *Sports Illustrated* 41 (14 October 1974): 98ff.

"Marching to a Different Drummer." *Sports Illustrated* 41 (4 November 1974): 38–40ff.

"Salvation in the Keys." *Esquire* 85 (June 1976): 152–53.

"A River Never Sleeps." *Esquire* 86 (August 1976): 6.

"Not at All Like Up Home in Michigan." *Sports Illustrated* 45 (25 October 1976): 54–56ff.

"Advertisement." *New York Times Book Review* (19 September 1982): 35.

"The Revenge Symposium." *Esquire* 99 (May 1983): 88.

"Fording and Dread." *Smoke Signals: New York Bookfair Special Edition,* 23 August 1984, 20. Reprinted in *Just Before Dark.*

"From the *Dalva* Notebooks, 1985–87." *Antaeus* 61 (autumn 1988): 208–14. Reprinted in *Just before Dark, 283–89.*

"History as Torment." Preface to *"What thou lovest well remains": 100 Years of Ezra Pound.* Boise, Idaho: Limberlost Press, 1986.

"Don't Fence Me In." *Condé Naste Traveler* 24.3 (March 1989): 114–25. Reprinted in *Just before Dark, 184–92.*

"Poetry as Survival." *Antaeus* 64 (spring 1990): 370–80. Reprinted in *Just before Dark, 294–305.*

Preface to *Russell Chatham: One Hundred Paintings.* Livingston, Mont.: Clark City Press, 1990.

"The Raw and the Cooked." *Esquire.* A monthly column that ran from 1991–92.

"Great Poems Make Good Prayers." *Esquire* 109 (October 1993): 146–47.

"Pie in the Sky." *Esquire Sportsman* 2.2 (fall-winter 1993): 33–34.

"Nesting in Air." In *Northern Lights: A Selection of New Writing from the American West,* edited by Deborah Clow and Donald Snow, 262–64. New York: Vintage, 1994.

"The Beginner's Mind." In *Heart of the Land: Essays on Last Great Places,* edited by Joseph Barbato and Lisa Weinerman, 136–50. New York: Pantheon Books, 1995.

"Squaw Gulch." In *Who's Writing This: Notations on the Authorial I with Self-Portraits,* edited by Daniel Halpern. Hopewell, N.J.: The Ecco Press, 1995.

"The Beginner's Mind." In *Heart of the Land: Essays on Last Great Places,* edited by Joseph Bednarik and Lisa Weinerman, 136–44. Foreword by Barry Lopez. New York: Pantheon Books, 1996.

Foreword to *Diggin' in and Piggin' Out: The Truth about Food and Men.* By Roger Welsch. New York: HarperCollins, 1997.

"First Person Female." *New York Times Magazine,* 16 May 1999, 100–01.

Book Reviews

"California Hybrid." Review of *The Fork,* by Richard Duerden, *Against the Silence to Come,* by Ron Lowinsohn, *The Process,* by David Meltzer, *Out Out* by Lew Welch, and *Hermit Poems,* by Lew Welch. *Poetry* 108 (June 1966): 198–201.

Review of *Dying: An Introduction,* by L.E. Sissman. *New York Times Book Review,* 28 April 1968, 6.

Review of *All My Friends Are Going to Be Strangers,* by Larry McMurtry. *New York Times Book Review,* 19 March 1972, 5, 26.

"Three Novels: Comic, Cute, Cool." Review of *Geronimo Rex,* by Barry Hannah. *New York Times Book Review,* 14 May 1972, 4.

"The Main Character in the Cold and the Snow." Review of *The Snow Walker,* by Farley Mowat. *New York Times Book Review,* 22 February 1976, 4–5. Reprinted in *Just before Dark,* 250–53.

Review of *The Monkey Wrench Gang,* by Edward Abbey. *New York Times,* 14 November 1976, 59.

"10,000 Successive Octobers." Review of *The Snow Leopard,* by Peter Matthiessen. *The Nation* 227.8 (16 September 1978): 250–51. Reprinted in *Just before Dark,* 253–56.

"Voice in the Wilderness." Review of *Sand River,* by Peter Matthiessen. *New York Times Book Review,* 17 May 1981, 1, 26.

*** A lengthy correspondence between Harrison and Thomas McGuane spanning twenty-five years is housed in Special Collections in the Michigan State University Libraries. Other of Harrison's papers are housed at the University of Arkansas.

Critical Sources Consulted

Abbey, Edward. *Confessions of a Barbarian: Selections from the Journals of Edward Abbey, 1951–1989,* edited by David Petersen. New York: Little, Brown, 1994.

———. *The Monkey Wrench Gang.* Philadelphia: Lippincott, 1975.

Abbott, Raymond. "Savages and Sioux." Review of *Dalva,* by Jim Harrison. *New York Times Book Review,* 12 June 1988, 28.

Adams, Carol J. "The Sexual Politics of Meat." In *Living with Contradictions: Controversies in Feminist Social Ethics,* edited by Alison M. Jaggar, 548–57. Boulder, Colo.: Westview Press, 1994.

Adorno, Theodor. *Negative Dialectics.* New York: Seabury Press, 1973.

Agee, Jonis. "The Macho Chronicles." Review of *Julip,* by Jim Harrison. *New York Times Book Review,* 22 May 1994, sec. 7, p. 41.

Alfrey, Shawn. *The Sublime of Intense Sociability: Emily Dickinson, H. D., and Gertrude Stein.* Lewisburg, Pa.: Bucknell University Press, 2000.

Allen, Walter. *The Urgent West: The American Dream and Modern Man.* New York: E.P. Dutton & Co., Inc., 1969.

Ames, Sanford. "Fast Food/Quick Lunch: Crews, Burroughs and Pynchon." In *Literary Gastronomy,* edited by David Bevan, 19–27. Amsterdam: Rodopi, 1988.

Anderson, Quentin. *Making Americans: An Essay on Individualism and Money.* New York: Harcourt, 1992.

Andriano, Joseph D. *Immortal Monster: The Mythological Evolution of the Fantastic Beast in Modern Fiction and Film.* Westport, Conn.: Greenwood Press, 1999.

Ashley, Kathleen, Leigh Gilmore, and Gerald Peters, eds. *Autobiography and Postmodernism.* Amherst, Mass.: University of Massachusetts Press, 1994.

Auer, Tom. "A Man Lit by Passion." *The Bloomsbury Review,* November/December 1990, 1, 16.

Auster, Paul. *Leviathan.* New York: Viking, 1992.

Bakhtin, Mikhail. *Problems of Dostoevsky's Poetics,* edited and translated by Caryl Emerson. Minneapolis: University of Minnesota Press, 1984.

Baldwin, Kenneth H., and David K. Kirby, ed. "Introduction." *Individual and Community: Variations on a Theme in American Fiction.* Durham, N.C.: Duke University Press, 1975.

Barillas, William David. "Place and Landscape in Midwestern American Literature." Ph.D. diss., Michigan State University, 1994.

Barnett, Louise K. *Authority and Speech: Language, Society, and Self in the American Novel.* Athens, Ga.: University of Georgia Press, 1993.

Barth, John. *The Floating Opera.* Garden City, N.J.: Doubleday, 1967.

———. "The Literature of Exhaustion." *Atlantic Monthly* 220.2 (August 1967): 29–34.

Bass, Rick. *The Lost Grizzlies: A Search for Survivors in the Wilderness of Colorado.* Boston: Houghton Mifflin Co., 1995.

Baym, Nina. *Feminism and American Literary History: Essays.* New Brunswick, N.J.: Rutgers University Press, 1992.

Bednarik, Joseph. "On Becoming a Tree: Talking with Jim Harrison." *Silverfish Review* 20 (spring 1991): 24–37.

———. "A Conversation with Jim Harrison." *Northwest Review* 33.2 (1995): 106–118.

Behler, Ernst. *Irony and the Discourse of Modernity.* Seattle: University of Washington Press, 1990.

Bell, Ian F. A., and D. K. Adams. *American Literary Landscapes: The Fiction and the Fact.* London: Vision Press, 1988.

Bell, Michael. *Literature, Modernism and Myth: Belief and Responsibility in the Twentieth Century.* Cambridge, England: Cambridge University Press, 1997.

Bellin, Joshua David. *The Demon of the Continent: Indians and the Shaping of American Literature.* Philadelphia: University of Pennsylvania Press, 2001.

Bennett, John W. *Human Ecology as Human Behavior: Essays in Environmental and Development Anthropology.* New Brunswick, N.J.: Transaction Publishers, 1992.

Berry, Wendell. *Home Economics.* San Francisco: North Point Press, 1987.

Bevan, David, ed. *Literary Gastronomy.* Amsterdam: Rodopi, 1988.

Bevier, Tom. "Author Falls for the Film Version of *Legends.*" *Detroit News,* 30 January 1995, 1C, 8C.

Biallas, Leonard J. *Myths: Gods, Heroes, and Saviors.* Mystic, Conn.: Twenty-Third Publications, 1986.

Bible. New King James Version. Nashville, Tenn.: Thomas Nelson Publishers, 1990.

Birkerts, Sven. *American Energies: Essays on Fiction.* New York: William Morrow and Company, 1992.

Blackburn, Sara. *New York Times Book Review,* 9 September 1973, 4,5.

Blades, John. "Untamed Characters: Jim Harrison's World Gets Hollywood Attention." *Chicago Tribune,* 16 May 1994, sec. 5: 2.

Blair, Walter. "Was *Huckleberry Finn* Written?" In *The Critical Response to Mark Twain's Huckleberry Finn,* edited by Laurie Champion, 108–12. New York: Greenwood Press, 1991.

Bloom, Harold, ed. *Mark Twain.* New York: Chelsea, 1986.

Bloomfield, Morton W. *Allegory, Myth, and Symbol.* Cambridge, Mass.: Harvard University Press, 1981.

Bluefarb, Sam. *The Escape Motif in the American Novel: Mark Twain to Richard Wright.* Columbus, Ohio: Ohio State University Press, 1972.

Bohy, Ric. "Jim Harrison, The Mad Poet Cools Off (a Little)." *Michigan: The Magazine of the Detroit News,* 9 February 1986, 8–10, 14, 16–18.

Bokina, John, and Timothy J. Lukes. *Marcuse: From the New Left to the Next Left.* Lawrence, Kans.: University Press of Kansas, 1994.

Bolle, Kees W. *The Freedom of Man in Myth.* Nashville, Tenn.: Vanderbilt University Press, 1968.

Bolles, Robert C., ed. *The Hedonics of Taste.* Hillsdale, N.J.: Lawrence Erlbaum Associates, Publishers, 1991.

Bonetti, Kay. *Conversations with American Novelists.* Edited by Kay Bonetti, Greg Michalson, Speer Morgan, Jo Sapp, and Sam Stowers, 39–55. Columbia: University of Missouri Press, 1997.

———. "An Interview with Jim Harrison." *Missouri Review* 8.3 (1985): 65–86.

———. "An Interview with Jim Harrison." Audiocassette. American Audio Prose Library, 1985.

Booth, David A. "Learned Ingestive Motivation and the Pleasures of the Palate." In *The Hedonics of Taste,* edited by Robert C. Bolles, 29–58. Hillsdale, N.J.: Lawrence Erlbaum Associates, Publishers, 1991.

Bourdieu, Pierre. *Distinction.* Cambridge, Mass.: Harvard University Press, 1984.

Bourjaily, Vance. "Three Novellas: Violent Means." Review of *Legends of the Fall,* by Jim Harrison. *New York Times Book Review,* 17 June 1979, 14, 27.

Brandt, Anthony. "Man of the Moment Jim Harrison: Season of the Wolf." *Men's Journal* (June-July 1994): 96–98, 137.

Brans, Jo. *Feast Here Awhile: Adventures in American Eating*. New York: Ticknor & Fields, 1993.

Brillat-Savarin, Jean Anthelme. *The Philosopher in the Kitchen*. New York: Penguin Books, 1981.

Brockway, Robert W. *Myth from the Ice Age to Mickey Mouse*. Albany, N.Y.: State University of New York Press, 1993.

Brooker, Peter, ed. *Modernism/Postmodernism*. London: Longman, 1992.

Brown, Sharon Rogers. *American Travel Narratives as a Literary Genre from 1542–1832: The Art of a Perpetual Journey*. Lewiston, N.Y.: Edwin Mellen Press, 1993.

Bruce, Ranald. "Less is More: Writers at the End of the Twentieth Century." *Millenium Studies* <http:\\www.millennaire.com\fds\ch3b1.htm>.

Bruni, Frank. "*Legends* Falls under the Weight of its Pretensions." *Detroit Free Press*, 13 January 1995, metro final ed.: 4D.

———. "*Wolf* Stalks Territory That's Unfamiliar." *Detroit Free Press*, 17 June 1994, metro final ed.: 1D.

———. "Writer's Wild Dream Comes Alive on Film." *Detroit Free Press*, 14 June 1994, metro final ed.: 1D.

Buege, Douglas J. "The Ecologically Noble Savage Revisited." *Environmental Ethics* 18 (1996): 71–88.

Buell, Lawrence. *The Environmental Imagination: Thoreau, Nature Writing, and the Formation of American Culture*. Cambridge, Mass.: Belknap Press of Harvard University Press, 1995.

Buettler, Bill. "Sensitive Look at Midlife Fuels Harrison's *Fireflies*." *Atlanta Journal-Constitution*, 26 August 1990, N8.

Burke, John Gordon. *Regional Perspectives: An Examination of America's Literary Heritage*. Chicago: American Library Association, 1973.

Burkholder, Robert E. *Dictionary of Literary Biography Yearbook 1982*. Edited by Richard Ziegfield. Detroit: Gale Research/Bruccoli Clark, 1983.

Busby, Mark. "The Significance of the Frontier in Contemporary American Literature." In *The Frontier Experience and the American Dream: Essays on American Literature*, edited by David Mogen, Mark Busby, and Paul Bryant, 95–103. College Station, Tex.: Texas A & M University Press, 1989.

Carafiol, Peter. *The American Ideal: Literary History as a Worldly Activity*. New York: Oxford University Press, 1991.

Carpenter, Scott. "Demythification in *Adventures of Huckleberry Finn*." *Studies in American Fiction* 15.2 (1987): 211–17.

Carr, Helen. *Inventing the American Primitive: Politics, Gender and the Representation of Native American Literary Traditions, 1789–1936*. Cork, Ireland: Cork University Press, 1996.

Carroll, Joseph. *Evolution and Literary Theory*. Columbia, Mo.: University of Missouri Press, 1995.

Carruth, Hayden. Review of *Letters to Yesenin,* by Jim Harrison. *Harper's,* June 1978, 87–88.

Carson, Rachel. *Silent Spring.* Boston: Houghton Mifflin, 1962.

Casey, John D. "American Settings." Review of *Warlock,* by Jim Harrison. *New York Times Book Review,* 22 November 1981, 14, 45.

Cather, Willa. *My Ántonia.* Foreword by Doris Grumbach. Boston: Houghton Mifflin, 1988.

Champion, Laurie. *The Critical Response to Mark Twain's Huckleberry Finn.* New York: Greenwood Press, 1991.

Chaplin, Gordon. "More Mad Dogs and Fewer Streetlamps." *Washington Post,* 2 March 1980, F1, F3–4.

Chenetier, Marc. "History in Contemporary American Fiction, or 'The Constrained Nightmare.'" In *History and Post-War Writing,* edited by Theo D'haen and Hans Bertens. Amersterdam: Rodopi, 1990.

Cheuse, Alan. "Jim Harrison's Misfits: A Fatherless Woman, an Upper Peninsula Rogue and a Victimized Academic." *Chicago Tribune,* 8 May 1994, sec. 14: 5.

Cioran, E. M. *The Trouble with Being Born.* Translated by Richard Howard. New York: Viking Press, 1976.

Claridge, Henry. "Writing on the Margin: E.L. Doctorow and American History." In *Essays on American Literature since 1970,* edited by Graham Clarke. London: Vision Press, 1990.

Cline, Sally. *Just Desserts: Women and Food.* London: Andre Deutsch, 1990.

Clough, Wilson O. *The Necessary Earth: Nature and Solitude in American Literature.* Austin, Tex.: University of Texas Press, 1964.

Clute, John. "Elegiac Heirs." Review of *Dalva,* by Jim Harrison. *Times Literary Supplement,* 24 March 1989, 299.

Coates, Joseph. "Bedrock Americana: Jim Harrison Speaks of Worlds Where Nature and Spirit Are One." *Chicago Tribune,* 12 August 1990, sec. 14:1+.

Collard, Andree, with Joyce Contrucci. "Shots in the Dark." In *Living with Contradictions: Controversies in Feminist Social Ethics,* edited by Alison M. Jaggar, 563–66. Boulder, Colo.: Westview Press, 1994.

Collins, Nancy. "Wolf, Man, Jack." *Vanity Fair* 57.4 (1994): 118–24, 166–70.

Colonnese, Tom. "Jim Harrison: A Checklist." *Bulletin of Bibliography* 39.3 (September 1982): 132–35.

Connor, Steven. *Postmodern Culture: An Introduction to Theories of the Contemporary.* London: Basil Blackwell, 1989.

Coughlin, Ruth. "Lord Jim." Review of *Julip,* by Jim Harrison. *Detroit News,* 18 May 1994, C3.

Coughlin, Ruth. "The Man Who Likes Empty Spaces." *Detroit News,* 14 August 1990, C1+.

Couser, G. Thomas. *Altered Egos: Authority in American Autobiography.* New York: Oxford University Press, 1989.

Cowart, David. *History and the Contemporary Novel.* Carbondale, Ill.: Southern Illinois University Press, 1989.

Cronon, William, ed. *Uncommon Ground: Toward Reinventing Nature.* New York: W.W. Norton & Company, 1995.

Cross, Robert. "Siren Song: Will Success Lure Poet-Novelist Jim Harrison Out of His Midwestern Lair?" *Chicago Tribune,* 30 August 1992, sec. 10: 14–18; 24.

Crow Dog, Mary. *Lakota Woman.* New York: HarperPerennial, 1990.

Darling, David. "An Interview with Jim Harrison: Thoughts on Independence in Publishing and Bookselling." *Independent Publisher* (March/April 1999): 8–11, 17.

Day, R. Morris. "Thief Treaties and Lie-Talk Councils." In *Forked Tongues and Broken Treaties,* edited by Donald E. Worcester. Caldwell, Idaho: Caxton Publishers, Ltd., 1975.

Debord, Guy. *The Society of the Spectacle.* Translated by Donald Nicholson-Smith. New York: Zone Books, 1994.

Delbanco, Nicholas. "A Perfect Union: Varied Novellas Are Connected by Harrison's Voice." *Detroit Free Press,* 12 August 1990, metro final ed.: 7Q.

Deloria, Vine, Jr. Foreword to *One Hundred Million Acres,* edited by Kirke Kickingbird and Karen Ducheneaux. New York: Macmillan, 1973.

DeMott, Robert J. *Steinbeck's Typewriter.* Troy, N.Y.: Whitston Publishing Co., 1996.

DeMott, Robert J., and Sanford E. Marovitz, eds. *Artful Thunder: Versions of the Romantic Tradition in American Literature.* Kent, Ohio: Kent State University Press, 1975.

Derwin, Susan. "Impossible Commands: Reading *Adventures of Huckleberry Finn.*" *Nineteenth-Century Literature* 47.4 (1993): 437–54.

Dettman, Marc. "Legends of the North." *Grand Rapids* 19.8 (August 1982): 30–34.

Deveson, Richard. "Call of the Wild." Review of *Sundog,* by Jim Harrison. *NS,* 23 August 1985, 28.

Dimock, Wai Chee, and Michael T. Gilmore, eds. *Rethinking Class: Literary Studies and Social Formations.* New York: Columbia University Press, 1994.

Docherty, Thomas, ed. *Postmodernism.* New York: Columbia University Press, 1993.

Douglas, Mary. *Implicit Meanings: Essays in Anthropology.* London: Routledge & Kegan Paul, 1975.

———. *Natural Symbols: Explorations in Cosmology.* New York: Pantheon Books, 1982.

————. *Purity and Danger: An Analysis of Concepts of Pollution and Taboo.* London: Routledge & Kegan Paul, 1966.

————, ed. *Constructive Drinking: Perspectives on Drink from Anthropology.* Cambridge, England: Cambridge University Press, 1987.

Douglas, Mary, and Aaron Wildavsky. *Risk and Culture: An Essay on the Selection of Technical and Environmental Dangers.* Berkeley, Calif.: University of California Press, 1982.

Duffy, Mike. "Flowery *Dalva* Salvaged Only by Fawcett's Beauty." *Detroit Free Press,* 1 March 1996, metro final ed.: 4F.

Edwards, Brian. *Theories of Play and Postmodern Fiction.* New York: Garland, 1998.

Eiseley, Loren. *The Immense Journey: An Imaginative Naturalist Explores the Mysteries of Man and Nature.* New York: Random House, 1957.

Elliott, Ira, and Marty Sommerness. "Jim Harrison: A Good Day for Talking: An Interview with the Author of *Wolf* and *Farmer.*" *October Chronicle* (29 October 1976): unpaginated. 8 pages.

Elsbree, Langdon. "Our Pursuit of Loneliness: An Alternative to This Paradigm." In *The Frontier Experience and the American Dream: Essays on American Literature,* edited by David Mogen, Mark Busby, and Paul Bryant, 31–49. College Station, Tex.: Texas A & M University Press, 1989.

————. *Ritual Passages and Narrative Structures.* New York: Peter Lang, 1991.

Ermarth, Elizabeth Deeds. *Sequel to History: Postmodernism and the Crisis of Representational Time.* Princeton, N.J.: Princeton University Press, 1992.

Falck, Colin. *Myth, Truth, and Literature: Towards a True Post-Modernism.* Cambridge, England: Cambridge University Press, 1989.

Fanning, Patrick. Review of *A Good Day to Die,* by Jim Harrison. *Library Journal,* 15 September 1973, 2570.

Farber, David, ed. *The Sixties.* Chapel Hill, N.C.: University of North Carolina Press, 1994.

Review of *Farmer,* by Jim Harrison. *New Yorker,* 30 August 1976, 90.

Review of *Farmer,* by Jim Harrison. *Library Journal,* 15 June 1976, 1446.

Review of *Farmer,* by Jim Harrison. *Publishers Weekly,* 31 May 1976, 191.

Feenberg, Andrew. "The Critique of Technology: From Dystopia to Interaction." In *Marcuse: From the New Left to the Next Left,* edited by John Bokina and Timothy J. Lukes, 208–26. Lawrence, Kans.: University Press of Kansas, 1994.

Fergus, Jim. "The Art of Fiction CIV: Jim Harrison." *Paris Review* 30 (1988): 52–97.

————. "Jim Harrison: Today's Hemingway?" *MD* (May 1985): 116, 118–19, 244–46.

——. "The Sporting Club." *Outside* (March 1989): 40–44; 112–117.

Ferrari-Adler, Jofie. "Lives Deeply Connected." Review of *The Road Home,* by Jim Harrison. *St. Petersburg (Fla.) Times,* 4 October 1998, 5D.

Fiedler, Leslie. *Love and Death in the American Novel.* New York: Stein and Day, 1966.

——. *No! in Thunder: Essays on Myth and Literature.* London: Lowe & Brydone, 1963.

Fieldhouse, Paul. *Food and Nutrition: Customs and Culture.* London: Croom Helm, 1986.

Fishkin, Shelley Fisher. *Lighting Out for the Territory: Reflections on Mark Twain and American Culture.* New York: Oxford University Press, 1997.

Fite, Gilbert. "Panel: The Realities of Regionalism." *South Dakota Review* 26.4 (1988): 83–86.

——. *Was Huck Black?: Mark Twain and African-American Voices.* New York: Oxford University Press, 1993.

Fowler, P. J. "The Contemporary Past." In *Landscape and Culture: Geographical and Archaelogical Perspectives,* edited by J. M. Wagstaff, 173–91. London: Basil Blackwell, 1987.

Franklin, Benjamin. *The Autobiography of Benjamin Franklin,* edited by Leonard W. Labaree, Ralph L. Ketcham, Helen C. Boatfield, and Helene H. Fineman. New Haven, Conn.: Yale University Press, 1964.

Franks, Jill. "The Regionalist Community." In *Regionalism Reconsidered: New Approaches to the Field,* edited by David Jordan, 87–103. New York: Garland Publishing, Inc., 1994.

Freeman, Judith. "Women's Intimations." Review of *The Woman Lit by Fireflies,* by Jim Harrison. *Los Angeles Times Book Review,* 19 August 1990, 1, 5.

Gallagher, Winifred. *The Power of Place: How Our Surroundings Shape Our Thoughts, Emotions, and Actions.* New York: Poseidon Press, 1993.

Garcia, Wilma. *Mothers and Others: Myths of the Female in the Works of Melville, Twain, and Hemingway.* New York: Peter Lang, 1984.

Gerstel, Judy. "A Vulnerable Predator: Jim Harrison Writes with a Keen, Compassionate Eye." *Detroit Free Press,* 15 August 1990, metro final ed.: 1D.

Gilligan, Thomas Maher. "Myth and Reality in Jim Harrison's *Warlock.*" *Critique: Studies in Contemporary Fiction* 25.3 (spring 1984): 147–53.

Gilmore, Leigh. "Policing Truth: Confession, Gender, and Autobiographical Authority." In *Autobiography and Postmodernism,* edited by Kathleen Ashley, Leigh Gilmore, and Gerald Peters, 54–78. Amherst, Mass.: University of Massachusetts Press, 1994.

Golze, Alfred R., ed. *Handbook of Dam Engineering.* New York: Van Nostrand Reinhold Co., 1977.

Review of *A Good Day to Die,* by Jim Harrison. *Publishers Weekly,* 16 July 1973, 108.

Review of *A Good Day to Die,* by Jim Harrison. *New York Times Book Review,* 9 September 1973, 4.

Gould, Eric. *Mythical Intentions in Modern Literature.* Princeton, N.J.: Princeton University Press, 1981.

Grant, Douglas. *Purpose and Place: Essays on American Writers.* New York: St. Martin's Press, 1965.

Green, Martin. *The Adventurous Male: Chapters in the History of the White Male Mind.* University Park, Pa.: Pennsylvania State University Press, 1993.

Greene, A.C. "The Man-God of the Michigan Jungles." Review of *Sundog,* by Jim Harrison. *New York Times Book Review,* 15 July 1984, 14.

Gross, Theodore L. *The Heroic Ideal in American Literature.* New York: The Free Press, 1971.

Gruen, Lori. "Dismantling Oppression: An Analysis of the Connection between Women and Animals." In *Living with Contradictions: Controversies in Feminist Social Ethics,* edited by Alison M. Jaggar, 537–48. Boulder, Colo.: Westview Press, 1994.

Gura, Philip F. *The Crossroads of American History and Literature.* University Park, Pa.: Pennsylvania State University Press, 1996.

Gurke, Leo. "Hemingway and the Magical Journey." In *Hemingway: A Revaluation,* edited by Donald R. Noble, 67–82. Troy, N.Y.: Whitson Publishing Company, 1983.

Gusfield, Joseph R. "Nature's Body and the Metaphors of Food." In *Cultivating Differences: Symbolic Boundaries and the Making of Inequality,* edited by Michèle Lamont and Marcel Fournier, 75–103. Chicago: University of Chicago Press, 1992.

———. "Passage to Play: Rituals of Drinking Time in American Society." In *Constructive Drinking: Perspectives on Drink from Anthropology,* edited by Mary Douglas, 73–90. Cambridge, Eng.: Cambridge University Press, 1987.

Guy, David. "Visiting Inner Worlds 'Just before Dark.'" *USA Today,* 25 July 1991, D8.

Hacker, David. "Of Bears, Bars and Books: Author Jim Harrison Looks down the Road at Writing." *Detroit Free Press,* 2 March 1988, metro final chaser: 3D.

Haesaerts, Paul. *James Ensor.* New York: Harry N. Abrams, Inc., 1959.

Haines, John. *Fables and Distances: New and Selected Essays.* Saint Paul, Minn.: Graywolf Press, 1996.

Halliburton, Richard. *Richard Halliburton: His Story of His Life's Adventure, As Told in Letters to His Mother and Father.* Indianapolis, Ind.: Bobbs-Merrill Company, 1940.

Hammill, James. "Wolf Recovery in Michigan." <http://metis.usa.net/Wolf Home/wolfrmic. html>.

Harper, Phillip Brian. *Framing the Margins: The Social Logic of Postmodern Culture*. New York: Oxford University Press, 1994.

Harpham, Geoffrey Galt. *The Ascetic Imperative in Culture and Criticism*. Chicago: University of Chicago Press, 1987.

Harrington, Maureen. "A Man's Man Has Knack for Sounding a Woman's Voice." *Denver Post*, 9 September 1990, E8.

Harris, Marvin. *Good to Eat: Riddles of Food and Culture*. New York: Simon and Schuster, 1985.

Harris, Marvin, and Eric B. Ross, eds. *Food and Evolution: Toward a Theory of Human Food Habits*. Philadelphia: Temple University Press, 1987.

Harrison, Alexander. "Seeking New Frontiers." Review of *Julip*, by Jim Harrison. *Times Literary Supplement*, 25 November 1994, 20.

Harrison, Jim. Interview. *American Literary History* 11.2 (summer 1999): 274–76.

———. Interview by Robert J. DeMott and Patrick A. Smith. Tape recording. Leelanau, Mich., 28–30 August 1997.

———. Interview by Robert J. DeMott and Patrick A. Smith. Tape recording. Leelanau, Mich., 24–26 July 1998.

Hassan, Ihab. *The Dismemberment of Orpheus: Toward a Postmodern Literature*. Madison, Wis.: University of Wisconsin Press, 1982.

Hayles, N. Katherine, ed. *Chaos and Order: Complex Dynamics in Literature and Science*. Chicago: University of Chicago Press, 1991.

Heidt, Edward R. *Vision Voiced: Narrative Viewpoint in Autobiographical Writing*. New York: Peter Lang, 1991.

Hillman, James. *A Blue Fire: Selected Writings*. Introduced and edited by Thomas Moore. New York: Harper & Row, 1989.

———. *The Dream and the Underworld*. New York: Harper & Row, 1979.

———. *Healing Fiction*. Barrytown, N.Y.: Station Hill, 1983.

Holman, David Marion. *A Certain Slant of Light: Regionalism and the Form of Southern and Midwestern Fiction*. Baton Rouge, La.: Louisiana State University Press, 1995.

Houston, Robert. "Love for the Proper Outlaw." *New York Times Book Review*, 16 September 1990, sec. 7: 13.

Howe, Parkman. "Two Novels Accent Self-Discovery." Review of *Farmer*, by Jim Harrison. *Christian Science Monitor*, 27 January 1977, 23.

Huey, Michael C. "Writing and Telling in Harrison's Latest." Review of *Dalva*, by Jim Harrison. *Christian Science Monitor*, 13 June 1988, 19.

Iggers, Jeremy. *The Garden of Eating: Food, Sex, and the Hunger for Meaning*. New York: Basic Books, 1996.

Inglis, James Gale. *Northern Michigan Handbook for Travelers, Including the Northern Part of Lower Michigan, Mackinac Island, and Sault Ste. Marie River, with Maps and Illustrations*. Petoskey, Mich.: Geo. E. Sprang, 1898.

Irons, Glenwood. *Gender, Language, and Myth: Essays on Popular Narrative.* Toronto: University of Toronto Press, 1992.

Israelsen, Orson W., and Vaughn E. Hansen. *Irrigation Principles and Practices.* 3d ed. New York: John Wiley and Sons, Inc., 1962.

Iyer, Pico. "Romancing the Home." *The Nation,* 23 June 1984, 767–71.

Jackson, Donald C. *Building the Ultimate Dam: John S. Eastwood and the Control of Water in the West.* Lawrence, Kans.: University Press of Kansas, 1995.

Jacobs, Naomi. *The Character of Truth: Historical Figures in Contemporary Fiction.* Carbondale, Ill.: Southern Illinois University Press, 1990.

Jaggar, Alison M. *Living with Contradictions: Controversies in Feminist Social Ethics.* Boulder, Colo.: Westview Press, 1994.

Jameson, Fredric. *Postmodernism: or, the Cultural Logic of Late Capitalism.* Durham, N.C.: Duke University Press, 1991.

Jerome, John. "Caution: Men Writing." *Washington Post,* 28 July 1991, WBK6.

Jezer, Marty. *The Dark Ages: Life in the United States, 1945–1960.* Boston: South End Press, 1982.

Jones-Davis, Georgia. "The Literary Seductions of a Macho Woman." Review of *Dalva,* by Jim Harrison. *Los Angeles Times Book Review,* 10 April 1988, 12.

Jordan, David, ed. *Regionalism Reconsidered: New Approaches to the Field.* New York: Garland Publishing, Inc., 1994.

Kakutani, Michiko. "Books of the Times." Review of *Sundog,* by Jim Harrison. *New York Times,* 21 May 1984, 17.

———. "Epic America in a Woman's Quest." Review of *Dalva,* by Jim Harrison. *New York Times,* 9 March 1988, C25.

———. "The Shapes and Textures of Three Lives." Review of *The Woman Lit by Fireflies,* by Jim Harrison. *New York Times,* 28 August 1990, C16.

Kartiganer, Donald M., and Malcolm A. Griffith. *Theories of American Literature.* New York: Macmillan, 1972.

Kass, Leon R. *The Hungry Soul: Eating and the Perfecting of Our Nature.* New York: The Free Press, 1994.

Kazin, Alfred. *A Writer's America.* New York: Alfred A. Knopf, 1988.

Keats, John. *Complete Poems and Selected Letters.* Edited by Clarence DeWitt Thorpe. New York: The Odyssey, Inc., 1935.

Kehoe, Alice Beck. *North American Indians: A Comprehensive Account.* Englewood Cliffs, N.J.: Prentice-Hall, 1981.

Kiell, Norman. *Food and Drink in Literature: A Selectively Annotated Bibliography.* Lanham, Md.: Scarecrow Press, Inc., 1995.

Killinger, John. *The Fragile Presence: Transcendence in Modern Literature.* Philadelphia: Fortress Press, 1973.

Kogan, Rick. "Alas, *Warlock* Casts No Spell to Hold Reader." Review of *Warlock,* by Jim Harrison. *Chicago Sun-Times,* 18 October 1981.

Kolodny, Annette. *The Lay of the Land: Metaphors of Experience and History in American Life and Letters.* Chapel Hill, N.C.: University of North Carolina Press, 1975.

Kotarba, Joseph, and Andrea Fontana, eds. *The Existential Self in Society.* Chicago: University of Chicago Press, 1984.

Kowalewski, Michael. "Bioregional Perspective in American Literature." In *Regionalism Reconsidered: New Approaches to the Field,* edited by David Jordan, 29–46. New York: Garland Publishing, Inc., 1994.

———. "Writing in Place: The New American Regionalism." *American Literary History* 6.1 (1994): 171–83.

Kravitz, Bennett. *Dreaming Mark Twain.* Lanham, Md.: University Press of America, Inc., 1996.

Krupat, Arnold. *The Turn to the Native: Studies in Criticism and Culture.* Lincoln, Nebr.: University of Nebraska Press, 1996.

Krystal, Arthur. "Jim Harrison: Three for the Road." *Washington Post,* 2 September 1990, WBK7.

Küchler, Tilman. *Postmodern Gaming: Heidegger, Duchamp, Derrida.* New York: Peter Lang, 1994.

Lamont, Michèle, and Marcel Fournier. *Cultivating Differences: Symbolic Boundaries and the Making of Inequality.* Chicago: University of Chicago Press, 1992.

Lannon, Linnea. "Readers Who Got Cross over *Bridges* Are Fewer." *Detroit Free Press,* 11 July 1993, metro final ed.: 6J.

Lauter, Estella, and Carol Schreier Rupprecht, eds. *Feminist Archetypal Theory: Interdisciplinary Re-Visions of Jungian Thought.* Knoxville, Tenn.: University of Tennessee Press, 1985.

Lawrence, D. H. *Studies in Classic American Literature.* Garden City, N.Y.: Doubleday, 1953.

Lee, A. Robert. *First Person Singular: Studies in American Autobiography.* London: Vision Press, 1988.

Review of *Legends of the Fall,* by Jim Harrison. *Atlantic Monthly,* September 1979, 92.

Review of *Legends of the Fall,* by Jim Harrison. *Publishers Weekly,* 19 March 1979, 87.

Legler, Gretchen. "Hunting: A Woman's Perspective." In *Living with Contradictions: Controversies in Feminist Social Ethics,* edited by Alison M. Jaggar, 560–63. Boulder, Colo.: Westview Press, 1994.

Lehmann-Haupt, Christopher. "Celebrations of the Natural." Review of *Farmer,* by Jim Harrison. *New York Times,* 26 July 1976, 21.

———. "The Woods Are Ugly, Cold, Wet." Review of *Wolf,* by Jim Harrison. *New York Times,* 24 November 1971, 33.

Levin, David. *In Defense of Historical Literature: Essays on American History, Autobiography, Drama, and Fiction.* New York: Hill and Wang, 1967.

Lévi-Strauss, Claude. *Anthropology and Myth: Lectures 1951–1982*. Translated by Roy Willis. London: Basil Blackwell, 1987.

———. *The Raw and the Cooked*. Translated by John and Doreen Weightman. Chicago: Chicago University Press, 1983.

Liebrum, Martha. "A Man of the Woods Writing about Women." *Houston Post*, 2 September 1990, C6.

Lockwood, Yvonne R., and William G. Lockwood. "Pasties in Michigan's Upper Peninsula: Foodways, Interethnic Relations, and Regionalism." *Creative Ethnicity: Symbols and Strategies of Contemporary Ethnic Life*, edited by Stephen Stern and John Allan Cicala. Logan, Utah: Utah State University Press, 1991.

Long, Timothy. "Chronicler of Macho Angst Takes a New Direction." *Boston Globe*, 5 August 1994, BG49.

Longyear, John Munro. *Landlooker in the Upper Peninsula of Michigan*. Marquette, Mich.: Marquette County Historical Society of Michigan, 1960.

Lopez, Barry. "The American Geographies." In *Finding Home: Writing on Nature and Culture from Orion Magazine*, edited by Peter Sauer, 116–32. Boston: Beacon Press, 1992.

Lopez, Barry Holstun. *Of Wolves and Men*. New York: Scribner's, 1978.

Loriggio, Francesco. "Regionalism and Theory." In *Regionalism Reconsidered: New Approaches to the Field*, edited by David Jordan, 3–27. New York: Garland Publishing, Inc., 1994.

Love, Keith. "Literary Voices in the Wilderness." *Los Angeles Times*, 12 April 1988, sec. VI: 1, 4–5.

Luke, Timothy W. "Marcuse and Ecology." In *Marcuse: From the New Left to the Next Left*, edited by John Bokina and Timothy J. Lukes, 189–207. Lawrence, Kans.: University Press of Kansas, 1994.

Lutholtz, M. William. "Tough Guy in Tender Times." Review of *Legends of the Fall*, by Jim Harrison. *Christian Science Monitor*, 5 September 1979, 19.

Lynch, Thomas. "Jim Harrison, Splendid Poet, Goes on a Spiritual Pilgrimage." *Detroit Free Press*, 20 October 1996

Lyons, Daniel. "Author Returns to Short Stories, but with Less Power than Before." *Detroit Free Press*, 20 March 1996, metro final ed.: 3C.

Lyotard, Jean-François. "Answering the Question: What is Postmodernism?" In *Postmodernism*, edited by Thomas Docherty, 38–46. New York: Columbia University Press, 1993.

———. "Note on the Meaning of 'Post-.'" In *Postmodernism*, edited by Thomas Docherty, 47–50. New York: Columbia University Press, 1993.

McClintock, James I. "Dalva: Jim Harrison's 'Twin Sister.'" *Journal of Men's Studies* 6.3 (spring 1998): 319–330.

McHale, Brian. *Postmodernist Fiction*. New York: Methuen, 1987.

McIntosh, Elaine N. *American Food Habits in Historical Perspective*. Westport, Conn.: Praeger, 1995.

McNamee, Thomas. "O Pioneers!" Review of *The Road Home,* by Jim Harrison. *New York Times Book Review,* 8 November 1998, 11.

McVay, Gordon. *Esenin: A Life.* Ann Arbor, Mich.: Ardis, 1976.

Magnusson, Paul. "Comic Parody of the Macho Image." *Detroit Free Press,* 18 October 1981, 5B.

Mallory, William E., and Paul Simpson-Housley, eds. *Geography and Literature: A Meeting of Disciplines.* Syracuse, N.Y.: Syracuse University Press, 1987.

Marowski, Daniel G., and Jean C. Stine, eds. "Jim Harrison." *Contemporary Literary Criticism.* Vol. 33. Detroit: Gale Research Company, 1985.

Martin, Lisa. "Feminism and Vegetarianism." In *Living with Contradictions: Controversies in Feminist Social Ethics,* edited by Alison M. Jaggar, 557–60. Boulder, Colo.: Westview Press, 1994.

Marx, Leo. *The Machine in the Garden: Technology and the Pastoral Ideal.* New York: Oxford University Press, 1964.

Matthieussent, Brice. *Jim Harrison, de A à W.* Paris: C. Bourgois, 1995.

McGuane, Thomas. *The Sporting Club.* New York: Farrar, Straus, and Giroux, 1968.

Meeker, Joseph W. *The Comedy of Survival: Studies in Literary Ecology.* New York: Scribner's, 1972.

Miles, Jonathan. "Jim Harrison: The Salon Interview." *Salon,* December 1998.

Mills, Jerry Leath. "Three Novellas, Three Lessons in Life." Review of *Julip,* by Jim Harrison. *Atlanta Journal-Constitution,* 22 May 1994, N12.

Mogen, David, Mark Busby, and Paul Bryant, eds. *The Frontier Experience and the American Dream: Essays on American Literature.* College Station, Tex.: Texas A & M University Press, 1989.

Moon, Michael, and Eve Kosofsky Sedgwick. "Divinity: A Dossier: A Performance Piece: A Little-Understood Emotion." *Discourse* 13.1 (1990–91): 12–39.

Morse, Jonathan. *Word by Word: The Language of Memory.* Ithaca, N.Y.: Cornell University Press, 1990.

Nash, Roderick. *Wilderness and the American Mind.* New Haven, Conn.: Yale University Press, 1973.

Newman, Charles. *The Post-Modern Aura: The Act of Fiction in an Age of Inflation.* Evanston, Ill.: Northwestern University Press, 1985.

Newth, Rebecca. "For Harrison, Writing a Matter of Shifting Gears." *Arkansas Democrat-Gazette,* 15 May 1994, 8J.

Noble, Donald R., ed. *Hemingway: A Revaluation.* Troy, N.Y.: Whitson Publishing Company, 1983.

Norris, Lisa. "The Sincere Self." <http://www.tc.cc.va.us/vabeach/Hum/Blackwater/Norris. htm>.

Norton, Mike. "A Peek at Jim Harrison's World: Flamboyant, Controversial Novelist Mellows—Just a Little." *Record-Eagle (Traverse City, MI),* date unknown, 1D-2D.

Nuwer, Hank. "The Man Whose Soul Is Not for Sale: Jim Harrison." *Rendezvous: Journal of Arts and Letters* 21.1 (fall 1985): 26–42.

Oates, Joyce Carol. "Going Places." Review of *Wolf*, by Jim Harrison. *Partisan Review* 37.3 (summer 1972): 463–64.

Opdahl, Keith. "Junk Food." Review of *Legends of the Fall*, by Jim Harrison. *Nation*, 7 July 1979, 23–24.

Packard, Robert. *Refractions: Writers and Places*. New York: Carroll & Graf Publishers, Inc., 1990.

Patai, Raphael. *Myth and Modern Man*. Englewood Cliffs, N.J.: Prentice-Hall, 1972.

Patnaik, Eira. "The Succulent Gender: Eat Her Softly." In *Literary Gastronomy*, edited by David Bevan, 59–74. Amsterdam: Rodopi, 1988.

Penzenstadler, Joan. "La frontera, Aztlan, el barrio: Frontiers in Chicano Literature." In *The Frontier Experience and the American Dream: Essays on American Literature*, edited by David Mogen, Mark Busby, and Paul Bryant, 159–79. College Station, Tex.: Texas A & M University Press, 1989.

Perlman, Bob. *The Trouble with Genius: Reading Pound, Joyce, Stein, and Zukofsky*. Berkeley, Calif.: University of California Press, 1994.

Phipps, Terry W. "Lord Jim: Jim Harrison: A Sense of Place." *Grand Rapids Magazine*, May 1998, 19–25.

Potter, Jeff. "A Drink with Jim Harrison." *Out Your Backdoor* (spring 1991): 12–13.

Prescott, Peter S. "The Macho Mystique." *Newsweek* 94 (9 July 1979): 72.

Prichard, Peter S. "Grace and Grit in Harrison's *Fireflies*." *USA Today*, 7 September 1990, D4.

Primeau, Ronald. *Romance of the Road: The Literature of the American Highway*. Bowling Green, Ohio: Bowling Green State University Popular Press, 1996.

Pryse, Marjorie. "Reading Regionalism: The 'Difference' It Makes." In *Regionalism Reconsidered: New Approaches to the Field*, edited by David Jordan, 47–63. New York: Garland Publishing, Inc., 1994.

Quantic, Diane Dufva. *The Nature of the Place: A Study of Great Plains Fiction*. Lincoln, Nebr: University of Nebraska Press, 1995.

Quick, Jonathan. *Modern Fiction and the Art of Subversion*. New York: Peter Lang, 1999.

Quirk, Tom. *Coming to Grips with Huckleberry Finn: Essays on a Book, a Boy, and a Man*. Columbia, Mo.: University of Missouri Press, 1993.

Raglon, Rebecca, and Marian Scholtmeijer. "Shifting Ground: Metanarratives, Epistemology, and the Stories of Nature." *Environmental Ethics* 18 (1996): 19–38.

Ravo, Nick. "Will Write for Food." *New York Times*, 17 April 1994, sec. 9: 8.

Reed, J. D. "Hick Gumshoe." *Time*, 9 November 1981, K12.

Reed, Julia. "After Seven Acclaimed Novels, Jim Harrison Is Finding It Harder to Elude Fame." *Vogue,* September 1989, 502, 506, 510.

Reeves, Richard. *American Journey: Traveling with Tocqueville in Search of Democracy in America.* New York: Simon and Schuster, 1982.

Reilly, Edward C. *Jim Harrison.* New York: Twayne Publishers, 1996.

———. "The Tragedy and the Folly: Harrison's *A Good Day to Die*—An Earlier Version." *Publications of the Mississippi Philological Association* (1986): 23–33.

Renza, Louis A. *"A White Heron" and the Question of Minor Literature.* Madison, Wis.: University of Wisconsin Press, 1984.

"Rewards of Revenge." *Esquire,* 8 May 1979, 5.

Ricci, Jim. "1-on-1 Iron Person Can Hold His Center." *Detroit Free Press* 1 August 1991, metro final ed.: 1F.

———. "Thoughtful Talk, Thoughtless Writing." *Detroit Free Press,* 8 August 1991, metro final ed.: 1D.

Richardson, Robert D., Jr. *Myth and Literature in the American Renaissance.* Bloomington, Ind.: Indiana University Press, 1978.

Rilke, Rainer Maria. *The Selected Poetry of Rainter Maria Rilke.* Edited and translated by Stephen Mitchell. New York: Vintage International, 1989.

Review of *The Road Home,* by Jim Harrison. <http://www.amazon.com>. 4 December 1998.

Review of *The Road Home,* by Jim Harrison. <http://www.crazio.com/~book cafe/andrea/ harrison.html>. 14 April 1999.

Roberson, William H. "'A Good Day to Live': The Prose Works of Jim Harrison." *Great Lakes Review* 8.2–9.1 (1982–83): 29–37.

———. "'Macho Mistake': The Misrepresentation of Jim Harrison's Fiction." *Critique* 29.4 (1988): 233–44.

Roemer, Michael. *Telling Stories: Postmodernism and the Invalidation of Traditional Narrative.* Lanham, Md.: Rowman & Littlefield, 1995.

Rohrkemper, John. "'Natty Bummpo Wants Tobacco': Jim Harrison's Wilderness." *Great Lakes Review* (fall 1982-spring 1983): 20–28.

Roorda, Randall. *Dramas of Solitude: Narratives of Retreat in American Nature Writing.* Albany, N.Y.: State University of New York Press, 1998.

———. "Sites and Senses of Writing in Nature." *College English* 59.4 (April 1997): 385–407.

Rosenberg, Kenyon C. Review of *Outlyer and Ghazals,* by Jim Harrison. *Library Journal,* 1 June 1971, 1986.

Rosenthal, M. L. "Outlyers and Ghazals." Review of *Outlyer and Ghazals,* by Jim Harrison. *New York Times Book Review,* 18 July 1971, 7+.

Ross, Jean W. "CA Interview." In *Contemporary Authors: New Series.* Vol. 8. Edited by Ann Evory and Deborah A. Straub, 227–29. Detroit: Gale Research, 1983.

————. "An Interview with Jim Harrison." In *Dictionary of Literary Biography Yearbook,* edited by Richard Ziegfeld, 275–76. Detroit: Gale Research/Bruccoli Clark, 1983.

Roth, Philip. *Reading Myself and Others.* Hammondsworth: Penguin Books, 1985.

Sagan, Carl. *Science as a Candle in the Dark: The Demon-Haunted World.* New York: Random House, 1996.

Salter, Christopher L., and William J. Lloyd. *Landscape in Literature.* Washington, D.C.: Association of American Geographers, 1977.

Sayre, Robert. "Rethinking Midwestern Regionalism." *North Dakota Quarterly* 62.2 (1994–95): 114–31.

Scambler, Graham. *Epilepsy.* London: Tavistock/Routledge, 1989.

Scannell, Vernon. "Willfully Waffling." Review of *Legends of the Fall,* by Jim Harrison. *Times Literary Supplement,* 21 March 1980, 326.

Schapiro, Barbara Ann. *Literature and the Relational Self.* New York: New York University Press, 1994.

Schapiro, Nancy. "Words Macho, Magical." *St. Louis Post-Dispatch,* 4 November 1990, C5.

Schneider, Jeremy. "From Wounded Knee to Capitol Hill: The History, Achievements, and Legacy of the American Indian Movement." <http://icarus.uic.edu/~jschne1/ wounded_knee.html>. 16 November 1997.

Schneiderman, Leo. *The Literary Mind: Portraits in Pain and Creativity.* New York: Human Sciences Press, Inc., 1988.

Schott, Webster. "Farmer." Review of *Farmer,* by Jim Harrison. *New York Times Book Review,* 10 October 1976, 32.

Review of *Selected and New Poems 1961–1981,* by Jim Harrison. *Publishers Weekly,* 25 June 1982, 114.

Shack, Neville. "The Biographical Entrails." Review of *Sundog,* by Jim Harrison. *Times Literary Supplement,* 16 August 1985, 907.

Sheehan, Marc J. "The Writer as Naturalist: Michigan Poet/Novelist Jim Harrison Talks about Food, Buddhism, Politics, and the Art of Writing." *Lansing Capital Times,* September 1990, 1, 18–19.

Shumaker, Wayne. *Literature and the Irrational: A Study in Anthropological Backgrounds.* Englewood Cliffs, N.J.: Prentice-Hall, 1960.

Siegal, Eric. "A New Voice from the North Country: A Portrait of the Prodigal Poet Who Came Home to Michigan." *Detroit Free Press Magazine,* 16 April 1972, 18–20.

Simonson, Harold P. *Beyond the Frontier: Writers, Western Regionalism and a Sense of Place.* Forth Worth, Tex.: Texas Christian University Press, 1989.

Sisyphus, Aloysius. "The Diddy Wah Diddy Interview: Jim Harrison." *Diddy Wah Diddy* 6.5 (October 1990): 6–7.

Skwira, Gregory. "Words from the Woods." *Detroit* (25 March 1984): 8–9, 11, 13–15, 16, 18–19.

Slethaug, Godron E. *The Play of the Double in Postmodern American Fiction*. Carbondale, Ill.: Southern Illinois University Press, 1993.

Slotkin, Richard. *The Fatal Environment: The Myth of the Frontier in the Age of Industrialization, 1800–1890*. New York: Atheneum, 1985.

———. *Gunfigther Nation: The Myth of the Frontier in Twentieth-Century America*. New York: Atheneum, 1992.

———. *Regeneration through Violence: The Mythology of the American Frontier, 1600–1860*. Middletown, Conn.: Wesleyan University Press, 1973.

Slovic, Scott. *Seeking Awareness in American Nature Writing: Henry Thoreau, Annie Dillard, Edward Abbey, Wendell Berry, Barry Lopez*. Salt Lake City: University of Utah Press, 1992.

Smart, J. J. C. "Man as a Physical Mechanism." In *Modern Materialism: Readings on Mind-Body Identity*. Edited by John O'Connor. New York: Harcourt, Brace & World, Inc., 1969.

Smiley, Jane. "Say It Ain't So, Huck: Second Thoughts on Mark Twain's 'Masterpiece.'" *Harper's* (January 1996): 61–67.

Smith, Carlton. *Coyote Kills John Wayne: Postmodernism and Contemporary Fictions of the Transcultural Frontier*. Hanover, N.H.: University Press of New England, 2000.

Smith, Patrick. Interview with Janet Burroway, 22 February 1999.

———. "A Man's World." Review of *The Beast God Forgot to Invent*, by Jim Harrison. *January Magazine*, 26 November 2000.

Smith, Paul. *Discerning the Subject*. Minneapolis: University of Minnesota Press, 1988.

Smith, Wendy. "*PW* Interviews Jim Harrison." *Publishers Weekly* 237.3 (3 August 1990): 59–60.

———. "Returning to the Earth." Review of *The Road Home*, by Jim Harrison. *New York Times Book Review*, 15 November 1998, 4.

Smyntek, John. "Michigan Author Will Do an Eat Column." *Detroit Free Press*, 15 January 1991, metro final ed.: 8F.

Snyder, Gary. *The Practice of the Wild: Essays*. San Francisco: North Point, 1990.

Spengler, Oswald. *The Decline of the West*. Translated by Charles Francis Atkinson. New York: Knopf, 1926.

Stafford, William, et al. "Panel: The Realities of Regionalism." *South Dakota Review* 26.4 (1988): 77–91.

Stegner, Wallace, et al. "The Writer's Sense of Place." *South Dakota Review* 26.4 (1988): 93–120.

Stevens, Joseph E. *Hoover Dam: An American Adventure*. Norman, Okla.: University of Oklahoma Press, 1988.

Stewart, Frank. *A Natural History of Nature Writing*. Washington, D.C.: Island Press, 1995.

Stielstra, Julie. "Real Men Get Struck by Lightning." Review of *Sundog*, by Jim Harrison. *Michigan Voice*, July-August 1984, 17.

Stocking, Kathleen. "Hard Cases: Conversations with Jim Harrison and Tom McGuane, Riders of the Purple Rage." *Detroit News Magazine,* 12 August 1980, 14–15ff.

———. *Letters from the Leelanau: Essays of People and Place.* Ann Arbor, Mich.: University of Michigan Press, 1990.

———. "Writer Jim Harrison: Work, Booze, and the Outdoor Life—and an Absolute Rage for Order." *Detroit Free Press,* 5 June 1977, 21–22, 24–26.

Stout, Janis P. *The Journey Narrative in American Literature.* Westport, Conn.: Greenwood Press, 1983.

Streitfield, David. Review of *The Road Home,* by Jim Harrison. *Washington Post Book World,* 13 December 1998, 15.

Streitfeld, David. "Thinking Small." *Washington Post Book World,* 16 June 1991, 15.

Strout, Cushing. *Making American Tradition: Visions and Revisions from Ben Franklin to Alice Walker.* New Brunswick, N.J.: Rutgers University Press, 1990.

———. *The Veracious Imagination: Essays on American History, Literature, and Biography.* Middletown, Conn.: Wesleyan University Press, 1981.

Stuewe, Paul. "Sex in Venice: Essays from Bloomsbury and Uris's Jerusalem." *Quill and Quire* (January 1982): 39.

Review of *Sundog,* by Jim Harrison. *Publishers Weekly,* 13 April 1984, 52.

Sypher, Wylie. *Comedy.* Baltimore: Johns Hopkins University Press, 1956.

———. *Literature and Technology: The Alien Vision.* New York: Random House, 1968.

Talbert, Bob. "A Few Questions if You Please." *Detroit Free Press,* 18 February 1996, metro final ed.: 6F.

———. "Jim Harrison's Wolf Movie Will Star Nicholson, Pfeiffer." *Detroit Free Press,* 18 April 1993, metro final ed.: 6F.

———. "Jim Harrison Screenplay Could Be 'Sues with Wolves.'" *Detroit Free Press,* 24 February 1991, metro final ed.: 5F.

———. "Showbiz Slant Skewed Olympic Coverage." *Detroit Free Press,* 13 August 1996, metro final ed.: 7D.

Technical Services Section of the Explosives Department. *Blaster's Handbook: A Manual Describing Explosives and Practical Methods of Using Them.* 12th ed. Wilmington, Del.: E. I. DuPont de Nemours & Company (Inc.), 1949.

Thompson, D'Arcy Wentworth. *On Growth and Form.* Cambridge, England: Cambridge University Press, 1943.

Thompson, William Irwin. *The American Replacement of Nature.* New York: Doubleday Currency, 1991.

Tillinghast, Richard. "From Michigan and Tennessee." Review of *Selected and New Poems 1961–1981,* by Jim Harrison. *New York Times Book Review,* 12 December 1982, 14, 31.

Tischler, Barbara L, ed. *Sights on the Sixties*. New Brunswick, N.J.: Rutgers University Press, 1992.

Torrey, Beef. "Collecting Jim Harrison: Untrammeled Renegade Genius." *Firsts: The Book Collector's Magazine* (May 1999): 38–47.

Trachtenberg, Stanley, ed. *Critical Essays on American Postmodernism*. New York: G.K. Hall & Co., 1995.

Treadwell, T. O. "Fantasist in the Shopping Mall." *Times Literary Supplement*, 15 January 1982, 48.

Turner, Frederick. *Beyond Geography: The Western Spirit against the Wilderness*. New York: Viking Press, 1980.

———. *Spirit of Place: The Making of an American Literary Landscape*. San Francisco: Sierra Club Books, 1989.

Turner, Jack. *The Abstract Wild*. Tuscon, Ariz.: University of Arizona Press, 1996.

Twain, Mark. *Adventures of Huckleberry Finn*. Berkeley, Calif.: University of California Press, 1985.

Tyson, Lois. *Psychological Politics of the American Dream: The Commodification of Subjectivity in Twentieth-Century American Literature*. Columbus, Ohio: Ohio State University Press, 1994.

Umphlett, Wiley Lee. *Mythmakers of the American Dream: The Nostalgic Vision in Popular Culture*. Lewisburg, Pa.: Bucknell University Press, 1983.

Utley, Robert M. *The Indian Frontier of the American West 1846–1890*. Albuquerque, N. Mex.: University of New Mexico Press, 1984.

Van Brunt, H. L. "Going Places." Review of *Wolf* by Jim Harrison. *Partisan Review* 37.3 (summer 1972): 463–64.

Vecsey, Christopher, and Robert W. Venables, eds. *American Indian Environments: Ecological Issues in Native American History*. Syracuse, N.Y.: Syracuse University Press, 1980.

Venables, Robert. "Twisted Footnote to Wounded Knee: Looking Back to Wounded Knee 1890." <http://dickshovel.netgate.net/TwistedFootnote.html>. 14 April 1997.

Vizenor, Gerald. *Fugitive Poses: Native American Indian Scenes of Absence and Presence*. Lincoln, Nebr.: University of Nebraska Press, 1998.

———. *Narrative Chance: Postmodern Discourse on Native American Indian Literatures*. Albuquerque, N. Mex.: University of New Mexico Press, 1989.

———. *The Trickster of Liberty*. Minneapolis, Minn.: University of Minnesota Press, 1988.

Walker, Cheryl. *Indian Nation: Native American Literature and Nineteenth-Century Nationalisms*. Durham, N.C.: Duke University Press, 1997.

Walker, Michael. "When the Wolf Howls." *Los Angeles Times/Calendar,* 12 June 1994, 8, 30–31, 34.

Review of *Warlock,* by Jim Harrison. *Publishers Weekly,* 11 September 1981, 60–61.

Wasserstrom, William. *The Ironies of Progress: Henry Adams and the American Dream.* Carbondale, Ill.: Southern Illinois University Press, 1984.

Watkins, Floyd C. *In Time and Place: Some Origins of American Fiction.* Athens, Ga.: University of Georgia Press, 1977.

Weber, Ronald. *The Literature of Fact: Literary Nonfiction in American Writing.* Athens, Ohio: Ohio University Press, 1980.

Wehr, Demaris S. "Religious and Social Dimensions of Jung's Concept of the Archetype: A Feminist Perspective." In *Feminist Archetypal Theory: Interdisciplinary Re-Visions of Jungian Thought,* edited by Estella Lauter and Carol Schreier Rupprecht, 23–45. Knoxville, Tenn.: University of Tennessee Press, 1985.

Westervelt, Linda A. *Beyond Innocence, or the Altersroman in Modern Fiction.* Columbia, Mo.: University of Missouri Press, 1997.

Westling, Louise H. *The Green Breast of the New World: Landscape, Gender, and American Fiction.* Athens, Ga.: University of Georgia Press, 1996.

White, Richard. "Are you an environmentalist or do you work for a living?: Work and Nature." In *Uncommon Ground: Toward Reinventing Nature,* edited by William Cronon, 171–85. New York: W.W. Norton & Company, 1995.

Whitmer, Barbara. *The Violence Mythos.* Albany, N.Y.: State University of New York Press, 1997.

Willingham, John R. Review of *Plain Song,* by Jim Harrison. *Library Journal,* 1 December 1965, 5286.

Wirth-Nesher, Hana. "The Literary Orphan as National Hero: Huck and Pip." *Dickens Studies Annual: Essays on Victorian Fiction* 15 (1986): 259–73.

Wolcott, James. Review of *Legends of the Fall,* by Jim Harrison. *Esquire,* October 1981, 23.

Woodbury, Dixon M., J. Kiffin Penry, and C. E. Pippenger, eds. *Antiepileptic Drugs.* 2d ed. New York: Raven Press, 1982.

Woods, William Crawford. "What a Strange Accomplishment." Review of *A Good Day to Die,* by Jim Harrison. *Washington Post,* 9 September 1973, 4.

Yardley, Jonathan. "Also Extravagantly Free-Male." Review of *Wolf,* by Jim Harrison. *New York Times Book Review,* 12 December 1971, 4, 38.

Young, Philip. *American Fiction, American Myth.* University Park, Pa.: Pennsylvania State University Press, 2000.

Zuckert, Catherine H. *Natural Right and the American Imagination: Political Philosophy in Novel Form.* Savage, Md.: Rowman & Littlefield Publishers, Inc., 1990.

Index